Subverting the System

Subverting the System

Gorbachev's Reform of the Party's Apparat, 1986–1991

JONATHAN HARRIS

ROWMAN & LITTLEFIELD PUBLISHERS, INC.
Lanham • Boulder • New York • Toronto • Oxford

ROWMAN & LITTLEFIELD PUBLISHERS, INC.

Published in the United States of America
by Rowman & Littlefield Publishers, Inc.
A wholly owned subsidiary of The Rowman & Littlefield Publishing Group, Inc.
4501 Forbes Boulevard, Suite 200, Lanham, MD 20706
www.rowmanlittlefield.com

P.O. Box 317, Oxford OX2 9RU, United Kingdom

British Library Cataloguing in Publication Information Available

Library of Congress Cataloging-in-Publication Data

Harris, Jonathan, 1935–
   Subverting the system : Gorbachev's reform of the party's apparat,
1986–1991 / Jonathan Harris.
     p. cm.
Includes bibliographical references and index.
  ISBN 0-7425-2678-X
  1. Kommunisticheskaia partiia Sovetskogo Soiuza—Reorganization.
2. Kommunisticheskaia partiia Sovetskogo Soiuza—Officials and
employees. 3. Gorbachev, Mikhail Sergeyevich, 1931– 4. Soviet
Union—Politics and government—1985–1991. I. Title.
  JN6598.K7H33 2004
  324.247'075'09048--dc22

                               2003019736

Printed in the United States of America

∞™ The paper used in this publication meets the minimum requirements of
American National Standard for Information Sciences—Permanence of Paper for
Printed Library Materials, ANSI/NISO Z39.48-1992.

This book is dedicated to the late
William O. McCagg Jr.

Contents

Preface

This study is an outgrowth of a long-standing interest in the ideological orientation and political activities of the leading full-time officials of the Communist Party of the Soviet Union (CPSU). An earlier analysis of the conflict between A. Zhdanov and G. Malenkov helped to develop a framework for understanding the euphemistic public discourse about the nature and scope of party officials' responsibilities. The same approach was used to understand the discourse of leading party officials during the first years of the Brezhnev-Kosygin regime in the mid-1960s.

This study uses the same framework to discuss the efforts of General Secretary Mikhail Gorbachev to redefine the function of party officials, their varied response to his initiatives, and the impact of this debate on the transformation of the political system. Gorbachev's support for glasnost made this ongoing political conflict accessible to the reader of the party's various publications. Moreover, Gorbachev's obvious unwillingness to use force meant that he had to use persuasion to win support for his position and allowed his opponents and critics to express their reservations and disagreement with growing confidence and less fear of retribution.

This study falls somewhere between the disciplines of political science and history. The emphasis on Gorbachev's efforts to transform the basic institutions of the political system reflects the concerns of what might be called "traditional" political science. But the approach to this process is essentially historical. Many political scientists would attempt to determine the "independent and dependent variables" that determine this process of change, but I regard the process as far too complex to be discussed in these terms.

This should not be interpreted to mean that this study is "atheoretical." It attempts to conceptualize the relationship between "the party" and "the state" in the political system differently from most Western scholarship on the USSR. Many Western scholars, following the terminological usage of the leaders of the USSR, refer to the relations between "party" and "state" as if they were independent bureaucratic entities. In fact, the membership of these bodies overlapped in significant fashion.

In order to avoid the distortions produced by this usage, this study makes use of the distinction made by George Orwell between an "inner" and "outer" party. The inner party, headed by the Secretariat of the Central Committee of the CPSU, is composed of full-time party officials with no administrative positions in the Soviet state. The "inner party" attempts to provide both supervision and leadership for the members of the "outer party"—those members of the CPSU who staff the Soviet state.

This study was not created in a vacuum but builds upon the extensive Western scholarship on the various elements of political change that occurred during Gorbachev's tenure as general secretary. I am deeply indebted to the authors of the monographs listed in the bibliography. While they present different interpretations of the driving forces for political change in the system, their efforts at understanding are extraordinarily complementary and provide an excellent foundation for detailed studies like my own.

I would also like to thank William Chase and Carmine Storella of the department of history at the University of Pittsburgh for their extensive and intelligent comments on an earlier more primitive version of this study. I am also particularly indebted to the referee for Rowman & Littlefield Publishers, Inc., for his extremely useful suggestions for the improvement of the original manuscript.

CHAPTER ONE

❧

Introduction

Western scholars have explained the transformation of the political system in the USSR under the leadership of General Secretary Gorbachev in a variety of ways. Many have focused on the general secretary as the major source of innovation for the political system. Others have given greater stress to the constraints imposed on the general secretary by the institutional arrangements of the past, what Philip G. Roeder has defined as the "constitution of Bolshevism."[1] Some have focused on the complex interactions between changes in the social and economic order and the initiatives of the political leadership, and others give greater stress to the "revolution from above."[2]

Despite differences of emphasis, all of these studies would agree on the overriding importance of certain fundamental institutional elements established by the "constitution of Bolshevism." All would support Gordon M. Hahn's conclusion that "without a strong party apparatus the Soviet regime would be rendered unstable. The party apparatus ensured the level of control needed for the regime to eschew terror and high mobilization and still maintain its stability."[3] In fact, all Western studies of perestroika have explicitly recognized that Gorbachev's weakening of the apparatus hastened the collapse of the regime.

While Western scholars have recognized the significance of this reform, they have not carefully examined the party leaders' *own* conception of this process. The following study attempts to determine what the leaders believed they were doing by examining the following elements of their public discourse: Gorbachev's own definition of the proper role for the party's full-time officials and their relationship with the Communists who manned the state; the nature and scope of his campaign to impose these definitions on members of the Secretariat of the CC/CPSU and subordinate party officials; the public criticism of the general secretary's campaign by orthodox members of the Secretariat and like-minded republican and regional party officials.

Western scholars have tended to ignore the importance of this public discourse because they did not always realize that party leaders' references to "the party" and the nature of its "leadership" had immense implications for the definition of officials' proper role. Western scholars ignored these implications because the leaders of the CPSU often failed to differentiate between "the party" and its apparatus in their most important comments on the role of the CPSU. For example, in mid-1989 the general secretary declared that "the party was elevated over everything and it controlled all the processes of state, economic, and ideological life, supplanting and crushing everything without exception, issuing incontestible directives and commands to state and economic agencies and public organizations."[4]

Since the leaders of all state, economic, and public organizations were members of the CPSU, this statement on its face is meaningless. But if the word "party" is replaced by the term "full-time party officials," Gorbachev's comment can be seen for what it was—an indirect but forceful denunciation of officials' previous policies. But Western scholars generally simply followed the lead of the general secretary and used the term "the party" when the term "apparat of full-time party officials" would have been more accurate. A recent study of perestroika concluded, "In general terms, as *Kommunist* argued in an editorial in January 1988, there should be a more restricted understanding of the party's role, involving a kind of 'division of labor' in which the party would stand aside from direct management of public affairs and confine itself to a much looser coordinating function."[5] In this instance *Kommunist*, the theoretical journal of the Central Committee of the CPSU, was actually providing guidance to the party's full-time officials.

This tendency to blur the difference between the full-time officials who held no position in the state and the thousands of Communist party members who staffed the Soviet governmental structure seemed to be particularly evident in those studies of perestroika that characterized the political system in the USSR as a "party-state." One such study concluded that "once he [Gorbachev] realized that he had to move to a system in which the market was the main regulator of economic life, he needed to deny the Communist party its economic functions and controls. Yet he still needed the Communist party as an instrument of implementation in the absence of any executive organs other than the economic ministries."[6] This formulation not only blurs the difference between the full-time party officials and the Communists under their supervision, but also implies that "the party" and the economic ministries of the state were completely distinct bureaucratic agencies. In fact, the ministries were headed by Communists subject to the party discipline imposed by the leading full-time officials of the CPSU.

The following study attempts to avoid this widespread confusion between the CPSU as a whole and its full-time officials by referring to them as the "inner party" and the Communists who manned the state as the "outer party."[7] The "inner party" was headed by the general secretary of the Central Committee of the CPSU and the Secretariat of the Central Committee of the CPSU and the "outer party" by the chairman of the Council of Ministers of the USSR, and the council itself. The leaders of both the Secretariat and the Council of Ministers were brought together, along with leaders of the most important republican parties, in the Politburo of the Central Committee of the CPSU. Local party officials and ministers were also brought together as members of the Central Committee.

Ever since Stalin's time, the leaders of the CPSU have consistently sought to disguise this fundamental difference between the members of the "inner" and "outer" parties. Public recognition that the apparatus of party officials formed the bureaucratic core of the CPSU that sought to lead and/or supervise Communists in the state would endanger the central political myth of the political system, or how "the party" led the country. As a result, the leadership's discussion of the proper relationship between the "inner" party and the "outer" party has generally been indirect (except during the last few years of Gorbachev's reign).

My analysis of this discussion suggests that it is possible to infer the leadership's views on officials' priorities from their public comments on the relative importance and nature of the "political" and "economic" work of the CPSU. To understand this debate, it is essential to understand the leadership's definition of these terms.

Stalin's brief comments on the relative importance of "party-political" (or "internal") work and "economic" work provided the framework for subsequent discussion of the role of party officials. In the 1920s and early 1930s Stalin had repeatedly described them as the "generals" of the CPSU responsible for leading its rank and file. But his conception of the nature of their leadership became less clear with the development of an increasingly complex state structure to administer the five-year plans in the 1930s. How were the "generals" of the CPSU to provide leadership of this massive state structure? In the late 1930s, Stalin seemed to argue that the Secretariat and the party officials subordinate to it could best lead by focusing on the various components of "party-political work" deemed essential for the party's continued vitality. These include (1) the recruitment, training, and assignment of personnel throughout the system, generally known as "work with cadres"; (2) the theoretical education of party members and a wide range of activities to promulgate the leadership's official line through control of the media, cultural life, and education, which was known as "ideological work"; (3) the efforts to mobilize Communists to fulfill the decisions of the leadership, known as "organizational work"; and (4) the "verification of fulfillment" of previously issued decrees and orders of the leadership.

In contrast, Stalin explicitly warned party officials not to give excessive attention to their "economic work," that is, their efforts to assure the implementation of the five-year plan by the government of the USSR. Stalin warned that party officials' "usurpation" of the authority of state officials threatened to undermine party officials' "vision" and make them neglect the party political work essential for the party's continued vitality.

To deal with the various elements of "political" and economic work, the Central Committee established a wide range of specialized departments under the direct control of the secretariat of the Central Committee of the CPSU and supervised by senior Secretaries of the Central Committee of the CPSU. (Many of them simultaneously held positions in the Politburo. This study will refer to them as the Politburo/secretaries.) The departments supervised the activities of local party officials and the activities of the central ministries within their particular sphere.[8]

Over the years, the departments of the CC/CPSU were reorganized a number of times. In the years between 1924 and 1930, before the development of the five-year plans, the departments of the Central Committee had been organized to focus on the major components of "political work." But the development of the first five-year plan led the leaders of the Secretariat to create special departments for various branches of the economy within the personnel department in 1930 to direct the thousands of new personnel needed to administer the plans. As Merle Fainsod concluded in his study of the apparat, the Secretariat proved to be "poorly adapted to enforce unified party control over the various branches of the economy and government."[9] As a result, in 1934 new branch departments independent of the department for personnel were established to provide more effective controls.

Stalin's comments on the relative importance of "political" and "economic work" evidently led to various important reorganizations of the departments of the CC/CPSU subordinate to the Secretariat in the late 1930s and 1940s. At the 18th Congress of the CPSU in 1939 the branch departments for industry established in 1934 were replaced by divisions for personnel management, ideological work, and verification of fulfillment—the key components of "political work." Two years later, at the 18th Conference of the CPSU, the leadership concluded that this arrangement had led party officials to neglect industry and called for the establishment of specialized secretaries responsible for industry and transport at all republic, regional, and city levels of the party's apparatus.[10] The industrial departments of the Central Committee were restored after Zhdanov's death in 1948.

During the last years of Stalin's reign, he seemed to prefer to govern the country through his position as chairman of the Council of Ministers of the USSR rather than as general secretary. As a result, the leaders of the Secretariat and its apparatus of subordinate full-time party officials seemed to play a secondary role in the Presidium of the Central Committee (which had replaced the Politburo in 1952). Immediately after his death, the Presidium was composed of eight ministers, the chairman of the Presidium of the USSR Supreme Soviet, and only one member of the Secretariat, N. S. Khrushchev.[11]

Once Khrushchev was named first secretary, he sought to change the relationship between the leaders of the "inner" and "outer" parties at the apex of the system by increasing the number of secretaries of the CC/CPSU within the Presidium and by giving primacy to party officials' "economic work." In his report on behalf of the CC/CPSU to the 20th Congress of the CPSU he derided those who had sought to differentiate between "pure party work" and state administration and who regarded theoretical education of party members as essential for practical success. He ordered party officials to improve their technical education and to focus on "economic work."

This definition of party officials' priorities had an important impact on the entire system of governance in the USSR. In 1957 First Secretary Khrushchev managed to replace the majority of the central ministries with regional economic councils in which local party officials were to play a major role in the development of all spheres of economic activity. Furthermore, once Khrushchev had overcome the efforts of the antiparty group (the majority of whom were ministers in the government of the USSR) to oust him from power, he managed to pack the Presidium with members of the Secretariat. The Presidium of December 1957 included eight secretaries of the Central Committee (in addition to First Secretary Khrushchev), the chairman of the party's control commission, and the first secretary of the Central Committee of the Communist Party of Kazakhstan and only three leading ministers.

But Khrushchev evidently had doubts about the Presidium's capacity to control the Council of Ministers of the USSR. In 1958 he assumed the position of chairman of the Council of Ministers of the USSR in order to establish more direct vertical controls over the leading members of the "outer party." But this extraordinary assumption of authority was evidently insufficient to protect his position. By all accounts Khrushchev suffered a severe setback after the "U-2" incident. In 1960 the number of secretaries in the Presidium was sharply reduced, and his opponents not only charged that Khrushchev's definition of officials' priorities had in fact led to a serious neglect of the party's "internal work," but also called for limitations on party officials' intervention in industrial administration. Not to be outdone, Khrushchev responded by carrying his views on the priority of officials' economic work to its logical conclusion. In the fall of 1962 he divided the entire apparatus into two separate divisions for industry and agriculture. This reform reportedly produced such immense confusion among party officials that it helped to hasten Khrushchev's demise.

The selection of Leonid Brezhnev as first secretary (general secretary after 1966) and Alexei Kosygin as chairman of the Council of Ministers to replace Khrushchev in the fall of 1964 seemed to indicate that Khrushchev's successors had repudiated his definition of party officials' priorities and sought to restore a demarcation of responsibilities between the "inner party" headed by the Secretariat and the "outer party" headed by the Council of Ministers of the USSR. The new leaders quickly restored the unity of the party apparatus, dismantled the regional economic councils, and resurrected the branch ministries. The leadership's first major public presentations seemed to indicate that the new leaders sought to give the government of the USSR greater authority over the administration of industry. In particular, Prime Minister Kosygin seemed to be given considerable leeway in the reform of the administration of industry while Brezhnev assumed responsibility for the reform of agriculture, the traditional bailiwick of the chief executive of the CPSU. At the same time, the veteran Secretary Suslov pressed for the restoration of theoretical education of party members and other elements of internal work.

Over the next two to three years Prime Minister Kosygin introduced a number of administrative reforms designed to lessen the branch ministries' control over their subordinate enterprises and allow them to respond to the market for their goods in the development of their plans for production. But by the end of the 1960s the ministries' resistance to these reforms, combined with the leadership's anxieties about their political implications, led to the abandonment of these experiments. Furthermore, the apparent failure of these reforms to increase production in key sectors evidently led the general secretary to favor an extension of party officials' "economic work." It seems highly likely that this process intensified after 1980 when the elderly Tikhonov replaced the ailing Kosygin as the chairman of the Council of Ministers. As a consequence, by the time Gorbachev was selected as general secretary in 1985 the Secretariat had become a "second Council of Ministers only more powerful."[12]

The following study attempts to demonstrate that Gorbachev sought to challenge his predecessors' definition of officials' priorities. In the years between 1986 and 1991 he not only sought to persuade subordinate party officials to give priority to the various elements of "political work," but also attempted to transform the nature of their approach to "economic work."

General Secretary Gorbachev modified the terminology used by his predecessors slightly during his reign as general secretary. In his report to the 27th Congress of the CPSU he used the terminology outlined above, but by mid-1986 he began to use the term "political methods of leadership" to describe party officials' "political" activities. He and his closest allies also used the term "political leadership" in different ways to describe the role and activities of various organs in the CPSU. They described the Politburo and Central Committee as "organs of political leadership" when they sought to highlight their responsibility for the development of policy in all areas of Soviet life. When they discussed the activities of local party officials they used the term "political leadership" to stress the capacity of party officials to coordinate a range of different activities in a particular region without losing their own strategic vision. In 1989, after the establishment of the Congress of Peoples' Deputies, Gorbachev also used this term to refer to party officials' role in the new world of electoral politics.

Gorbachev persisted in his campaign to change the orientation of party officials throughout his reign. Although he did retreat at various times in the face of orthodox opposition to his definitions, his efforts proved to be largely successful until 1990. He launched his campaign rather hesitantly at the 27th Congress of the CPSU in 1986, and worked assiduously to impose his views upon his subordinates until the 28th Congress of the CPSU in mid-1990, when he transferred his authority over the Secretariat to the newly appointed deputy general secretary, V. A. Ivashko.

This study will attempt to demonstrate that the general secretary's success in the years between 1987 and 1990 proved to be disastrous for the political system in a number of ways. First of all, the implementation of his definitions hampered the capacity of the members of the "inner party" to provide coherent and effective direction to the members of the "outer party" and thereby seriously undermined the fundamental basis of "party leadership" of the Soviet state. In particular, the success of Gorbachev's campaign not only seriously undermined party officials' authority in the major spheres of "political work"—their control over personnel, and the various elements of "ideological work—but also transformed the nature of their "economic work."

Second, Gorbachev's campaign produced deep divisions within the leadership of the CPSU. His orthodox opponents increased their attack on his formulations as the implications of his definitions became more obvious. Finally, and most important, his orthodox opponents engaged in a major campaign to restore the authority of party officials in many areas after the 28th Congress of the CPSU in mid-1990 when Gorbachev handed direct control of the Secretariat to V. A. Ivashko.

In the period from the 28th Congress until the abortive coup against the president in August 1991 Gorbachev seemed to use his authority as general secretary sporadically and to regard his new position as president of the USSR as the more effective instrument to lead the country. During the last year of his reign, the president was increasingly preoccuppied with the government's economic policy, the establishment of a new type of federation for the USSR, and the threat to his authority and to the USSR posed by Boris Yeltsin, who had been elected as the chairman of the Supreme Soviet of the Russian republic in the spring of 1990. Unfortunately for President Gorbachev, these three issues became hopelessly intertwined. But it would be a mistake to conclude that Gorbachev totally discarded his authority as general secretary during this period. He continued to use it as a base for his attempts to redefine official ideology and to counter the efforts by the deputy general secretary and other secretaries of the CC/CPSU to restore party officials' lost authority.

The following summary of Gorbachev's campaign to persuade party officials to focus on their "political work" is designed to provide an introduction for the more detailed examination in the following chapters. During his first year as general secretary, from March 1985 until the 27th Congress of the CPSU in February/March 1986, Gorbachev did not make any public criticism of party officials. During this period, he seemed willing to grant the Council of Ministers of the USSR greater autonomy in the implementation of industrial policy. In September 1985 he appointed his close colleague N. Ryzhkov as the chairman of the Council of Ministers and seemed to endorse Chairman Ryzhkov's conception of the role of the government of the USSR in the management of industry. At the same time he focused on the major elements of "political work." He gave vast attention to personnel management and increasingly portrayed himself as the chief ideologist of the CPSU whose numerous pronouncements were to be regarded as the major source of direction for the entire process of perestroika.

Gorbachev made his first public comments on party officials' proper role in his report to the 27th Congress of the CPSU in March 1986. He implied (in rather tentative fashion) that they should give more attention to "political work" and should stop their interference in the administration of economic affairs and in "public agencies." The general secretary did not merely seek to limit officials' intervention in industrial administration but sought to persuade them to be more responsive to the rank-and-file Communists in state and Soviet agencies and to the pressing needs of Soviet citizens. His comments prompted a public debate at the 27th Congress among important leaders of the "inner party" over party officials' responsibilities which continued unabated until the abortive coup against Gorbachev.

The opening round of the debate was between Ligachev and Yeltsin. On the one hand, Yegor Ligachev, who was the unofficial "second secretary" from 1985 until 1988, totally ignored Gorbachev's critique of party officials' alleged "interference" in the state's administration of industry and vigorously insisted that party officials were and should be responsible for virtually all spheres of Soviet life. Ligachev repeatedly defended this position until his retirement from the Politburo and Secretariat at the 28th Congress of the CPSU. On the other hand, Boris Yeltsin, who was head of the Moscow *gorkom* and named a candidate member of the Politburo at the end of the 27th Congress, attacked Ligachev's position (without naming him directly) with considerable vehemence. He discarded the standard euphemisms to assail the departments of the Central Committee for their excessive interference in the Council of Ministers' administration of industry and their inadequate management of personnel. Yelstin demanded a fundamental reform of the Secretariat and he reiterated his assault on the Secretariat and its subordinate officials in the period between 1986 and 1991.

In the months immediately after the 27th Congress, the leadership of the CPSU was distracted by the immense crisis created by the explosion of a nuclear power plant in Chernobyl and found it difficult to define its immediate priorities. But in June 1956, Gorbachev had evidently clarified his views on officials' priorities. In his report to the members of the Central Committee in June 1956 he moved beyond the hesitant formulations in his report to the 27th Congress to an overt attack on party officials' alleged interference in administrative matters. Gorbachev now began to mobilize his most loyal deputies to promote his campaign. G. P. Razumovsky, who had been named by Gorbachev to direct the Central Committee's department of organizational-party work, which was responsible for the management of personnel, was dispatched to the provinces to persuade local party officials to follow their general secretary's lead. But by the end of 1986, the general secretary evidently had concluded that his numerous changes in leading personnel had not yet had the desired effect. He reportedly decided to reform the "entire cadre system" and convened the Central Committee to discuss the issue in January 1987.

Gorbachev's dramatic report to the Central Committee in January 1987 marked a fundamental shift in the direction of reform. Gorbachev not only discussed personnel management, but also made a fundamental assault on the entire theoretical and practical legacy of the Stalinist system. Within this context, Gorbachev presented a more precise definition of party officials' priorities. He now urged them to focus on "political leadership" in order to make them more responsive to the social and economic needs of Soviet citizens. He recognized that party officials' intervention in the administration of industry had been needed to deal with its rigidity, but he now insisted that the proposed efforts to grant enterprises considerable autonomy would eliminate the basis for officials' "usurpation." The following month he explicitly urged the officials who led both *gorkom* and *raikom* to focus on personnel management, ideological and organizational work and effective "work with people," and not attempt to engage in economic administration.

Gorbachev's report to the Central Committee not only defined party officials' role with greater clarity, but also had immense implications for the development of the CPSU's official ideology. Although he did not assail Stalin by name, his critique of the major characteristics of the Stalinist system set the stage for a massive assault on orthodox ideological formulations and practices and the increased representation of his own formulations on every subject as the official ideology of the CPSU. Gorbachev's closest ally, A. Yakovlev, worked with immense vigor to propagate the general secretary's views. Gorbachev had named Yakovlev the head of the propaganda department of the Central Committee in 1985. Yakovlev was promoted to the position of secretary of the Central Committee at the end of the 27th Congress and named a candidate member of the Politburo in January 1987. The general secretary and Secretary Yakovlev proceeded to redefine the substance of official ideology and the nature of "ideological work" in ways that quickly undermined party officials' control over the media and the country's intellectual and cultural life.

This process had an immense impact on the relationships between the secretaries of the CC/CPSU and on the political conflicts within the Politburo. In 1987 and 1988 Secretary Yakovlev and Secretary Ligachev became locked in a bitter struggle for control of the propaganda, educational, and cultural departments of the Central Committee. Yakovlev's appointment of liberal editors to a wide range of party and nonparty journals, and the lifting of control over films and other cultural venues created conditions for an increasingly open critique of the Soviet past and present. Ligachev countered with increasingly gloomy warnings about the subversive impact of this policy on the cohesiveness of both the CPSU and the society as a whole, but he proved unable to stem the tide of cultural and intellectual liberalization. Furthermore, Yakovlev's promotion to full membership in the Politburo in mid-1987 intensified conflicts within that body over the definition of official ideology and over the direction and control of the media and culture. These questions continued to divide the Politburo until its total transformation after the 28th Congress of the CPSU.

Gorbachev's redefinition of party officials' role also helped to foster discord within the Politburo and the Secretariat over the reform of the Council of Ministers' administration of industry. Gorbachev's effort to limit party officials' interference in the government's administration of industry encouraged Chairman Ryzhkov and other ministers to conclude that their own views would provide the basis for reform. But the general secretary revealed that he did not consider himself bound by his own strictures against "usurpation," and he repeatedly sought to impose his own radical views about the decentralization of industry on the leaders of the Soviet government. This produced a series of conflicts between Gorbachev and Ryzhkov over the proper way to organize the administration of industry.

During the same period, local party officials expressed their resistance to the general secretary's definitions. For years local party officials had played a very active role in industrial management by intervening to provide local enterprises with scarce resources and using their connections among their counterparts in other regions of the country to help the implementation of the five-year plans. Comments by party officials published in late 1987 in *Partiinaia Zhizn'* (the Central Committee's major journal for party officials) revealed that many of them preferred to continue to work this way.

This public resistance may have been encouraged by the apparent slackening in the general secretary's campaign on behalf of officials' "political work" during the last months of 1987 and the first months of 1988. Circumstantial evidence suggests that this shift reflected the general secretary's effort to respond to the internal party crisis created by Boris Yeltsin's blunt assault on the slow pace of reform. Gorbachev not only attacked Yeltsin in sharp terms, but also seemed to mute his own reformist formulations and to revert to more orthodox definitions in his public commentary. In this context his critics were able to express their orthodox criticism of the transformation of party officials' "ideological work" fostered by Yakovlev and his colleagues. Secretary Ligachev's report on problems of education to a meeting of the Central Committee in February 1988 reflected this orientation.

The proceedings of this meeting of the Central Committee in February 1988 seemed to indicate that a deadlock had been reached between Gorbachev and his critics. But within the next three months the general secretary moved vigorously to assure the implementation of his conception of officials' proper role. At the 19th Conference of the CPSU in June 1988 the general secretary explicitly ordered party officials to stop giving orders to state and Soviet agencies. He told them to replace their "command style methods with organizational, personnel and ideological work" and called for a complete reform of the Secretariat and apparatus to achieve this objective. At the same time he sought to make party officials more responsive to their various constituencies in two important ways. First of all, he insisted that they stand for election as party officials by their respective party committee. Second, he strongly suggested that they stand for election as the chairman of the executive committee of the local soviet.

These pointed suggestions reflected the general secretary's effort to "democratize" both the CPSU and the Soviet state by the introduction of competitive elections. Gorbachev had begun his campaign to have party officials elected by their committees at the Central Committee meeting in January 1987, but his suggestion had not been supported by the Central Committee and action on this issue was not taken until the 19th party conference in mid-1988. The general secretary's insistence that party officials also seek election as chairman of the local soviet was an outgrowth of his effort to restore "all power to the soviets." In his report to the Conference, the general secretary had denounced the "governmentalization" of life in the USSR and insisted that the extension of the authority of the soviets at all levels would fulfill the founding fathers' dream of a state based on popular participation. He called for granting soviets "full independent authority" in their respective regions and insisted that the Supreme Soviet of the USSR be transformed into a genuine legislative body. He also sought to assure his own authority over a rejuvenated Supreme Soviet by recommending the indirect election of a new chairman of that body with broad executive and legislative powers.

Gorbachev's proposals dealing with party officials' role did not go unanswered. Secretary Ligachev supported an all-inclusive definition of their responsibilities for all sectors of Soviet life in his own address to the Conference and to the Gorkii gorkom the following month. But in the fall of 1988 Gorbachev was powerful enough to brush aside these objections and to reorganize the departments of the Central Committee directed by the Secretariat and the apparatus of subordinate party organizations. The industrial departments of the Central Committee were eliminated and replaced with a department for social and economic questions. At the same time, six new commissions headed by Politburo/secretaries and staffed by members of the Central Committee were formed to deal with the most significant elements of party officials' work. Ligachev later charged that this reorganization was designed to destroy the Secretariat as a collective decision-making body, but this has proved difficult to verify, since the Secretariat continued to issue binding decrees. Whatever the exact status of the Secretariat, the new commissions began to play a more active role in policy making in the winter of 1989.

The reform of the departments of the Central Committee and the extension of the legislative authority of the elected soviets created an immense challenge to party officials at all levels of the apparatus. The decision to replace the centralized appointment of local party officials with their election by local party committees threatened to seriously undermine the Secretariat's traditional control over its key subordinates. Although the proposed electoral terms were quite long (four to five years), the party officials would clearly be obliged to become more responsive to their local constitutents than in the past in order to retain their authority. At the same time, the elimination of industrial departments at all levels of the system would limit officials' capacity to play their previous role in supervising the industrial establishments within their own bailiwick. (The departments for agriculture remained in place.)

Furthermore, by this time party officials' "ideological work" had been reduced to a shambles by Gorbachev's frontal assault on orthodox ideology and his growing embrace of important elements of both "social democratic" and "bourgeois democratic" ideology and practice. Party officials responsible for ideological work continued to portray the general secretary's numerous pronouncements as sources of guidance for all members of the CPSU. But his growing tendency to blur the lines between socialist and nonsocialist theory and practice and his eclectic definition of socialism destroyed the coherence of official ideology and enraged orthodox members of the leadership. Finally, with the transformation of the soviets into genuine legislative bodies, Gorbachev gave increasing attention to the "parliamentary role" of the CPSU. This shift raised serious questions about the continued political function of local party officials and their relationship to the Communists elected as deputies.

But it would be a mistake to conclude that the elimination of the industrial departments of the Central Committee had eliminated the authority of the Secretariat and its subordinate officials in dealing with economic affairs. General Secretary Gorbachev insisted that party officials should apply "political methods of leadership" to the solution of pressing social-economic problems rather than give direct orders to state officials as in the past. This rather vague formulation allowed local party officials to develop a number of rather ingenious ways to focus on the solution of citizens' immediate economic difficulties. In early 1989 *Partiinaia Zhizn'* began to publish articles by local party officials that demonstrated their capacity to interpret Gorbachev's formulations in ways that allowed them to retain authority in dealing with a range of social and economic issues. Finally, in mid-1989 the general secretary himself suddenly called on republican and regional party officials to develop "their own" programs of social and economic development responsive to local conditions rather than wait for guidance from the center.

Furthermore, the establishment of the commissions of the Central Committee provided a framework for the continued involvement of leading party officials in various spheres of economic activity. First of all, Secretary Ligachev's commission on agricultural policy attempted to improve the agricultural sector in a variety of ways and made use of the local agricultural departments in traditional fashion. Second, Secretary Sliunkov, who headed the new commission on social economic questions from 1988 until 1990, worked vigorously to assure that both his commission and the new social economic departments of local party units would assume responsibility for a wide variety of social-economic questions. In 1988–1989 he repeatedly urged them to focus on raising the standard of living of Soviet citizens, to assure the introduction of economic reforms, and to broaden the role of the primary party organizations (PPO) in enterprises to assure the fulfillment of these objectives. Furthermore, with the establishment of the Congress of Peoples' Deputies/Supreme Soviet as the USSR's legislature, Sliunkov broadened the scope of his commission's responsibilities. In 1989–1990 he openly criticized the various economic programs presented by the Council of Ministers of the USSR and called for their modification.

But in February 1990 the general secretary delivered a serious blow to his subordinates' remaining authority. After repeated assertions throughout 1989 that the USSR did not need a multiparty system, Gorbachev reversed his position and urged the members of the Central Committee to give up the CPSU's monopoly of political power. This decision destroyed the ideological basis for party officials' efforts to provide leadership for Communists in state agencies, and threw many officials into a state of confusion. During the next five months, the Secretariat and local officials seemed unable to provide a coherent conception of the role of party officials in a "multiparty" political system and focused almost exclusively on the preparations for the forthcoming 28th Congress of the CPSU.

But the Secretariat and its subordinates were saved by the reform of both the Politburo and Secretariat endorsed by the 28th Congress. The new Politburo was formed without any representatives of the Council of Ministers of the USSR, and their place was taken by the first secretaries of the Communist parties of all of the member republics of the USSR. The new Politburo seemed designed to coordinate the activities of the republican parties and reportedly was convened with less and less frequency over the following year.

In contrast, the reform of the Secretariat led to its reemergence as a vigorous leader of the apparat of party officials. The new party rules adopted by the Congress named the deputy general secretary the head of the Secretariat. With Ivashko's selection for this post, the Secretariat moved vigorously to restore the power of the apparat. The Secretariat was enlarged and proceeded to issue decrees that were clearly designed to restore officials' responsibilities and their capacity to provide direction for the Communists in state and Soviet agencies.

The reemergence of the Secretariat's authority was facilitated by the general secretary's absorption with other issues. During the last year of his reign Gorbachev was increasingly preoccupied with the challenges to both the USSR and the CPSU posed by Boris Yeltsin, who had been elected chairman of the Supreme Soviet of the RSFSR by the new Congress of Peoples' Deputies of the RSFSR in May 1990. In June the new parliament declared the Russian republic to be sovereign and in the following month a radical program for rapid transition to capitalism within the RSFSR (the so-called "500 days" program) was published. While the general secretary/president attempted to respond to these challenges, the Secretariat moved aggressively to broaden its own responsibilities. In October 1990 a number of new commissions of the Central Committee were established to deal with nationality questions, the regeneration of the primary party organizations, and other issues. During the following months these commissions and the departments of the Central Committee provided an increasing number of recommendations for action by the Secretariat. During the last months of 1990 and the first half of 1991, the Secretariat issued a series of decrees to local party officials that were designed to restore their responsibilities for both economic and ideological issues. By the middle of 1991 the Secretariat had become a major center of orthodox opposition to the general secretary and it fully supported the attempted coup against him in August of 1991.

The following analysis of Gorbachev's campaign to redefine party officials' responsibilities is based primarily on the following official publications of the CPSU.

(1) The published record of the leaders' pronouncements at the periodic meetings of the Congresses and Conferences of the CPSU, of the Central Committee of the CPSU, of various special convocations of party officials and others, and after 1989, of the Congress of Peoples' Deputies of the USSR. During the period from 1986 until 1991 the leaders generally followed the implicit provisions of what might be called the "etiquette" of internal party discussions. In the interests of maintaining an aura of party unity, the leaders were never to be attacked by name and disagreements were to be

expressed indirectly. Gorbachev's opponents expressed their disagreements with his formulations either by not repeating them in their own pronouncements, by modifying them in various ways, or by endorsing orthodox definitions. However, it must be emphasized that the public discussion of officials' responsibilities became less euphemistic over time as the limitations on speech were increasingly lifted. But there was considerable variation in the degree of various leaders' frankness. For example, Poltiburo/Secretary Yakovlev seemed to discard virtually all euphemisms after 1989, while Politburo/Secretary Ligachev did not.

Within this context, the clarity of the general secretary's own public statements varied considerably. His initial attempt to redefine party officials' priorities and responsibilities in his report to the 27th Congress of the CPSU in 1986 was rather muted and unclear. But as the campaign to persuade party officials to give more attention to "political work" gained momentum, he sometimes discarded his vague references to the role of "the party" to speak explicitly about party officials' responsibilities. When the campaign seemed to falter, either in the face of his opponents' resistance or because of the demands of more immediate pressing issues, his public comments became far less clear. He sometimes simply temporarily discarded his own reformist formulations or bracketed them with more orthodox definitions in an apparent effort to appease his critics. But at times his public comments were contradictory or confused to the point of incoherence. We regard these lapses as indications of his own unwillingness or inability to directly confront the unintended consequences of his own policies. In short, his discourse revealed that he sometimes did not know what to do and sought to disguise his own indecision with a variety of rhetorical devices.

In contrast, his major opponents did not seem to suffer from such difficulties. Yeltsin never disguised his conclusion that the party officials' authority had to be sharply curtailed, if not totally eliminated, and Ligachev consistently defended the view that party officials' responsibilities could not be curtailed without destroying the basis of "party leadership" of both state and society.

(2) The decrees and resolutions of the Congresses and Conferences of the CPSU, of the Central Committee, Politburo, and Secretariat. These decrees were usually based on detailed reports of the departments of the CC/CPSU that provided an analysis of the situation, the shortcomings to be overcome, and an outline of remedial measures. The decrees themselves often incorporated these suggestions or modified them.

The decrees were not only binding directives for all subordinate members of the CPSU, but also an important means to maintain the semblance of party unity. The formulations incorporated into these decrees reflected the "balance of forces" between the general secretary and his opponents at a particular time. As a result, when a deadlock developed between Gorbachev and his opponents, these decrees became so contradictory that they may have lost their value as a coherent source of direction. It is impossible to determine the extent to which these decrees were actually implemented, particularly after the growing divisions within the leadership after 1989. However, they did reflect the extent to which the general secretary's formulations were supported by other leaders at a particular time. The most important decrees were published in the annual *Spravochnik partiinogo rabotnika* through 1990.

(3) The materials published in the Central Committee's major journals *Partiinaia Zhizn'* and *Izvestiia TsK KPSS*. *Partiinaia Zhizn'* published major decrees and resolutions, summaries of the activities of the Politburo and Central Committee, and detailed articles by both party officials and specialists on all components of "party work." Its lead editorials reflected the state of play between Gorbachev and his opponents. When the general secretary was clearly "in command" the lead editorial would repeat his formulations verbatim. At other times the editorials reflected either the ascendancy of his opponents or the existence of some deadlock between them and the general secretary.

Most important, *Partiinaia Zhizn'* published lengthy essays by local party officials on their activities. These articles not only demonstrated the extent of their authors' support for the general secretary's definitions, but also illustrated how local officials actually sought to implement the leadership's formulations and the decrees of the Politburo, Secretariat, and Central Committee. These articles became increasingly outspoken in their criticism of the general secretary's views with the slackening of internal party discipline.

Shortly after the reform of the apparatus in the fall of 1988, the CC/CPSU launched a new journal, *Izvestiia TsK KPSS*. During the first year and a half of its existence, it seemed to serve as a "house organ" for the general secretary and his closest allies. Gorbachev was the chairman of the editorial committee that included both Medvedev and Yakovlev. Its summaries of the activities of the Central Committee seemed to endorse Gorbachev's formulations and many of the articles (but not all) by local party officials followed suit. It not only published all important resolutions by the leading organs of the CPSU, but also included fairly detailed reports of the deliberations of both the departments and newly formed commissions of the CPSU. By 1990 it had come to replace *Partiinaia Zhizn'* as the major "discussion journal" for the CPSU. (In 1990 *Partiinaia Zhizn'* changed its format in a way that made it difficult to determine its orientation.)

With the revival of the Secretariat after the 28th Congress of the CPSU, *Izvesttia TsK KPSS* shifted its direction. Deputy General Secretary Ivashko replaced Gorbachev as the chairman of the journal's editorial board and both Medvedev and Yakovlev were replaced by secretaries of the CC/CPSU with an orthodox orientation. From mid-1990 until the abortive coup against Gorbachev in August 1991, the journal became the major organ of the resurgent Secretariat and seemed to give preference to materials critical of the general secretary and his views.

Unfortunately for the student of politics in the USSR, these official publications do not make easy reading. The discourse is flat, unemotional, and bureaucratic in tone, and the discussion of significant issues is often conducted in euphemistic and indirect fashion. Many official declarations seem to be composed of contradictory formulations that were probably designed to placate warring factions. Sometimes significant formulations are buried in a sea of self-congratulatory rhetoric. As a result these materials are not easy to interpret without a clear sense of the central issues being discussed. But this was the discourse used by the officials in the CPSU. (Their memoirs and the archival materials used in recently published monographs reveal that the officials used the same discourse in their secret discussions, although they did seem to express their views more forcefully in these settings.) This study quotes extensively from published materials in order to demonstrate the significant differences between officials over the question of their role and responsibilities. As a result, the text is not always as dramatic as the issues under discussion.

This study also makes fairly extensive use of recently published memoirs by members of the leadership. This text uses the memoirs by the general secretary, by Politburo/Secretaries Medvedev and Ligachev, and by V. I. Boldin. (Boldin served as Gorbachev's personal assistant from 1985 until 1987 and then became the head of the general department of the Central Committee that was responsible for organizing the Politburo's agenda.) This study also makes extensive use of the detailed memoirs by N. I. Ryzhkov, who served as the chairman of the Council of Ministers of the USSR from 1985 until 1990.

I initially and rather naively hoped that it would be possible to reconstruct a coherent narrative of the leaders' secret deliberations on party officials' role from these memoirs. While the memoirs by Medvedev and Ryzhkov proved to be extremely helpful in this regard, the memoirs by other leaders provided contradictory accounts of the same discussions that could not be clearly resolved. Furthermore, the memoirs were often so vague and unclear about the timing of specific events that a fully coherent narrative could not be constructed. However, when the memoirs are read in conjunction with contemporaneously published material, they often helped to reveal the internal debates that lay behind the public discourse on these issues.

These materials indicate that the conflict between Gorbachev and his opponents over the definition of party officials' responsibilities in the period between 1986 and 1991 was never fully resolved. The issue was salient during most of the period under review but at times General Secretary Gorbachev seemed willing to drop the issue (at least in public) in the face of more pressing problems or to maintain at least a semblance of "party unity." For example, in the second half of 1987, when he seemed to focus on the reform of the administration of industry, the vigorous campaign to shift officials' priorities came to a temporary halt. It is at least possible that Gorbachev muted the campaign in order to win support for his efforts to decentralize the administration of industry. In the first half of 1990, when the general secretary called on party officials to focus on the preparations for the 28th Congress of the CPSU, the public discussion of officials' role seemed to be suspended. Moreover, at the congress itself, the leaders seemed to agree to limit their public discussion of the divisive issue in the interests of the unity of the CPSU.

The debate over the responsibilities of party officials was clearly influenced by the reform of major economic and political institutions in the period from 1985 until 1991. The efforts to decentralize the government's administration of industry and to introduce various elements of a "market economy" influenced the definition of "economic work" in dramatic fashion. Party officials were increasingly urged to help enterprises to introduce self-financing, various types of leasing arrangements, and to help to eliminate widespread "prejudices" against the market among Soviet citizens. These orders produced serious divisions among officials at all levels of the system. Some seemed to comply, while others openly criticized the entire effort to move toward the "market." At the same time, the transformation of the soviets into legislative bodies with genuine authority, and the general secretary's tendency to define the CPSU as a "parliamentary party," produced immense difficulties for local party officials in defining the scope of "political work."

Notes

1. Philip G. Roeder, *Red Sunset: The Failure of Soviet Politics* (Princeton, N.J.: Princeton University Press, 1993).

2. Compare Jerry Hough, *Democratization and Revolution in the USSR 1985–1991* (Washington, D.C.: Brookings Institution Press, 1997) with Gordon Hahn, *Russia's Revolution from Above* (New Brunswick, N.J.: Transaction Publishers, 2002).

3. Hahn, *Russia's Revolution from Above*, 18.

4. *Pravda*, July 19, 1989, 1.

5. Stephen White, *Gorbachev and After* (London: Cambridge University Press, 1991), 38.

6. Archie Brown, *The Gorbachev Factor* (London: Oxford University Press, 1996), 131.

7. Martin Malia reports that this distinction was made by George Orwell. See Martin Malia, *The Soviet Tragedy* (New York: The Free Press, 1994), 389.

8. The most detailed outline of these responsibilities is found in Jerry Hough and Merle Fainsod, *How the Soviet Union Is Governed* (Cambridge, Mass.: Harvard University Press, 1979), 412–417.

9. Merle Fainsod, *How Russia Is Ruled* (Cambridge, Mass.: Harvard University Press, 1953), 167–168.

10. Ibid., 172–174.

11. Ibid., 280.

12. V. I. Boldin, *Krushenie pedestala* (Moscow: Izdatelstvo Respublika, 1995), 202.

CHAPTER TWO

⬥

Gorbachev Campaigns for "Political Work" Forward and Back: 1986–1987

During his first year as general secretary, Gorbachev did not comment publicly on the role and responsibilities of the full-time party officials in the CPSU. But his actions suggest that he was moving toward the conclusion that the Secretariat and its subordinates should give greater attention to their "political work" and allow the Council of Ministers of the USSR under Chairman Ryzhkov greater responsibility for "economic work."

While it is difficult to conclude exactly why Gorbachev came to this conclusion, it is possible that his own early career may have created a predisposition toward this definition of officials' priorities. Gorbachev had always been a full time official in the CPSU, had never held a position in the state structure (except for his brief stint in the prosecutor's office), and had therefore never held direct responsibility for production. After his return to his home district of Stavropol in 1955, he worked for many years as a leader in the Komsomol movement. His first major appointment in the apparatus in 1962 gave him responsibility for "work with cadres"; in 1966 he was named first secretary of the Stavropol *gorkom*; and in 1970 the first secretary of the *kraikom*. All of these positions gave him vast experience in supervising and directing the activity of Communists in state and other agencies responsible for a wide variety of programs. A man of great personal charm, he may have concluded that his own successful "political work" might serve as an appropriate model for all party officials.

Whatever the impact of this early experience, Gorbachev did focus on personnel management and the modification of official ideology during his first year as general secretary. But he did not discuss party officials' responsibilities publicly until the 27th Congress of the CPSU. In his report to the Congress, Gorbachev launched his public campaign (in rather tentative fashion) to shift party officials away from direct and overt intervention in the administration of industry. (The responsibility of party officials for agriculture was evidently never in dispute.) Gorbachev's comments led to a serious division within the leadership of the "inner party" that continued throughout Gorbachev's tenure as general secretary.

Shortly after the 27th Congress, Gorbachev made his orientation far more explicit, and the campaign proceeded vigorously until shortly after a meeting of the CC/CPSU in January 1987. At this juncture the general secretary seemed to revert to a more orthodox position. While the reasons for this shift are not clear, it did encourage orthodox officials to express their views more openly. Public debate continued until mid-1987 when the Central Committee met to deal with the thorny issue of the administration of industry. In this context, Gorbachev seemed to focus his attention on the decentralization of industrial administration and the campaign to shift officials' priorities seemed to come to a temporary halt. In the aftermath of the meeting of the Central Committee, orthodox voices seemed to prevail.

As noted above, during the first year of his reign Gorbachev did not comment publicly on the role of party officials. But in the first months of his tenure he acted to bolster his own authority in the institutions that controlled them—the Politburo and Secretariat. First of all, he quickly established his own personal "brain trust" that included his closest allies in both bodies as well as a number of personal advisers and associates who held no such official position. The membership of this inner circle varied over time with the nature of the issues under discussion, but it did not include those members of the Politburo and Secretariat who were known to be opposed to or skeptical of the general secretary's position as well as all members of the Council of Ministers of the USSR. As a result, from the very beginning of his reign both the Politburo and the Secretariat were effectively divided between those who were also members of the "brain trust," such as Yakovlev and Medvedev, and those who were systematically excluded from its deliberations, such as Ligachev, Ryzhkov, and others.

Gorbachev not only excluded Ligachev from his inner circle, but also sought to limit his authority within the Secretariat. As the so-called "second secretary," Ligachev generally chaired the meetings of the Secretariat and he regarded himself as the leading authority on the management of personnel and control over the various elements of "ideological work." But it is important to remember that just a few months after being named general secretary,

Gorbachev named his own allies to head the departments of the Central Committee that were directly responsible for these spheres of activity. Gorbachev named Yakovlev as the director of the propaganda department and Razumovsky as the director of the organizational–party work department. These appointments did not change the institutional arrangements at the apex of the system, but they clearly made it increasingly difficult for Ligachev to assert his own authority in these areas and helped to intensify subsequent conflicts within both the Politburo and Secretariat.

From 1985 until 1990, the Politburo included the leaders of the "inner party" and the "outer party." The former included the Politburo/secretaries who provided the personal link between the Politburo and the Secretariat and who generally supervised a number of departments of the CC/CPSU. The leaders of the "outer party" included the chairman of the Council of Ministers of the USSR and other high ranking members of the council as well as the ministers responsible for foreign affairs, defense (sometimes as a candidate member), and the chairman of the KGB. The other members included the first secretaries of important republican and/or urban party organizations.

Although there were areas of disagreement over policy between these two groups, their relationship initially seemed to have been harmonious. The general secretary worked assiduously to name "like-minded" personnel to the Politburo, the Secretariat, the Central Committee, and the Council of Ministers, and seemed willing to grant primary responsibility for the administration of the five-year plans to the Council of Ministers headed by his comrade Chairman Ryzhkov.

During the first months of the regime, the Politburo/secretaries seemed to be sufficiently united in purpose to impose their preferences on the leaders of the Council of Ministers. In particular, the Politburo/secretaries evidently agreed on the need for a series of radical measures to deal with the problem of rampant alcoholism and were able to override the objections of the more cautious and pragmatic Politburo/ministers.[1]

Despite these disagreements, the general secretary and the chairman of the Council seemed to agree on a wide range of economic issues. First of all, they clearly decided to continue the reforms of industrial administration that had been instituted during the reign of Y. Andropov as general secretary. During the last years of Brezhnev's reign, the leadership had realized that the pace of economic growth had slowed and that the quality of both producer and consumer goods had sharply deteriorated. When Andropov succeeded Brezhnev as general secretary, he had encouraged a number of experiments in the administration of industry that were designed to grant enterprises greater autonomy from ministerial control and to help them become "self-financing" on the basis of their response to the market for their products. Gorbachev and Ryzhkov had worked together in the development of these reforms when they had both served as secretaries of the Central Committee under Andropov's leadership. Gorbachev explicitly endorsed these reforms in mid-1985, and he reports in his memoirs that the Politburo had agreed to extend them to the entire economy by early 1987.[2]

Gorbachev and Ryzhkov also initially shared the view that technological progress was the key to the modernization of Soviet industry. In fact, they had worked together to plan a Central Committee conference on technological progress before Gorbachev had become general secretary. When the conference was convened in mid-1985, it was attended by a wide range of governmental officials who were responsible for planning and administration. Its deliberations seemed to have a direct impact on Gorbachev's definition of priorities. Immediately after the conference, Gorbachev called for a massive investment in an "entire program of scientific-technological progress" focusing on the modernization of machine tools and the accelerated development of computer and information technology, robotics, biotechnology, and genetic engineering. This extraordinarily ambitious program was to be based on cooperation with the most advanced enterprises in the peoples' democracies in Eastern Europe and the establishment of joint enterprises with Western firms, particularly in the Federal Republic of Germany.[3]

Finally, Gorbachev shared Ryzhkov's conviction that the country's modernization could be accelerated by the bureaucratic reorganization of the state's administration structure. For example, the general secretary evidently concluded that the machine tool industry could be modernized by the establishment of a special bureau for machine tool construction in the Council of Ministers. Although he subsequently declared in his memoirs that this approach had been "one sided," he adopted a similar approach to the administration of agriculture at the same time. In November 1985 the Politburo endorsed the establishment of a superministry for agriculture to coordinate the activities of a number of ministries responsible for that sector. Headed by a deputy chairman of the Council of Ministers, it absorbed a number of specialized agricultural ministries and established its own subordinate units at the republican and local levels.

While Gorbachev seemed willing to grant considerable authority to Ryzhkov on these issues, he also evidently regarded himself as the "leader" of the USSR who transcended bureaucratically defined authority. During the second half of 1985 Gorbachev sought to bolster his popular support by travelling throughout the country and by unprecedented use of personal appearances on television. During these appearances, Gorbachev dramatized the stark differences between himself and his aged and infirm predecessors and represented himself as the courageous defender of the people against the indifference and insensitivity of local officials.

The general secretary not only represented himself as the "good tsar" defending the people against the bureaucracy, but also as the ideological leader of the CPSU. His subordinates in the propaganda department worked assiduously to assure that all of his pronouncements were repeatedly represented as having immense ideological and practical significance for all members of the CPSU. This became particularly evident after the 27th Congress of the CPSU convened in February 1986.

Gorbachev made his first public comments on the proper role of party officials in his detailed and elaborate report to the 27th Congress of the CPSU on behalf of the Central Committee. His comments on the economy seemed quite conventional, while some of his remarks on ideological questions verged on the heretical. He declared that the application of science and technology was the key to progress in every sector of the economy, endorsed the continuation of the experiments in industrial administration begun under Andropov, and called for serious improvements in the production of goods and services for the population as a whole.

But some of his ideological formulations were extremely unorthodox. He urged the CPSU to give up its claims to infallibility and engage in "criticism and self-criticism" and to improve its responsiveness to the real needs of Soviet society. These comments not only implied that the official version of Marxism-Leninism, which was ostensibly the basis for all the actions of the CPSU, was not only open to question, but also had diverted the party from its proper concern with the society's welfare. In the same spirit, he repeatedly criticized the continued tendency within the CPSU to discuss the country's problems in euphemistic fashion and implied that it was not very useful to blame these difficulties on the baneful influence of "bourgeois ideology." All of these statements implied that the nature and substance of "ideological work" would have to be changed.

Gorbachev also stressed other elements of the party's "internal" work. He called for the restoration of internal party democracy, urged party members to engage in more extensive criticism and self-criticism, and to live up to the formidable demands provided by the party's own rules. He also called on members of the CPSU to be more candid and open in discussing both plans and decisions and to show more modesty and humanity in their dealings with others.

But Gorbachev's initial comments on the role of party officials were far less assured. On the one hand, his references to "the party" and its local committees implied that full-time officials should limit their interference in both "state and public" agencies and instead focus on the management of personnel and the "verification of fulfillment" of state agencies under their supervision. On the other hand, he took great care to qualify his criticism of undue intervention by recognizing that party officials had difficulty distinguishing between the proper level of supervision and inappropriate "petty tutelage" and "confusion of functions."[4]

It is extremely difficult to determine why Gorbachev decided to raise this issue in this ambiguous way at this particular juncture. His extensive visits to various regions of the USSR in 1985–1986 may have convinced him that party officials' preoccupation with the demands of industrial production had made them neglect the pressing social and economic needs of the population. It is also possible that Gorbachev hoped to cement a cooperative relationship with Chairman Ryzhkov who deeply resented party officials' intervention in the government's implementation of the five-year plan. It is also possible that the ambiguity of his definitions may have been designed to placate more orthodox members of the leadership.

While Gorbachev's motives are not clear, his comments marked the beginning of conflict over the definition of officials' priorities that continued for the next five years. Most important, this conflict produced a sharp division between the general secretary and some of the secretaries of the CC/CPSU that was to plague him until the abortive effort to oust him. The opening round of this dispute came in the sharp exchange between Politburo/Secretary Ligachev and Boris Yeltsin, who was the first secretary of the Moscow *gorkom* and a candidate member of the Politburo at this time. Yeltsin did not mince words and clearly regarded Gorbachev's remarks as legitimizing a full-scale assault on party officials' alleged obsession with production. He charged that "party agencies have become so deeply enmeshed in economic affairs that they have sometimes begun to lose their positions as agencies of political leadership. It is no accident that the structure of the Central Committee departments has gradually become all but a copy of the ministries. Many people in the departments have simply forgotten what true party work is. There is complete duplication of the State Planning Committee and the Council of Ministers."[5]

Yeltsin singled out the department of organizational-party work, which was under Ligachev's supervision, for particularly sharp attack. He complained that it had become so engrossed in immediate economic problems that it had ignored the "degeneration of cadres." Yeltsin charged that the department's failures had contributed to a series of economic disasters in a number of critical regions. Yeltsin explicitly called for a complete reform of the Secretariat to meet the "new conditions" of perestroika.

In contrast, Ligachev vigorously defended the position that party officials were responsible for all of the important issues of the day. He ignored Gorbachev's comments about the "confusion of functions" between party officials and state agencies and defended an orthodox definition of party officials' responsibilities by emphasizing the "unity of the ideological, theoretical, organizational and entire practical work of the party." Ligachev also disagreed with the general secretary on ideological questions. He did not second the general secretary's comments about the fallibility of the CPSU, stressed the continued significance of party members' theoretical education, and balanced his praise for the media's exposure of "shortcomings" with praise for its positive portrayal of Soviet reality. Most important, he chastised *Pravda* for going too far in its discussion of the shortcomings of Soviet life.[6]

It is important to recognize that Gorbachev's views did not prevail at the 27th Congress. The wording of the new program for the CPSU that was adopted at the end of the Congress suggests that a temporary compromise had been reached between orthodox and reformist leaders over the definition of officials' priorities. The new program bracketed Ligachev's inclusive definition of party officials' responsibilities with a watered down version of Gorbachev's comments and reaffirmed the importance of Marxist-Leninist theory as the basis for the party's activity.[7]

But within a few months, the general secretary seemed able to brush aside orthodox objections and to provide a more coherent definition of party officials' priorities. In his report to a Central Committee meeting on June 16, 1986, Gorbachev moved beyond the ambiguous formulations of his report to the 27th Congress to complain that party officials had ignored the Congress's stress on the mastery of "political methods of leadership" and had continued to take on administrative functions. He now dropped his euphemisms to speak directly about party officials' role. He charged that they could "talk forever about production campaigns" but repeatedly failed to provide political analysis of social processes or to focus on emerging social-economic and scientific technological problems. He called for the elimination of "administrative approaches" at all levels of the apparatus and declared that only "thorough political, organizational and ideological work at all levels of party leadership" could solve the problems raised by the Congress.[8]

Gorbachev's "model" party official would be far more responsive to local conditions than the model official in the CPSU. He would be able to both assess and respond to changes in the mood and morale of local citizens, to become far more sensitive to their immediate social and economic needs. To achieve these objectives, he would have to move out of his office to "work with people" in a humane and compassionate fashion, and to investigate all aspects of Soviet life. Gorbachev may well have hoped that if officials would be able to act in this fashion they would help to provide the CPSU with a "human face" and thereby bolster citizens' faith in the CPSU and its leadership. Moreover, it is at least possible that Gorbachev regarded his own behavior, with its emphasis on a personal response to the solution of immediate problems, as a model for all party officials.

Gorbachev's remarks at the meeting of the Central Committee marked the beginning of a concerted campaign in support of his definitions. Published sources suggest that he delegated the leadership of this campaign to his loyal lieutenant and ally, G. Razumovsky. Razumovsky had been named a secretary of the Central Committee at the end of the 27th Congress, and he seemed to emerge as the major spokesman for the general secretary on this issue in June 1986. Writing in *Partiinaia Zhizn'* on the changes in the party's rules adopted by the 27th Congress, Razumovsky sharply condemned party officials' continued interference in administrative activity and urged them to act as "political leaders" dealing with the most pressing problems in their own regions.[9] He repeated the same argument later that month in his address to the graduating class of the Academy of Social Science of the Central Committee, one of the party's leading schools for its own officials.[10] In July *Partiinaia Zhizn'* endorsed this position in its lead editorial[11] and by the fall of 1986 a number of *obkom* secretaries described how they had fostered the development of "political methods of leadership" within their own regions.[12]

During the same period, the public discussion of various elements of "ideological work" suggests that the general secretary had sought to undercut Ligachev's authority by granting Yakovlev more responsibility in this sphere of activity. Yakovlev had been promoted to the position of secretary of the Central Committee at the 27th Congress in March 1986 and he began to appear in public along with Ligachev at various important cultural events.[13] But the media coverage of these events implied that Ligachev had retained a dominant position in dealing with the major elements of ideological work throughout the last half of 1986. While the two secretaries often appeared together in public, Ligachev's pronouncements were given more extensive attention by the media. For example, in April 1986 when both secretaries appeared at a conference of the country's leading theatrical workers, Ligachev's warnings about the ideological dangers of cultural liberalization were given extensive coverage. Ligachev lashed out against the "one-sided" portrayal of Soviet life that had appeared in recent theatrical works and he urged playwrights to give far more attention to the struggle against "bourgeois ideology" and the horrors of capitalist life.[14] In late June he stressed the overriding importance of a Marxist-Leninist worldview and a "class approach" to histori-

cal developments in his keynote address to a conference on education sponsored by the Central Committee.[15] In September he fulminated against the
ideological threats to Soviet youth from abroad in an address to the heads of
social science departments in higher education.[16]

While Yakovlev did appear with Ligachev at important cultural events, his
published remarks did not openly challenge Ligachev's position. For example,
his report on a conference on music sponsored by the Central Committee in
October 1986 carefully balanced orthodox and reformist formulations. On the
one hand, he explicitly opposed any ban against Western popular music or to
identify it as "low culture" as Ligachev and other conservative officials responsible for culture probably would have preferred. On the other hand, he
defined Western mass culture as "ideological-psychological aggression" designed to "dehumanize the masses" and insisted that Soviet music, as well as
all other cultural pursuits, should foster *ideinost*, patriotism, proletarian internationalism, and civic spirit among Soviet youth.[17]

Ligachev's continued authority over ideological questions was particularly
apparent in his selection to present the report marking the anniversary of the
Bolshevik revolution in November 1986. In his address Ligachev balanced
his general endorsement of reform with orthodox formulations stressing the
vast difference between socialism and capitalism and with fulsome praise for
the achievements of the USSR.[18]

But in late 1986 the general secretary directly challenged Ligachev's authority by an open assault on the existing system of personnel management—the key element in party officials' "political work." In his memoirs
Gorbachev claims that by the end of 1986 he had concluded that piecemeal
changes in personnel had not produced sufficient change in policy and that
the "entire cadre system" had to be reformed. Gorbachev reports that he had
ordered the organizational–party work department to provide a thorough
analysis of the "cadre question." He claims that he had been so dissatisfied
with the report, which had been produced under the supervision of Ligachev,
that he created a special working group to deal with the question. The group
was dominated by his closest supporters and evidently excluded members of
Ligachev's staff despite his generally recognized responsibility for supervising
personnel management.[19]

Medvedev, who was a member of this inner group, reports in his memoirs that he joined Yakovlev and Boldin in supporting a fundamental reform of the apparatus that moved far beyond the debate over priorities to
challenge the very basis of the Secretariat's control over local officials. He
claims that they had agreed that the centralized appointment of the first
secretaries of party committees had made them too powerful and therefore

had recommended that the officials should henceforth be elected by local committees from alternative candidates. This radical proposal threatened to undercut the Secretariat's control over its subordinates, to transform the relationship between the officials and their respective committees, and thereby threaten the capacity of party officials to provide "party leadership" at all levels of the system. As Medvedev subsequently recognized, this reform would transform the CPSU from being "an element in state power" into a genuine political party.[20]

In January 1987, the Central Committee was convened to discuss this issue and other aspects of personnel management. But the general secretary's report to the Central Committee moved far beyond the question of "work with cadres" to make a scathing assault on the legacies of the Stalinist regime. Gorbachev did not mention Stalin by name, but he now attributed all of the errors of his own predecessors to their continued support of Stalinist definitions of socialism. Gorbachev now argued that their "theoretical rigidity" had made it impossible to eliminate outmoded methods of economic administration, to correct obsolete attitudes toward property, to overcome the underestimation of the importance of economic levers, and to introduce socialist democracy. In addition, the general secretary charged that the previous regime's failure to improve the standard of living, to prevent the growth of social dislocation, consumerism, corruption, and its indifference to social questions had produced a massive gap between the world of everyday life and the world of "phony well-being."[21]

Gorbachev discussed party officials' responsibilities in this context. Most important, he now endorsed Yeltsin's earlier assertion that their preoccupation with production had a baneful impact on their management of personnel. He now charged that those officials responsible for the assessment and assignment of cadres had placed so much emphasis on their technical capacities that they had ignored essential qualities of leadership, such as the "breadth of insight" moral principle, and the capacity to persuade people to act. Gorbachev charged that this approach to cadre management had produced a "technocratic administrative pressure style of work" that had severely undermined officials' capacity to "work with people." The general secretary now insisted that this should be the "main element" of party work.

Gorbachev did acknowledge that party officials' absorption with industrial administration had reflected the rigidities of the existing system, but he insisted that the forthcoming economic reform would grant enterprises far greater autonomy and eliminate the party officials' temptation to "usurp" the authority of state administrators. The general secretary insisted that a focus on "political leadership" would make party officials more responsive to the social implications of economic policy and more aware of the social and economic needs of Soviet citizens.[22]

The Central Committee explicitly endorsed Gorbachev's position on this issue. Its resolution called on "party organs" to give up inappropriate administrative functions, to end their usurpation of "soviet organs, economic and social organizations," particularly at the *raikom* and *gorkom* levels.[23] It defined party committees as "organs of political leadership" that would make "concern with man"—the living and working conditions and ideological orientation of Soviet citizens—the center of their attention.

But the Central Committee did not adopt the recommendation to introduce the genuine election of party officials by their respective committees that had been supported by Gorbachev's more radical advisers and colleagues. The refusal of the Central Committee to adopt this position is often attributed to its members' opposition, but it must be emphasized that Gorbachev himself had approached this issue with great caution at the meeting of the Central Committee. He subsequently claimed in his memoirs that he and other members of the Politburo had endorsed the election of party officials on the eve of the meeting of the Central Committee, but his report to the Central Committee was in fact much more tentative on the issue. In his report he had characterized the proposal to elect officials as a "suggestion" that had emerged during previous discussions of internal party matters and he seemed to reassert the Secretariat's traditional prerogatives by adding that the personnel decisions of higher party bodies remained binding.[24] Whatever the basis for Gorbachev's caution on this issue, he did achieve genuine success at a meeting of the CC/CPSU. The Central Committee not only endorsed his view of officials' priorities, but also allowed him to make significant changes in the composition of the Politburo, which Medvedev later asserted had led to a "revitalization" of that body.[25]

But immediately after the meeting of the Central Committee, the general secretary seemed to tilt toward a more orthodox definition of officials' responsibilities. He now explained that the turn to "political leadership" did not demand a shift to "purely political activity" or reduce officials' responsibilities for economic and other questions, and he insisted that party officials should provide "leadership" for all specialized organs of administration.[26]

It is not clear why Gorbachev seemed to shift his position at this particular juncture. He may well have been responding to some shift of orientation within the Politburo, or he may have retreated temporarily on this issue in order to win support for more immediate priorities. But whatever the reason, his shift seems to have encouraged more orthodox officials to express their reservations about his initial position. In the spring of 1987 clear divisions of opinion reappeared among leading officials. While Secretaries Razumovsky and Yakovlev continued to campaign for far greater concern with "political work," regional leaders such as I. K. Polozkov, the first secretary of the Krasnodar *kraikom*, adopted a more orthodox position.

In the spring of 1987, Secretary Razumovsky gave the keynote address to a conference on the education of party officials sponsored by the Central Committee. He charged that the Brezhnev regime's preoccupation with production had led to a massive neglect of party officals' "party-political" education and that the faculty of the party's leading internal schools had ignored the decisions on this subject of both the 27th Congress and the Central Committee meeting of January 1987. He claimed that the problems created by party officials' "supplanting" of soviet and economic agencies had been overlooked by current faculty members and he recommended that they be replaced to ensure that officials would be trained to become "positive models in the political, cultural and moral sense."[27]

In April 1987 Secretary Yakovlev took the campaign to the republican Communist parties. In an address to the Central Committee of the Communist Party of Tadzhikistan, Yakovlev lashed out at local officials' failure to curtail their perennial intervention in the state's administration of the economy and to give sufficient stress to the "political leadership" demanded by the general secretary.[28]

Razumovsky repeated his critique in an address to a conference of personnel officers from the ruling Communist parties in Eastern Europe in May 1987. He insisted that the proposed extension of enterprise autonomy and the broadening of local soviet authority demanded that party officials adopt a "totally different approach" to these organizations to be based on personnel management, verification of fulfillment, and effective "work with people." At the same time, Razumovsky resumed the campaign for the election of party officials by their respective party committees.[29]

But I. K. Polozkov adopted a more orthodox stance. In early 1987 Polozkov had already expressed his reservations about the trajectory of reform. He had sharply questioned the media's growing criticism of the USSR's shortcomings in his address to the Central Committee in January 1987,[30] and his subsequent public comments on that meeting had ignored Gorbachev's critique of the Stalinist system.[31] His detailed discussion of the development of perestroika in his own region, published in the spring of 1987, balanced reformist and orthodox definitions of party officials' responsibilities in a particularly skillful fashion.[32] Moreover, in an elaborate essay published in *Partiinaia Zhizn'*, Polozkov ignored Gorbachev's strictures against officials' intervention, praised his own *kraikom*'s efforts to assure that state agencies fulfilled their targets, and explicitly declared that *gorkom* and *raikom* officials were responsible for all policies within their respective regions. He called for the establishment of special groups in both local committees and primary party organizations to assure the fulfillment of the targets set by the *kraikom*.[33]

This disagreement over party officials' priorities was paralleled by a growing dispute within the Secretariat between Secretary Ligachev and Secretary Yakovlev over both the nature of official ideology and the scope of party officials' "ideological work." This conflict had been prompted by Gorbachev's assault on Stalinist theory and practice in his report to the Central Committee in January 1987. In his report, Gorbachev had given considerable attention to the discussion of social sciences, which played a key role in the elaboration of official ideology. Gorbachev had charged that his predecessors' theoretical rigidity had forestalled "objective scientific analysis," produced useless "scholastic theorizing," and prevented the advancement of new ideas. His comments on cultural policy were equally blunt. He complained that cultural productions were often mediocre, and criticized the various unions of creative workers (writers, filmmakers, etc.) for their failure to support genuine talent and their "administrative interference" in cultural life.[34] The general secretary's criticism of the various unions of creative workers was an indirect assault on their supervisors in the cultural department of the Central Committee led by Secretary Ligachev.

Ligachev responded vigorously to Gorbachev's critique in the first months after the Central Committee meeting. In late February he told a conference of television officials to emphasize the positive aspects of Soviet life and expose "bourgeois" propaganda as well as criticize existing "shortcomings" in the USSR.[35] In March he told a meeting of members of the intelligentsia in Saratov that it was inappropriate to "criticize everything," reminded them that fine works of art and literature had been produced even during the period of "stagnation," and once again lauded the triumphs of revolution, socialist construction, and World War II.[36] In a second address in Saratov, he reemphasized the overriding importance of the "ideological content" of literary and artistic works, and derided the growing enthusiasm for literary works "previously unknown to the general public."[37] At the end of March he told a conference of media officials sponsored by the Central Committee that he strongly opposed the portrayal of the USSR's past as a "chain of mistakes and disappointments."[38]

But in April 1987 Ligachev seemed to lose the dominant position which he had enjoyed before the Central Committee meeting of January 1987 and Yakovlev seemed to emerge at least temporarily to take Ligachev's place. In early April Yakovlev gave the keynote address to a conference of media officials in which he vigorously endorsed Gorbachev's analysis of the Stalinist system and adopted a particularly liberal view of the role of the press.[39] In an address to representatives of the Tadzhik intelligentsia a few weeks later, Yakovlev launched a full-scale assault on the "dogmatism" of those who opposed reform. In the process, he defined the objectives of the USSR's cultural and intellectual life in strikingly humanistic terms. Yakovlev essentially dismissed the concept of a state-controlled cultural life, and called for a "humanist" review of technical industrial questions to assure that social needs were not neglected. Most startling, he asserted that society was in such constant flux that all social knowledge had become "non-axiomatic," a conclusion that clearly implied that virtually all existing "Marxist-Leninist" propositions were open to question. Yakovlev acknowledged as much by calling for the development of a "new theoretical approach" to be based on an analysis of perestroika in action.[40]

Yakovlev elaborated on his critique in a lengthy report to a conference of social scientists sponsored by the Academy of Sciences of the USSR in mid-April. He criticized them for their dogmatic opposition to such advances as cybernetics and mathematical modeling in economics, their "mindless support" for centralized economic management of the economy, and their ideological rationalization of the entire period of stagnation. He urged social scientists to discard their justifications of the status quo and their euphemistic portrayal of the USSR and instead provide "truthful" assessments of both the Soviet past and present. He heaped particular scorn on the ideological legacy of the Brezhnev era, which had emphasized the growing harmony and uniformity of Soviet society. Insisting that "contemporary socialism must first get to know itself," he urged social scientists to confront the country's problems rather than comment on pronouncements by the leadership and to revise interpretations of the past.[41]

The vast differences in orientation between Ligachev and Yakovlev had a profound impact on the entire process of reform; they made it impossible for the leadership to sustain a coherent program of "ideological work." From this point onward the party's "ideological workers" were confronted with two dramatically different ideological orientations within the leadership of the CPSU. Each secretary presented his own conception of the nature of the USSR's past, the very purpose of the various elements of "ideological work," the extent of the dangers posed by "bourgeois ideology," and the utility of the official tenets of Marxism-Leninism. While Ligachev continued to insist that the party leadership based its activities on "Marxism-Leninism," Yakovlev claimed that the practice of perestroika itself would provide the basis for a "new ideology." Ligachev clearly favored vigorous intervention by the departments of the Central Committeee concerned with ideological and cultural issues, while Yakovlev was bent on limiting the authority of these agencies. In these circumstances, party officials responsible for ideological work became so deeply divided that they were no longer able to support a single agreed-upon line. To make matters worse, in June 1987 Yakovlev was promoted to full membership in the Politburo. As a result, the fierce differences between the two secretaries spilled over into the meetings of the Politburo and intensified the conflicts within that body over the nature and scope of the party's ideological position.

It has proved impossible to determine Gorbachev's orientation toward this deep ideological cleavage. Boldin claims in his memoirs that Gorbachev had attempted to manipulate the two secretaries by throwing his support from one to the other on a variety of ideological issues.[42] Gorbachev gives this issue very little attention in his own memoirs. He clearly recognizes the conflict between the two and reports that he later named Ligachev to another position to lessen his alleged "domination" of ideological questions, but does not explore the issue in any detail.[43]

Whatever the case, as the party's "ideological work" fell into growing disarray, the general secretary began to focus on a fundamental reform of the state's administration of industry. Gorbachev's proposals for reform proved as divisive as the conflicts between Ligachev and Yakovlev. They undermined the alliance between the leaders of the "inner party" and "outer party" that had been created by the general secretary's redefinition of officials' priorities in 1986–1987. His insistence that party officials should limit their interference in industrial administration had initially seemed to imply that the Council of Ministers of the USSR would henceforth enjoy greater control over the administration of industry. But the general secretary and his closest supporters in the Politburo and Secretariat, all of whom had enjoyed successful careers in various sectors of "party political work," obviously did not regard themselves as constrained by the general secretary's injunctions against party officials' "interference" in state administration. As a result, throughout the discussion of the reform of industrial administration, which continued throughout 1987, the reformist leaders of the "inner party" sought to impose their views on the leaders of the "outer party."

Medvedev reports that the leadership's discussion of industrial administration began in early 1987 when sudden shortfalls in industrial production prompted the general secretary to search for some new ways to improve industrial performance. Gorbachev worked assiduously to broaden his own knowledge of economics and consulted with a wide range of academic specialists in the process. At the same time he convened an advisory group that included members of his own "brain trust" and a number of leading party and state officials, including Chairman Ryzhkov, to prepare the "basic concept" of the needed reform.[44]

Medvedev reports that sharp disagreement between the reformist leaders of the "inner party" and the leaders of the "outer party" developed immediately over the role of the state administration in the planning of industrial production. The leading governmental officials sought to retain traditional indicators of output and were extremely skeptical about further extension of autonomy to industrial enterprises and the reduction of state controls over both supply and prices. In contrast, the "theoreticians" (which included both the academic economists and the leading officials responsible for "political work") sought to eliminate traditional indicators of gross output, to introduce "economic methods" of planning and to reform the price system in ways which would allow individual enterprises to become genuinely "self-financing."

Medvedev's memoirs indicate that these basic differences were exacerbated by the method chosen to prepare proposals for discussion by both the Politburo and the Central Committee. Two groups were formed to work out these proposals. The first group, headed by Secretary Medvedev, was composed of academic economists and unidentified staff from the Central Committee and was held responsible for the preparation of "theses" that would provide the "general conception" of the reform. The second group, headed by Secretary Sliunkov, who was responsible for the supervision of industry, included a group of government officials and was charged with the demanding task of preparing draft decrees which would reform the systems for finance, supply, and prices. These proposals were to be submitted to Medvedev's group for its approval.[45]

This division of labor made it almost impossible to overcome the resistance of the leaders of the Council of Ministers to any proposal that threatened to undermine their role in the administration of industry. Medvedev reports that Chairman Ryzhkov strongly opposed any effort to eliminate the existing control figures or the state orders imposed on enterprises by ministries, and that other ministers paid "lip service" to the terminology used by the academic economists but followed their chairman's lead. Gorbachev subsequently complained that Gosplan, the Ministry of Finance, and the Ministry of State Supply regarded the establishment of self-financing enterprises as a threat to their control over the planning process.[46]

This conflict seriously undermined the relationship between General Secretary Gorbachev and Chairman Ryzhkov. Ryzhkov had evidently been pleased with Gorbachev's efforts to limit party officials' interference in the administration of industry, but he could hardly be expected to support the effort to undermine the Council of Ministers' prerogatives. While Ryzhkov was evidently willing to go along with the Politburo's endorsement of the "general theses" on the reform, he simply refused to endorse the specific proposals when they were submitted to the Central Committee for discussion and approval in June 1987.[47]

In the face of Ryzhkov's resistance, in late June 1987 the Central Committee finally hammered out a complicated and contradictory law on state enterprises that simultaneously seemed to grant individual enterprises greater autonomy from ministerial control and to emphasize the importance of state orders! The failure to resolve this fundamental contradiction helped to foster deep divisions at the apex of the political system. On the one hand, the general secretary was to blame the Council of Ministers and its chairman repeatedly for the alleged failure to implement the legislation.[48] On the other hand, the chairman of the Council of Ministers dates his disenchantment with the general secretary from this dispute over the administration of industry. In his memoirs Chairman Ryzhkov charged that Gorbachev's conception of an economic system composed of self-regulating independent enterprises was unworkable because it envisioned the elimination of the branch ministerial system without establishing any coherent system of management to take its place. Ryzhkov reports that he had initially believed that Gorbachev adopted this position because he simply did not understand the complexity of the branch ministerial system, but later came to the conclusion that Gorbachev had his "own line" and could not be convinced to change his views under any circumstances. Ryzhkov added that it was extremely difficult to counter the general secretary's reforming zeal even though he had no coherent sense of an alternative system of administration.[49]

Ryzhkov reports that the conflict over the decentralization of authority over industry divided the leadership into two warring camps. He claimed that the members of the Politburo who had experience in the administration of industry or agriculture had adopted a "realistic view" of the possibilities for administrative reform while those who had come to power through the "komsomol-party official path" adopted a radical orientation that ultimately led to the destruction of the economy.[50]

Ryzhkov charged that Gorbachev sided with the "ultra-radicals" in the Politburo (whom he identified as Yakovlev, Medvedev, and Shevardnadze) who seemed to believe that the establishment of a system based on fully independent enterprises would "work everything out." While Gorbachev joined this group, Ryzhkov and other members of the Politburo (he included Vorotnikov, Sliunkov, Zaikov, and Nikonov, and did not refer to Ligachev) shared the "reasonable position" of the factory directors who had worked on the government's own program of reform. Ryzhkov adds that when he asked Gorbachev why he repeatedly supported the views of radicals whose knowledge of economics was purely academic and ignored the views of those with practical experience, the general secretary had no reply![51]

The approval of the decentralization of the state's management of industry by the Central Committee in late June seemed to have a direct impact on the debate over party officials' priorities. As noted above, Gorbachev's apparent retreat from his reformist position after the meeting of the Central Committee in January 1987 had allowed orthodox voices on this issue to be heard. Gorbachev did not comment on this issue during the meeting of the Central Committee in June and the public campaign urging party officials to adopt "political methods of leadership" was temporarily muted. More orthodox views on officials' responsibilities and the nature of official ideology were given greater coverage.

This shift is not easy to explain. While the contemporary published sources do not provide any useful clues, Gorbachev later charged that the "majority" of local party officials had proved to be either unwilling or unable to adjust both to glasnost and the decentralization of industrial administration.[52] It is possible that this resistance may have been sufficiently strong to block temporarily the general secretary's campaign to shift party officials' priorities. It is also possible that Gorbachev muted this campaign in order to win party officials' support for the decentralization of industrial management. Whatever the reason, after the meeting of the CC/CPSU in June 1987 Gorbachev's major spokesman on this issue felt obliged to give more attention to orthodox formulations. In July 1987, Secretary Razumovsky, who had led the campaign to shift officials' orientation, now muffled his reformist stance. In an address to the graduates of the Central Committee's Academy of Social Sciences he now characterized perestroika as an outgrowth of the leadership's commitment to Marxism-Leninism, rather than as a radical break with the past, muted his previous insistence that party officials act as "political leaders," and seemed to embrace the view that they were responsible for all sectors of public policy within their jurisdictions.[53]

While Razumovsky muffled his earlier position, Secretary Ligachev's orthodox views were given prominent attention. In an extensive discussion with the editors of Sovetskaia Kultura he energetically defended the concept of party and state direction of the country's cultural life, explicitly sided with a group of orthodox writers who had condemned the reluctance of many of their colleagues to even refer to the CPSU, and urged editors to give more attention to the leadership's views on cultural matters.[54]

The revival of attention to orthodox formulations continued into the summer and fall of 1987 when both Gorbachev and Yakovlev retreated from public view in order to write Gorbachev's book on perestroika. Their absence coincided with the emergence of debate over the proper interpretation of the Stalinist regime. This had become an increasingly important ideological issue with the approach of the celebrations for the seventieth anniversary of the Bolshevik revolution.

In Gorbachev's absence, Ligachev moved quickly to question the need for a full reappraisal of Stalin and his legacy. In an address to a conference on education in August 1987, Ligachev had insisted that the 20th Congress of the CPSU had already resolved the question of the "cult of personality," and he had described the 1930s in strikingly positive terms. He declared that this decade had not only brought industrialization and collectivization to the USSR, but had carried the country to new heights in culture, education, and other areas. Ligachev had evidently sought to play down the significance of the purges by asserting that the "majority" of those who had suffered repression had remained "true to socialism." Ligachev also provided a far more positive appraisal of the Brezhnev/Kosygin regime than the general secretary by claiming that he had enjoyed a "great life" in the 1960s and 1970s in Western Siberia despite the regime's failure to cope with the system's various problems.[55] He repeated his call for a more "balanced" view of the USSR's past accomplishments in his address to a conference on the seventieth anniversary sponsored by the Central Committee the following month.[56]

In this context, *Partiinaia Zhizn'* now followed Ligachev's orthodox lead in its discussion of the education of party members and the responsibilities of party officials. Its editorial on the system of political and economic education repeatedly stressed "Marxist-Leninist education" as the key to the mobilization of society and to the realization of the potential of the "human factor."[57] Furthermore, the journal of the Central Committee published articles by local party officials which described their constant intervention in the details of industrial development in very positive terms.[58] The rare discussion of "political methods" of leadership focused exclusively on the importance of the selection, appointment, and education of cadres.[59]

As the seventieth anniversary of the Bolshevik revolution approached, the general secretary clearly understood that he would have to confront the entire issue of Stalin and Stalinism in his report. Indeed, in his memoirs he claims that he had already begun work on this report before his extensive vacation.[60] To prepare his address, which would help to restore a clear sense of direction for the confused "ideological workers," Gorbachev established a small working group composed of his most radical advisers. Medvedev reports that it included himself, Yakovlev, Frolov, and Cherniaev.[61] Medvedev reveals that the draft prepared by this working group, which was highly critical of Stalin and his policies, was criticized sharply by orthodox members of the Politburo when it was submitted to the Politburo for discussion and approval. Medvedev claims that he and Yakovlev and Shevardnadze were the only members of the Politburo to support the original draft while the majority wanted a more celebratory version of the USSR's history.[62]

In October 1987 the Central Committee convened to hear the report of the general secretary. On October 21, 1987, after Gorbachev had finished outlining the major elements of his draft report on the anniversary of the revolution, Boris Yeltsin was allowed to speak. In a brief and confusing speech, Yeltsin charged that perestroika had not yet brought concrete benefits to the population, that enthusiasm for reform had begun to wane, and that Soviet citizens would lose faith in the CPSU unless the process of change was quickened. He claimed that "some members" of the Politburo had tended to glorify the general secretary and warned that this tendency could have negative consequences for the country as a whole.[63] Yeltsin also complained bitterly about the Politburo's alleged failure to promote him to full membership in that body and his ongoing conflicts with Ligachev. He implied that he should be allowed to give up his position as a candidate member of the Politburo, and he suggested that the Moscow party organization be permitted to determine his fate as first secretary of the *gorkom*.

Yeltsin's remarks produced an uproar of reproach at the Central Committee meeting. The general secretary and many other members of the Central Committee attacked Yeltsin in strikingly orthodox terms and the Central Committee officially condemned his remarks as "mistaken."[64]

This surge of orthodoxy in the Central Committee seemed to convince Gorbachev that he would have to retreat from his reformist position on a variety of important ideological issues. This shift in orientation became particularly evident when he presented his final report on the anniversary of the Bolshevik revolution in early November 1987. Gorbachev now provided a far more "balanced" portrayal of Stalin than envisioned by his original radical working group. He did condemn the purges of the CPSU in the 1930s, as Khrushchev had done in both 1956 and 1961, and he made an unprecedented attack on the immense human cost of collectivization in the early 1930s, which Khrushchev had ignored. But he made no reference to Lenin's well-known "testament" of 1923 (as Khrushchev had done in his address to the 20th Congress of the CPSU), and he explicitly represented Stalin as a vital and effective counterweight to Trotsky in the 1920s. Finally, Gorbachev lauded the policies of state-led industrialization and collectivization carried out under Stalin's direction and he warmly defended both Stalin's pact with Hitler in 1939 and his leadership of the country during World War II.[65]

Gorbachev also retreated to a more orthodox position later that month when he met with the secretaries of the Central Committee and the heads of its departments in late November 1987. The published report of this meeting indicated that Gorbachev did not even mention Stalin by name in his discussion of the USSR's past,[66] and his definition of party officials' priorities was now far more "balanced" than his earlier pronouncements on the subject. Gorbachev reportedly had declared that the growing democratization of the society and the radical economic reform demanded a "reconceptualization" of the role of the CPSU as the "political vanguard" of the society. He also had insisted that the introduction of *khozraschet* in enterprises would make it impossible for officials to command "in the old way." But he did not criticize party officials for "supplanting" state and soviet officials, urge them to give more attention to "political leadership," or imply that they had to be elected by their respective committees. In fact, his ambiguous comments on the role of "the party" seemed to imply that its officials were responsible for the co-ordination of a wide range of activities and should give more attention to the activities of the primary party organizations. He was completely clear on one point—the need to instruct all party members about the forthcoming intro-duction of "self-financing" and the "new economic mechanism."[67]

Gorbachev also adopted a more orthodox position in regard to party offi-cials' control over the media. The published report on his meeting with the leaders of the Secretariat revealed that many of them had called for more su-pervision of the media by party officials. Gorbachev now seemed to adopt this position as his own. He not only implied that the journalists' coverage of the activities of local party officials' had been inadequate, but overtly called for more explicit "cooperation" between the two groups.[68] The general secretary retained this position in the first months of 1988. In early January, he warned a group of editors and cultural leaders that there were "limits" to glasnost and urged them not to engage in recriminations against those who might hold "outmoded" views but who still worked for reform. He concluded that "we are for glasnost in the interests of socialism" and assailed any drift toward "bourgeois liberalism."[69]

Gorbachev's retreat toward orthodoxy may have been designed to placate those members of the Politburo who had assailed Secretary Yakovlev for un-dermining party officials' control over the media.[70] Gorbachev later revealed that a conservative coalition in the Politburo (it included Ligachev, Solo-mentsev, Chebrikov, Yazov, and later Ryzhkov) had charged that Yakovlev had allowed the publication of far too much criticism of both party and state officials and had demanded the restoration of greater controls over both the press and television.[71]

Gorbachev's sensitivity to orthodox opinion on this issue did not constrain him from acting vigorously to extend the scope of economic reform. Ligachev reports in his memoirs that in the last weeks of 1987 the general secretary essentially browbeat Chairman Ryzhkov and other members of the Politburo to accept the extension of the autonomy of enterprises far beyond that envisioned in the law on state enterprises. Ligachev charges that Gorbachev insisted that enterprises be allowed to sell significant portions of their output without central control. In Ligachev's view, this established the basis for a "market economy" in some sectors (while leaving others under state direction) which led to the subsequent disintegration of the entire planning system.[72]

Despite this victory in imposing his reformist views on economic administration on other members of the Politburo (which was not made public at the time), the general secretary remained responsive to orthodox views on ideological issues. This became apparent during the Central Committee's discussion of the reform of higher education in February 1988. Ligachev gave the main report, which clearly implied that he remained the leading authority on the subject. In his discussion of "party guidance" of educational reform Ligachev charged that many Soviet youths had become indifferent to politics, had embraced "bourgeois" conceptions of morality, and had fallen under the influence of "primitive" religious views and nationalist orientations. He repeated his criticism of "one-sided" interpretations of the history of the USSR and portrayed Gorbachev's report on the seventieth anniversary of the revolution as a model of correct historical analysis. He insisted that "mastery of theory" was essential to understand current developments, lashed out against those who had used glasnost to ignore the achievements of the past, and he called on all party members to "uphold the honor and dignity of the trailblazers of socialism."[73] Finally, Ligachev warned against the dangers of drifting toward "bourgeois liberalism," and demanded more thorough "ideological vigilance" and a more "class conscious" educational system.

Gorbachev's own report to the Central Committee meeting[74] made a number of significant concessions to orthodox opinion. He indirectly acknowledged the legitimacy of orthodox complaints by admitting rather ruefully that the recent economic reforms (the introduction of cooperatives, the legalization of a limited range of private economic activity, and greater autonomy for enterprises) had produced significant ideological and organizational confusion within the CPSU. He also incorporated some of Ligachev's strictures about the dangers of "rewriting history" into his own report. He balanced his call for an "examination of current reality" and the elimination of "outmoded definitions" with a very sharp attack on those who had incorrectly portrayed the USSR's history as a series of "bloody crimes."[75]

The public coverage of this meeting of the Central Committee indicated that a deadlock may have developed within the top leadership of the CPSU over ideological issues. *Pravda's* coverage of the deliberations of the Central Committee gave roughly equal coverage to the reports by Ligachev and Gorbachev.[76] Furthermore, Yakovlev's briefing on the meeting seemed to be designed to disguise the evident gains made by Gorbachev's critics. He did not even refer to Ligachev's report, focused on practical issues of educational reform, and totally ignored Gorbachev's lapses into orthodoxy.[77]

This deadlock in the Politburo evidently encouraged the most ardent critics of the general secretary and his program to launch a concerted attack against perestroika. On March 13, 1988, *Sovetskaia Rossiia* published a letter from N. A. Andreeva, a teacher in Leningrad, that cited Ligachev's report to the Central Committee (without direct attribution) in support of its political orthodoxy. This broadside not only assailed the widespread criticism of Stalin and his regime, but also implied that the critics of the USSR's past and present were the offspring of discredited "anti-Soviet" elements from the past. This letter made a savage attack on the so-called "left liberal socialists" whose "indifference" to the achievements of the USSR and criticism of past leaders had undermined the prestige of the current leadership of the CPSU.[78]

Boldin claims that Gorbachev had initally given little attention to this letter until prodded by Yakovlev, who was clearly a major target of this critique. Gorbachev then insisted that the letter be discussed in the Politburo. His summary of this discussion in his memoirs reveals that the majority of its members were either indifferent or sympathetic toward the letter and that Yakovlev, Zaikov, and Shevardnadze were the only members of the Politburo who agreed that it deserved public condemnation.[79] This low level of support for the general secretary may help to explain the delay in the leadership's public response to the letter. It was not until early April that *Pravda* argued that it was essential to criticize the Stalinist past to prevent its return.[80]

Notes

1. The memoirs by the leading participants involved in this decision differ sharply over the attribution of responsibility. Gorbachev argues that the entire Politburo supported the policy and ignores the proposals made by the leading ministers in the Council of Ministers. Ryzhkov stresses the limited proposals made by the government to deal with the crisis. Boldin holds the general secretary responsible for the excesses in the implementation of policy. Compare Mikhael Gorbachev, *Zhizn' I reformy* (Moscow: Novosti, 1995), vol. 1, 340–341 with N. I. Ryzhkov, *Desiat let velikikh potriasenii* (Moscow: Assositsiatsiia KPM, 1995), 110, with Boldin, *Krushenie*, 141–142.

2. Gorbachev, *Zhizn'*, 342.

3. Ibid., 337.

4. *Current Soviet Policies*, vol. 9 (Columbus, Ohio: Current Digest of the Soviet Press, 1986), 40.

5. Ibid., 66.

6. Ibid., 74–76.

7. Ibid., 157.

8. See the text of his report in *Partiinaia Zhizn'*, no. 13 (1986), 24.

9. G. Razumovsky, "Ustav kpss-nezyblemi zakon zhizn' partii," *Partiinaia Zhizn'*, no. 12 (1986), 16. Approved for publication June 10, 1986.

10. *Pravda*, June 28, 1986, 2.

11. "Energichno vesti perestroiku partiinoii raboty," *Partiinaia Zhizn'*, no. 14 (1986), p. 16. Approved for publication July 8, 1986.

12. A. Khomiakov, "Osvaivat politicheskie metody rukovodstva, otkazyviat'siia ot administrativno-komandogo stiliia," *Partiinaia Zhizn'*, no. 19 (1986), 29–31, approved for publication September 23, 1986. V. Sitnikov, "Partiinyi komitet: osvaivat politicheskie metody rukovodstva," *Partiinaia Zhizn'*, no. 23 (1986), 11–14, approved for publication November 25, 1986.

13. See the materials published in *Spravochnik partiinogo rabotnika 1986* (Moscow: Politizdat, 1987), 215–218.

14. Ligachev's remarks were published in full in *Teatr*. A condensed version of this report appears in *Current Digest of the Soviet Press* (CDSP) 38, no. 44, 1–2.

15. *Spravochnik partiinogo rabotnika*, 235–236.

16. *Pravda*, October 2, 1986, 2.

17. *Spravochnik partiinogo rabotnika*, 262–265.

18. *Pravda*, November 7, 1986, 1–3.

19. Gorbachev, *Zhizn'*, 306.

20. Vadim Medvedev, *V komande gorbacheva* (Moscow: bylina, 1994), 45.

21. M. S. Gorbachev, *Izbrannye rechi i stat'i* (Moscow: politizdat, 1987), vol. 4, 305.

22. Ibid., 333–334.

23. *Partiinaia Zhizn'*, no. 4 (1987), 51.

24. Gorbachev, *Izbrannye*, 322.

25. Medvedev, *V komande*, 41.

26. For the text of his remarks see *Partiinaia Zhizn'*, no. 6 (1987), 4.

27. *Pravda*, April 4, 1987, 2; G. Razumovsky, "Sovershenstvovat podgotovki I perepodgotovkii rukovodiashchikh kadrov partii," *Kommunist*, no. 9 (1987), 3–4. Approved for publication May 21, 1987.

28. A. N. Yakovlev, "Glavny v perestroike segodniia-prakticheskie dela i konkretny rezultaty," *Partiinaia Zhizn'*, no. 19 (1987), 7–16.

29. G. Razumovsky, "Partiinuiu raboty-na uroven zadachi perestroiki," *Partiinaia' Zhizn'*, no. 12 (1987), 6–10.

30. Gorbachev, *Zhizn' I reformy*, 310.

31. *Pravda*, February 11, 1987, 2.

32. I. Polozkov, "Ne dliia parada," *Idet perestroika* (Moscow: Politizdat, 1987), 81, 97–98.

33. I. Polozkov, "Organizatsiia proverka ispol'neniia," *Partiinaia Zhizn'*, no. 11 (1987), 9–17. Approved for publication May 26, 1987.

34. Gorbachev, *Izbrannyi rechi i stat'I*, vol. 4, 334.

35. *Pravda*, February 24, 1987, 2.

36. *Pravda*, March 3, 1987, 2.

37. *Pravda*, March 6, 1987, 2.

38. *Pravda*, March 24, 1987, 2.

39. *Pravda*, April 1, 1987, 2.

40. *Pravda*, April 19, 1987, 3.

41. Yakovlev's report was summarized in *Pravda*, April 10, 1987, and published in incomplete form in *Kommunist* in May. See A. N. Yakovlev, "Dostizhenie kachestvennogo novogo sostoianiia sovetskogo obshchestva I obshchestvennye nauki," *Kommunist*, no. 8 (1987), 4–20.

42. Boldin, *Krushenie*, 162.

43. Gorbachev, *Zhizn'*, vol. 1, 410.

44. Medvedev, *V komande*, 48.

45. Ibid., 49–50.

46. Gorbachev, *Zhizn' i reformy*, vol. 1, 352.

47. Ibid., 356–357.

48. Ibid., 357–360.

49. Ryzhkov, *Desiat*, 195.

50. Ibid., 198–199.

51. Ibid., 200.

52. Gorbachev, *Zhizn'*, vol. 1, 367–368.

53. *Pravda*, July 28, 1987, 3.

54. Excerpts from Ligachev's report in *Sovetskaia kultura* (July 7, 1987) were published in the *CDSP* 39, no. 34, 15.

55. *Pravda*, August 27, 1987, 2.

56. *Pravda*, September 17, 1987, 2.

57. "Politicheskaia I ekonomicheskaia ucheba trudiashchikhsiia: sluzhit delu revoliutsionnogo obnovleniia obshchestva," *Partiinaia Zhizn'*, no. 19 (1987), 14–20. Approved for publication September 29, 1987.

58. V. Egovkin, "Gorkom partii: v tsentre vnimaniia rekonstrukysiia proizvodstva," *Partiinaia Zhizn'*, no. 18 (1987), 36–40. Approved for publication September 8, 1987.

59. Z. Borovika, "Raikom: desitvovat politicheskimi metody," *Partiinaia Zhizn'*, no. 22 (1987), 53–54. Approved for publication November 10, 1987.

60. Gorbachev, *Zhizn'*, vol. 1, 365–367.

61. Medvedev, *V komande*, 59.

62. Ibid., 60–62.

63. For the full text of Yeltsin's address see *Izvestiia TsK KPSS*, no. 2 (1989), 240–241.

64. For the most detailed discussion of this speech and its aftermath, see Leon Aaron, *Yeltsin: A Revolutionary Life* (New York: St. Martin's Press, 2000), 202–217.

65. *Pravda*, November 3, 1987, 2–3.

66. "Byt v avangarde, rabotat po-novomu. Soveshchanie v TsK KPSS," *Partiinaia Zhizn'*, no. 23 (1987), 6–7. Approved for publication November 24, 1987.

67. Ibid., 10.

68. Ibid., 10–11.

69. *Pravda*, January 13, 1988, 1.

70. Yakovlev had not attended the meeting between Gorbachev and the editors. See *Pravda*, January 9, 1988, 1.

71. Gorbachev, *Zhizn'*, vol. 1, 378.

72. Yegor Ligachev, *Inside Gorbachev's Kremlin* (New York: Pantheon Books, 1993), 339–342.

73. *Izvestiia*, February 18, 1988, 4.

74. In his memoirs, Gorbachev claims that he had decided to present his own report to the Central Committee to balance Ligachev's report without "interfering" in Ligachev's preparations of his own report. See Gorbachev, *Zhizn'*, 378.

75. *Pravda*, February 19, 1988, 3.

76. *Pravda*, February 18–21, 1988.

77. *Pravda*, February 27, 1988, 2.

78. For excerpts from the text see *CDSP* 11, no. 13, 1–2.

79. Gorbachev, *Zhizn'*, vol. 1, 381–386.

80. *Pravda*, April 5, 1988, 1.

~⊛~

The 19th Conference of the CPSU and the Reform of the Party's Apparat: 1988

Gorbachev had clearly made concessions to his orthodox critics at the meeting of the Central Committee in February 1988. But in the following months he revived his campaign to persuade party officials to adopt "political methods of leadership" in preparation for the 19th Conference of the CPSU scheduled for June 1988. In his elaborate and radical report to the Conference, Gorbachev combined this campaign with an effort to broaden the authority of both the executive and legislative branches of the central government and an attempt to elaborate a "new definition of socialism" to replace the orthodoxies of the past.

The general secretary proved to have sufficient authority to persuade the delegates to the Conference to endorse his position despite considerable overt criticism from orthodox officials. As a result, he was able to force through a fundamental reform of the departments of the Central Committee in the fall of 1988. The reform was overtly designed to force party officials to end their "interference" in industrial administration and give primacy to "political methods of leadership" by eliminating all of the industrial branch departments of the CC/CPSU except the defense department and by creating new commissions of the Central Committee. (The departments for agriculture were not eliminated.)

But the reform of the departments of the Central Committee did not end conflict over the definition of party officials' role and responsibilities. Gorbachev and his allies proved unwilling or unable to provide a coherent definition of "political methods of leadership," and this failure allowed party officials at various levels of the system to respond in a variety of ways. The secretaries of the Central Committee who headed the new commissions for agriculture and for social-economic affairs continued to focus on the details of "economic work." At lower levels of the apparatus some officials openly expressed their confusion about the implementation of the reform and others continued to act "in the old way" or attempted to establish new institutions that would allow them to deal with economic problems in a less intrusive fashion. Most important, many leading orthodox officials portrayed this confusion as a vindication of their criticism of the general secretary.

The other major reforms endorsed by the 19th Conference also produced a variety of unintended consequences. The extension of the authority of the Council of Ministers prompted leading officials such as Chairman Ryzhkov to press for more independence than envisioned by the general secretary. And as will be discussed in detail below, the transformation of the soviets into legislatures with genuine authority produced a series of headaches for party officials at all levels of the system. Finally, Gorbachev's efforts to develop a "new definition of socialism" produced nothing but further confusion in the party's "ideological work." In his report to the 19th Conference, Gorbachev lumped together revisionist and orthodox formulations in a contradictory pastiche. His eclecticism made it impossible for Secretary Medvedev, the new head of the Central Committee's ideological commission, to formulate a coherent ideological position for the CPSU.

The incoherence of official ideology became alarmingly obvious in the fall of 1988 when the leadership of the CPSU was suddenly forced to deal with a sudden surge of nationalist sentiment in the Baltic and other republics of the USSR. The leaders quickly discovered that the "new definition of socialism" could not provide any guidance for dealing with this unprecedented challenge. Nor could it help party officials to orient themselves to the new world of electoral politics opened up by the elections for the Congress of Peoples' Deputies of the USSR in the first months of 1989.

As noted above, in the first months of 1988 Gorbachev was preparing to launch a major assault against his orthodox opponents at the forthcoming 19th Conference of the CPSU. Medvedev reports that in January 1988 the general secretary had already named an enlarged "brain trust" dominated by his most reformist colleagues and advisers to prepare for the Conference.[1] Materials published in *Partiinaia Zhizn'* in March indicated that the general secretary had decided to revive his campaign to persuade party officials to give more attention to their political work. The lead editorial in *Partiinaia Zhizn'* no. 6 (1988) repeated verbatim the formulations used by Gorbachev in January 1987 on the need for party officials to provide "political leadership," and now extended the definition of this term to embrace criticism and self-criticism, internal democratization, and glasnost.[2] *Partiinaia Zhizn'* reminded its readers that party bodies should act as organs of "political leadership" rather than as organs of economic administration, condemned party officials for acting in the name of their committees without sufficient consultation with them, and represented the election of party officials by their respective committees as essential to the democratization of the CPSU.[3]

Shortly afterward, local party officials joined the campaign. For example, in April 1988, V. Novikov, a secretary of the Moscow *obkom*, urged party officials to focus on "organizational, upbringing, and ideological work" and defined "political leadership" as cadre work, improved supervision, and the coordination of efforts by soviet, trade union, and economic organs to solve social economic problems.[4] At the same time *Partiinaia Zhizn'* published a suggestion that the industrial branch departments at the *gorkom* and *raikom* be eliminated in order to end continued "substitution" by party officials.[5] During the same period, Gorbachev personally sought to bolster support for his program among party officials. He claims in his memoirs that he met with 150 local party officials in the last months before the 19th Conference and discovered that they were deeply divided. Some of them supported his orientation, but many others had distributed or republished the letter from Andreeva in the local party press.[6] These divisions became all too evident in the discussion of his report to the 19th Conference in June 1988.

In his report Gorbachev revised major tenets of official ideology in a fundamental way. While he continued to define the CPSU as a "vanguard" party, he also endorsed various elements of "bourgeois democratic" theory and practice that had been repeatedly reviled in the past. After attacking Stalin's reign in particularly vigorous terms (he now asserted that the "political deformation" of the Soviet system after the revolution had led to the "absolute power" of Stalin and his entourage),[7] he explicitly defined the extension of freedom of expression and freedom of religion as major goals of the Soviet system and proudly listed a series of improvements in citizens' civil liberties achieved under his reign. At the same time, he gave considerable attention to the need for a "law based state" that would provide a legal framework for all political institutions including the CPSU, and the overriding importance of elections to assure the democratization of both party and state.

In his discussion of party officials' role, the general secretary returned to his reformist position with a vengeance. Although he once again couched his definition of officials' role in terms of the role of "the party," the implications of his remarks were clear. He now insisted that "the party" renounce "command style methods once and for all and conduct its policy by means of organizational, personnel, and ideological work," and called for a total reform of the apparat to fulfill these functions. At the same time he explicitly de-clared that party officials should be elected by their respective committee and act as their agents.[8]

Gorbachev not only sought to limit party officials' interference in indus-trial administration and the activities of the soviets, but he also sought to broaden the power of both the executive and legislative bodies of the Soviet state. He now declared that the Politburo and the Central Committee would act as "agencies of political leadership" that would not usurp the authority of state agencies. He added that the Supreme Soviet of the USSR and the USSR Council of Ministers would act independently, and that all policies of the CPSU would be implemented through the Communists within state agencies.[9] He defined the Council of Ministers as "the supreme executive and administrative body of power," insisted that local soviets be granted "full independent authority," and the Supreme Soviet of the USSR be trans-formed into a genuine legislative body with broad authority. He also sought to assure his own authority over a revitalized Supreme Soviet by calling for the indirect election of a new Chairman of the Supreme Soviet with consid-erable legislative and executive power.

But what would be the relationship between the party's full-time officials and the newly empowered soviets in a "democratized" political system? Gor-bachev attempted to resolve this problem by suggesting that the first secretaries of the local party organizations be "recommended" for the position of chairman of the soviet in their respective regions. Gorbachev's rationale for this arrange-ment indicated that he was either unwilling or unable to define a coherent di-vision of authority between the party officials and the elected soviets. Gor-bachev claimed that this reform would simultaneously help to "demarcate" the function of party and state agencies, lend the soviets the prestige of the party, improve the party's monitoring of the chair of the soviet and his executive committee, and place party officials under more popular control.[10]

It was obviously impossible to fulfill these totally contradictory objectives by allowing a single individual to occupy the positions of first secretary of the party organization and chairman of the soviet at the same time. It is not sur-prising that Gorbachev's verbal gymnastics managed to alienate his various critics and opponents. Orthodox party officials saw the proposal as an effort to undermine their own authority while the radical proponents of "all power to the Soviets" regarded it as a transparent effort to protect the authority of party officials.

In the discussion of Gorbachev's report at the 19th Conference, many re-gional party leaders expressed their misgivings about various aspects of his program. Some were outraged at the media's unrelenting assault on party officialdom; others charged that glasnost had stimulated the growth of anti-party sentiment and undermined the CPSU's capacity to lead and called for greater discipline to counter the disruptive consequences of internal democratization. But it was Ligachev who provided the most coherent defense of an orthodox definition of officials' responsibilities. While he recognized that the Secretariat was overburdened with economic issues, he did not support Gorbachev's criticism of party officials' perennial intervention in industrial management, his suggestion that the apparat be reorganized, or his conclusion that the first secretaries of local party organizations should stand for election as chairman of the local soviet.[11]

Despite this opposition, the general secretary's recommendations were incorporated into the Conference's final resolutions and in the decrees adopted by the Central Committee.[12] A decree of July 29, 1988, explicitly called for a strict demarcation of function between party committees and state and economic organs in order to eliminate "parallelism" and "duplication" of effort, insisted that the party officials serve as the instrument of party committees in the implementation of "political, organizational and upbringing" activities, and announced that the Politburo would soon reform the structure of the entire apparatus.[13] On August 12, 1988, the Central Committee issued detailed instructions for the election of party officials by their respective committees. Small primary party organizations were to hold elections on a yearly basis, large PPOs were to hold elections every two to three years, and all other party committees were to elect their officials for five-year terms.[14] On August 13, 1988, the Central Committee chastised all those who had allegedly underestimated the significance of Marxist-Leninist education as a means to master "political methods of leadership."[15]

But the Central Committee's decrees did not end the debate within the leadership. For example, Ligachev directly challenged the general secretary in an address to the *aktiv* of the *obkom* in Gorkii in August 1988. While he seemed at first glance to endorse Gorbachev's view that party officials should no longer engage in "inappropriate functions," he forcefully defended an inclusive definition of their responsibilities. He implied that their traditional role in industrial management would not be hampered either by the proposed extension of soviet authority or the new stress on their "political" leadership. He also declared that "party control" over industry remained essential to counter the baleful influence of market forces, which Ligachev regarded as subversive to socialism in the USSR. Ligachev's detailed discussion of the Gorkii *obkom*'s varied activities clearly implied that the full-time officials of the CPSU were responsible for every sphere of social, economic, and cultural activities in their regions.[16]

To counter Ligachev's critique, the loyal Razumovskii was dispatched to the provinces to explain the meaning of "political leadership" to local party leaders. In an address to the party *aktiv* in Novosibirsk (where Ligachev had spent much of his early career) he stressed the importance of the activities of primary party organizations. He urged them to focus on their "ideological educational role" to develop a creative approach to new methods of labor organization and oppose evidence of "bureaucratism" and "conservativism" in their work place.[17]

But many local party officials openly expressed their confusion about the actual meaning of "political leadership." For example, A. Gerasimov, the first secretary of the Leningrad *gorkom*, complained that the leadership of the CPSU had failed to provide a coherent "theoretical base for party-political methods" and that it was therefore proving difficult to eliminate local officials' "commandism" and to focus their attention on social economic problems of the people, particularly at the level of the primary party organizations.[18] He claimed that the existing party literature on "political leadership" had been written during the period of "stagnation" and was therefore of little use under the "new conditions." He urged the Central Committee's party school to provide adequate guidance on the subject.[19]

Sometime in August the Politburo began to discuss the details of the reform of the Secretariat and its subordinate officials that had been approved in general terms by the 19th Conference of the CPSU. Medvedev reports that the Politburo was deeply divided over this issue. He revealed that he joined with Yakovlev and Shevardnadze in advocating the elimination of all of the Central Committee's departments that did not fulfill the party's "political role" and that other members of the Politburo after initially resisting this orientation finally felt obliged to follow the guidelines of the 19th Conference.[20] Gorbachev himself, in a memo to the Politburo on August 24, 1988, announced that the industrial departments in both the Central Committee and in local party organs would be eliminated and replaced by new departments for social-economic questions. In his explanation of this drastic change he insisted that he wanted the government of the USSR to have full control over the administration of industry.[21]

In the end, in addition to the new department for social-economic questions, the Central Committee retained departments for ideology, party construction and cadre policy, agriculture, state and law, defense, international affairs, general (internal communications), and administrative affairs. A Politburo decree of September 10, 1988, outlined the reorganization in detail. All of the above departments except international affairs were established for republic, *krai*, and *oblast* party organizations. Party committees at the city and lower levels would have departments for party construction, ideology, and social-economic questions (in larger cities) and departments for the defense industry where appropriate.[22] The decree defined party committees as "organs of political leadership," stressed the need to eliminate "substitution," commandism, and a technocratic orientation and to recruit officials into the apparat who were themselves capable of "political methods of work."[23]

Three weeks later, the final element in the reform was put in place. In his report to the 19th Conference, Gorbachev had called for the establishment of specialized commissions in the Central Committee to allow its members to participate more actively in the development of policy in the intervals between its regular meetings.[24] A Central Committee resolution of September 30, 1988, established six commissions headed by senior Politburo/secretaries. Yakovlev was named director of the commission on international affairs, and Ligachev was named to direct the commission on agriculture. Razumovsky was appointed the head of the commission on party construction and cadres, Medvedev to head the ideological commission, Sliunkov to direct the commission on social-economic questions, and Chebrikov was named to direct the commission on legal affairs.[25]

The leaders of the CPSU subsequently explained the formation of these commissions in very different ways. Gorbachev later claimed that it had been designed at least in part to eliminate the disruptive conflicts between Yakovlev and Ligachev over ideological and cultural matters and to limit Ligachev's range of responsibility without forcing him from the leadership. In contrast, Ligachev later charged that the commissions had been established to prevent the Secretariat from meeting as a collective decision-making body and thus deprive subordinate officials of any coherent guidance.[26] He clearly implied that the Commissions had been designed to take the place of the Secretariat. Whatever the accuracy of Ligachev's charges, there is no doubt that the number of decrees that appeared over the Secretariat's name seemed to decrease considerably from the time of the reform until the dramatic revival of its activities after the 28th Congress of the CPSU in mid-1990.[27]

While the reform of the apparatus was a major victory for the general secretary, some of the public commentary on these extraordinary changes suggests that at least some party officials were not very enthusiatic about it. For example, a lengthy article in *Partiinaia Zhizn'* balanced its praise for the reform with renewed stress on the "unity of political and economic work," on the role of "the party" in working out the country's economic policy, training cadres, and assuring party control over enterprise activity. It provided doctrinal support for this position by citing Lenin's injunction not to permit any "breach" between political work and economic problems.[28]

Partiinaia Zhizn' also published essays by orthodox party officials claiming that the general secretary's campaign to introduce the election of local party officials had serious negative consequences. For example, I. V. Polozkov, the first secretary of the Krasnodar *kraikom*, complained that the internal democratization of the CPSU had begun to undermine party officials' control over personnel. While he pointed with considerable pride to his own *kriakom's* support for multiple candidates for a wide range of positions, he sharply criticized work collectives and unnamed party organizations that had rejected the nominations provided by higher party bodies and had elected "their own candidates." He complained that some of these were "dangerous unprincipled leaders and babblers," and clearly implied that higher party organs had to retain full control over the electoral process to assure the effectiveness of their "political leadership."[29]

Although the new commissions of the Central Committee were not actually convened until early 1989, some of their leaders were assigned important tasks immediately after their appointment. In particular, V. Medvedev, the leader of the new commission on ideology, was charged with the elaboration of a "new definition of socialism." This proved to be an impossible task because of the general secretary's increasingly enthusiastic support for critical elements of both "bourgeois" and "social democratic" theory and practice. Medvedev sought to cope with this problem by simply lumping orthodox and revisionist formulations together without any effort to resolve the obvious contradictions between them. On the one hand, he argued that the CPSU's capacity to provide guidance for the system as a whole was based on its grasp of Marxism-Leninism. On the other hand, he also declared that the CPSU could learn a great deal about the defense of working class interests from social democratic theory and practice![30] In November 1988 he declared that the CPSU remained loyal to its "socialist choice" and insisted that the introduction of nonsocialist property relations and the use of the market were essential to overcome the low productivity and alienation of the working class. He also argued that Soviet ideologists had assailed "bourgeois democracy" too harshly in the past and concluded that it would be "sectarian" not to use its electoral practices in the USSR.[31]

While Medvedev fumbled toward the development of a "new definition of socialism," the leadership proved either unwilling or unable to provide coherent guidelines for local party officials on the nature of "political methods of leadership." *Partiinaia Zhizn'*, the major journal of "discussion" for party officials, now proved to be useless as a source of guidance. In early November it recognized that it was extremely difficult to end party officials' interference in both state and soviet agencies but did not indicate how this problem was to be overcome.[32] And the roundtables on the subject sponsored by the Central Committee's own educational institutions were not much help. Their participants urged party officials to focus on the "analysis, prediction, and evaluation" of the economic performance of enterprises rather than interfering in their activities.[33]

The leadership's evasiveness prompted *Partiinaia Zhizn'* to publish open complaints that the leaders of the CPSU had failed to provide a coherent definition of "political leadership." For example, leaders of primary party organizations charged that party officials at both the *obkom* and *gorkom* levels talked a great deal about it but had been unable to provide any coherent definition of its content. These leaders charged that local party officials' "style of leadership" had remained unchanged because they did not know how to convince people rather than simply order them around.[34]

Local party officials were not the only ones who did not grasp the meaning of "political methods of leadership." The members of the faculty at the Central Committee's Academy of Social Sciences, one of the party's leading training programs for party officials, were evidently no more well informed. Sometime in late 1988 the Central Committee's departments for ideology and for party construction and cadres had investigated the academy's various programs. Their report had charged that the faculty had failed to provide their students with a clear understanding of the "implementation" of the party's leading role, of the division of function between "party" and "state," and of the proper use of "political methods of work with the masses." The departments demanded immediate improvement of the curriculum.[35]

Most important, some orthodox party officials openly challenged the implications of the general secretary's emphasis on "political methods of leadership." For example, I. Polozkov, who had been named to Ligachev's commission on agriculture in late November, recognized the importance of "political methods of leadership" but insisted that the extension of authority to local soviets would not diminish responsibility of party officials for all activities within their respective regions.[36] Furthermore, in an interview published in *Kommunist* in early 1989, Polozkov charged that the local party officials who had been trained to operate within the system of industrial departments had become totally confused by the new stress on "political leadership," and that the leadership of the CPSU had failed to provide them with adequate guidance to work under "new conditions."[37]

But if party officials were confused by the stress on party officials' "political leadership" and the elimination of most of the industrial branch departments of the Central Committee (the department for defense industry was retained), the leaders of the Council of Ministers of the USSR were not.

The reforms adopted by the 19th Conference implied that the Council of Ministers of the USSR should enjoy greater autonomy in the administration of industry. In fact, the resolution adopted by the 19th Conference of the CPSU had explicitly defined the Council of Ministers as the "supreme executive and administrative body of power" accountable to the Supreme Soviet of the USSR for the implementation of all plans for social and economic development.[38]

Chairman of the Council of Ministers Ryzhkov subsequently revealed that he had acted quickly to demonstrate the government's new independence but that the general secretary vigorously resisted his efforts. Ryzhkov established new governmental agencies for information independent of the Secretariat, invited representatives from the media to meetings of the Presidium of the Council, and used television to publicize the government's activities.[39] Ryzhkov charged that the "ever unstable Gorbachev" not only worked with Yakovlev and Medvedev to prevent the Council of Ministers of the USSR from publishing its own materials, but also repeatedly attempted to block its initiatives and to make it the scapegoat for lapses in his own judgment. Ryzhkov claimed that the general secretary had become obsessed with retaining his own paramount authority after the 19th Conference of the CPSU and had become increasingly jealous of the growing independence of both the Council and its chairman.[40]

Gorbachev's subsequent discussion of the government's economic policy after the 19th Conference of the CPSU gives credence to Ryzhkov's complaints. In his memoirs the general secretary consistently holds the Council of Ministers responsible for all of the USSR's growing economic difficulties. He complains that the government gave way to "populist pressure," abandoned control over wages, established "excessive" social programs, lost control over the process of inflation, and did not act swiftly enough to cope with the growing shortage of consumer goods.[41]

While Ryzhkov sought to extend the authority of the Council of Ministers of the USSR, the general secretary was devoting considerable time and energy to the reform of the moribund system of soviets at the central, republican, and local levels. His report to the 19th Conference had indicated that he sought to transform them into genuine legislative bodies with vast powers. In the fall of 1988 he acted to assure that he would be in a position to direct this reform. On October 1, 1988, he replaced Gromyko as the chairman of the Presidium of the Supreme Soviet of the USSR. This allowed him to lead the discussion in the Supreme Soviet of the new electoral laws and constitutional changes needed to establish the proposed Congress of Peoples' Deputies/Supreme Soviet.

But the very discussion of constitutional change helped to prompt a dramatic challenge to the federal system in the USSR. During the late 1980s nationalist and increasingly anti-Soviet political movements had developed in the Baltic republics. By 1988 many Baltic nationalists had come to the conclusion that the constitutional amendments under discussion would limit the rights of the republics to secede from the USSR, which had been provided, however formally, by Article 72 of the constitution adopted in 1977. These anxieties contributed to the formation of national fronts in all of the Baltic republics in October 1988. Their growing influence became evident on November 16, 1988, when the Supreme Soviet of the Estonian republic declared the republic to be sovereign and passed a constitutional amendment that subordinated the legislation of the USSR to its own.[42]

The response of the leadership of the USSR to this challenge indicated that its "new definition of socialism" had not produced any change in the orthodox analysis of the "nationality question" in the Soviet Union. On November 18, 1988, the Presidium of the Supreme Soviet, headed by Chairman Gorbachev, declared the legislation of the Supreme Soviet of the Estonian republic to be null and void. In his remarks to the Presidium, Gorbachev denounced this action as retrograde and totally contrary to the process of reform.[43]

At this juncture Gorbachev and his lieutenants seemed to conceptualize the "national question" as simply another "ideological" issue. In November 1988, the general secretary sent the head of the new ideological commission of the Central Committee to Latvia in a hopeless effort to bolster the local Communist Party against the national front that had been established in the previous month. Medvedev's public comments indicated that the leadership had been unable to determine a "new" approach to this vital issue. Medvedev simply denounced the Latvians' striving for independence and lashed out at the local Communists for giving way to that sentiment, but provided no coherent advice for them other than to rally local support for "internationalism" and perestroika.[44]

Upon his return to Moscow, Medvedev was assigned the unenviable task of responding to the increasingly impatient criticism of the regime's economic policies. By the end of 1988 it had become increasingly obvious that the leadership's efforts to broaden the autonomy of enterprises and production units at the expense of both the central ministries and local party officials and the attempts to encourage cooperative and private economic activity had produced immense confusion in economic administration, declines in production, and shortages in important consumer goods. Medvedev later asserted in his memoirs that the economic reform of 1987 had become so tangled in a "bureaucratic quagmire" that the proposed changes had never actually been implemented![45]

Medvedev's comments on the economic situation revealed that the "new definition of socialism" could not provide any guidance on economic issues. Medvedev not only refused to acknowledge the leadership's growing confusion on economic policy but reverted to a euphemistic discussion of the country's problems. He insisted that the leadership did have a coherent economic strategy and that perestroika was threatened not by the regime's policy but by the polarization created by its various critics. He lashed out at "conservative dogmatic elements" for favoring a return to the discredited "command administrative system" and for opposing both the establishment of cooperatives and the decentralization of industrial administration. At the same time he attacked "radicals" who were so "impatient and adventurous" that they ignored the regime's accomplishments and confused people with their "negativism and demagoguery."[46]

Gorbachev's own major pronouncements at this critical juncture were no more coherent. He had been under increasing assaults from both orthodox Communists and "radical democrats" about the pace and nature of reform in the USSR. In January 1989 he sought to respond to his critics in a lengthy address to a meeting of members of the Central Committee with various leading cultural and scientific figures in the USSR. While Gorbachev promised repeatedly to introduce measures to improve the economy, his speech indicated that he had no clear conception of how to cope with the economic and political problems facing the USSR.[47]

Nevertheless, Gorbachev's confusing and contradictory remarks were portrayed as a major source of inspiration and direction for the party as a whole. A Politburo decree of January 24, 1989, declared that the general secretary's speech had "principled significance" for the "ideological-political work" of the party, and ordered the ideological department of the Central Committee to assure its widespread distribution and to convene a conference on the "theory and practice" of perestroika as soon as feasible. It also ordered the ideological commission to convene a conference of the heads of all local ideological departments in February 1989.[48]

On January 25, 1989, the commission on ideology convened for the first time since its formation in October/November 1988. Its published report criticized ideological workers for their failure to respond effectively to the "problems" created by the decline in citizens' living standards and to make adequate preparations for the forthcoming elections for the Congress of Peoples' Deputies of the USSR. While the commission's report concluded that the changing situation demanded a "new approach" to ideological work based on a "modern conception of socialism," it failed to provide any such conception on its own. The commission's own vague declaration that this "new conception" would stress socialist pluralism, criticism of the Stalinist system, and defend "socialist values and ideas," was of little use to the hard-pressed ideological workers in the field.[49]

In early February, the commission convened a meeting of the directors of ideological departments down to the *gorkom* level, and the directors of media outlets and of other ideological institutions to discuss the problems of "ideological work." The report by A. S. Kapto, the head of the ideological department of the Central Committee, and the published summary of the discussion indicated that the leadership had no clear conception of a "new approach" to ideological work other than publicizing the general secretary's pronouncements. The participants in this meeting clearly recognized that the economic and political reforms had transformed the context of their work and seemed to portray Gorbachev's banal address to the Central Committee in January 1989 as a source of guidance for future action. But the report also indicated that the ideological workers had all but given up on their previous efforts to shape public opinion. It noted that the coming elections for deputies to the Congress of Peoples' Deputies and the coming meeting of the Central Committee on agriculture deserved considerable attention but provided no coherent guidelines to deal with these developments. Instead it concluded that the activities of ideological workers would henceforth be based on awareness of public attitudes and on a "realistic" assessment of current difficulties.[50]

While Medvedev and his commission on ideology struggled to define their role and activity, Ligachev, the chairman of the new commission on agricultural affairs, was operating in a very traditional fashion. Party officials had always controlled this sector of the economy and the departments for agriculture in the Central Committee and in local party organizations had *not* been eliminated by the reform of the apparatus in 1988. In this context, Ligachev was therefore able to largely ignore the strictures about the importance of "political methods of leadership" and to focus his commission and subordinate party officials on the perennial difficulties of agricultural production.

Ligachev later revealed that he had not taken on his new position "voluntarily,"[51] but he clearly took his responsibilities very seriously. During his first months as chairman, Ligachev travelled throughout the country speaking on agricultural policy. In an address to the Rostov *obkom* in late December 1988, Ligachev charged that the nation's perennial agricultural problems reflected the regime's inability to deal with the agricultural sector as a whole. He called for massive capital investments to raise the technological level of all segments of the "agro-industrial complex," to improve rural social and economic conditions, and to transform the existing state and collective farms into a network of lease-based cooperatives. He also gave particular attention to the long-neglected food processing industry, assailing its technological backwardness and the inappropriate placement of processing plants in cities, and recommended the construction of new and smaller plants closer to the fields.[52]

In February 1989 the commission on agriculture, which included both party officials from the major agricultural regions of the USSR and a number of ministers concerned with agriculture, was convened for the first time. Ligachev made it clear that he regarded the commission as the major supervisory organ for all state agencies concerned with agriculture.[53] In his remarks to the commission, Ligachev urged both party and soviet agencies to cooperate to assure that regional industrial centers would focus on the modernization of agricultural production, the improvement of storage and processing facilities, and the broadening of cultural and intellectual life in their respective adjacent rural regions.[54]

Politburo/Secretary Sliunkov, who headed the new commission for social-economy policy (which included both party officials and a number of ministers), clearly sought to assure that the commission and its subordinate departments for social-economic policy would play a major role in the development of economic policy. In March 1989 the commission was convened for the first time to discuss the problem of pension reform and other issues. After discussing a series of legislative proposals to improve the existing system of pensions, the commission urged the appropriate state ministries and departments of the Central Committee to coordinate their efforts in working out the details of the law. Most important, the report on its first meeting made it clear that the commission intended to deal with a very broad range of economic problems. These included the implementation of the programs for social and economic development in the thirteenth five-year plan, the effectiveness of investment in the construction industry, ecological questions, the progress of economic reform, financial difficulties, and the pace of scientific-technological progress.[55]

Furthermore, materials published in *Partiinaia Zhizn'* suggest that the elimination of the industrial branch departments of the CC/CPSU had not ended authoritative support for party officials' intervention in industrial administration. *Partiinaia Zhizn'* now urged party officials to coordinate the activities of the primary party organizations in industrial enterprises in order to assure the implementation of economic reform. In the process, *Partiinaia Zhizn'* now represented the local party officials as the advocates of self-financing for all production units and as the defenders of their autonomy against the central ministries' ostensible efforts to regain control over them.[56]

While the commissions headed by Ligachev and Sliunkov focused on economic questions, Secretary Razumovsky, who headed the Central Committee's new commission on questions of party construction and cadre policy, was attempting to implement the decrees of the Central Committee on the election of party officials. In February 1989, the commission, which was composed almost entirely of powerful local party leaders, met for the first time. Razumovsky's report to the commission indicated that he remained totally loyal to the general secretary and his program. He explicitly endorsed the general secretary's views on the importance of the "democratization" of the CPSU and the election of its officials by their respective committees.[57] But his report also indirectly recognized that the commission had failed to prepare party officials for the most important new element in their "political work"—the elections for deputies for the Congress of Peoples' Deputies held in March 1989. Ligachev subsequently revealed that Razumovsky had been assigned the responsibility for organizing and directing party officials' participation in the election process but had proved unwilling or unable to provide them with any coherent direction.[58]

But Razumovsky was hardly the only leading official of the CPSU who was unable to help party officials to respond to the new sphere of "political work." For example, Medvedev's public discussion of the role of "the party" in the elections for the Congress of Peoples' Deputies could hardly have been useful to party officials. Medvedev followed his usual path: he simply lumped together contradictory formulations without resolving the differences between them. He defined the CPSU as the country's "political vanguard" but insisted that it would cooperate with other organizations on an "equal basis." He denied that the leadership had a "blueprint" for the development of socialism but insisted that its long-range objectives would be worked out on the basis of unfolding practice.[59] Such obfuscations could hardly help party officials to cope with the new world of electoral politics.

Notes

1. Medvedev, *V komande*, 72.
2. "Raikom, gorkom partii v perestroike," *Partiinaia Zhizn'*, no. 6 (1988), 11. Approved for publication March 22, 1988.
3. Ibid., 12.
4. V. Novikov, "Potentsial kooperatsii-uskoreniiu sotsialno-ekonomicheskogo razvitiia," *Partiinaia Zhizn'*, no. 9 (1988), 49–53. Approved for publication April 19, 1988.
5. Ibid., 48.
6. Gorbachev, *Zhizn'*, vol. 1, 388.
7. *Current Soviet Policies*, vol. 10, 11.
8. Ibid., 22–23.
9. Ibid., 24.

10. Ibid., 14.

11. *Pravda*, July 2, 1988, 2.

12. *Current Soviet Policies*, vol. 10, 79–81.

13. *Parttiinaia Zhizn'*, no. 16 (1988), 29–30.

14. See *Spravochnik partiinogo rabotnika*, 1989, 300–301.

15. Ibid., 326–237.

16. *Pravda*, August 6, 1988, 2.

17. *Pravda*, August 18, 1988, 1–2.

18. A. Gerasimov, "Oblagevat novym stylem rukovodstva. Uchit'siia destvovat v novykh usloviiakh," *Partiinaia Zhizn'*, no. 17 (1988), 15–21. Approved for publication August 23, 1988.

19. Ibid., 21.

20. Medvedev, *V komande*, 78–79.

21. Gorbachev's memo was published in the new Central Committee journal *Izvestiia TsK KPSS*, no. 1 (1989), 81–86.

22. *Spravochnik partiinogo rabotnika* 1989, 307–308. Cherniaev reports that Gorbachev wanted to keep the agricultural department until the food crisis had been solved. Cherniaev, *Shest let s Gorbachevym* (Moscow: Progress, 1993), 235. For an excellent discussion of the reforms, see Gordon M. Hahn, "The First Reorganization of the CPSU Cerntral Committee Apparat under Perestroika," *Europe-Asia Studies* 49, no. 2 (Spring 1997), 281–302.

23. *Spravochnik partiinogo rabotnika* 1989, 309.

24. *Current Soviet Policies*, vol. 10, 23.

25. *Pravda*, October 1, 1988, 1.

26. Ligachev, *Inside Gorbachev's Kremlin*, 109–111.

27. *Spravochnik partiinogo rabotnika*, 1990.

28. N. Miakinnik, "Partiinoe rukovodstva ekonimiki," *Partiinaia Zhizn'*, no. 21 (1988), 5–13. Approved for publication October 25, 1988.

29. I. Polozkov, "Na konkursnoi sostiazatel' noiosnove," *Partiinaia Zhizn'*, no. 22 (1988), 30–32. Approved for publication November 4, 1988.

30. *Pravda*, October 5, 1988, 4.

31. V. Medvedev, "K poznaniiu sotsializma.otvety na voprosy zhurnala kommunist," *Kommunist*, no. 17 (1988), 3. Approved for publication November 17, 1988.

32. "Demokratizatsiia-rukovodiashchiu deiatel'nost i vnutrennyi zhizn' partii," *Partiinaia Zhizn'*, no. 22 (1988), 7–8. Approved for publication November 4, 1988.

33. *Partiinaia Zhizn'*, no. 23 (1988), 19–25.

34. V. Pokrovov, "Obladevat politicheskimi metodami rukovodstva," *Partiinaia Zhizn'*, no. 1 (1989), 30–32. Approved for publication December 20, 1988.

35. The report was published in *Spravochnik partiinogo rabotnika* 1990, 154–159.

36. *Pravda*, December 22, 1988, 3.

37. I. Polozkov, "Politicheskoe rukovodstvo ot slov k delu," *Kommunist*, no. 2 (1989), 12–21. Approved for publication January 17, 1989.

38. *Pravda*, July 5, 1988, 2.

39. Ryzhkov, *Desiat*, 282–283.

40. Ibid., 288.

41. Gorbachev, *Zhizn'*, vol. 1, 362.

42. White, *Gorbachev and After*, 159.

43. Gorbachev, *Zhizn'*, vol. 1, 511–513.

44. *Pravda*, November 13, 1988, 3; November 15, 1988, 4.

45. Medvedev, *V komande*, 87.

46. *Pravda*, December 26, 1988, p. 2.

47. See *Current Digest of the Soviet Press* 41, no. 1, 1–10.

48. The Politburo decree was published in *Spravochnik partiinogo rabotnika* (1990), 142–144.

49. The report of the commission appeared in *Spravochnik partiinogo rabotnika* (1990), 145–147.

50. *Spravochnik partiinogo rabotnika* (1990), 147–149.

51. *Pravda*, July 11, 1990, 6.

52. *Pravda*, December 25, 1988, 2.

53. For the report of the commission, see *Izvestiia TsK KPSS*, no. 2 (1989), 24–27.

54. *Pravda*, February 9, 1989, 2.

55. For the report of the commission, see *Spravochnik partiinogo rabotnika* (1990), 184–187.

56. "Prioritet-delovytost khoziaistvennoi initsiative," *Partiinaia Zhizn'*, no. 5 (1989), 3–8.

57. *Izvestiia TsK KPSS*, no. 3 (1989), 44–45. *Pravda*, February 28, 1989, 2.

58. Ligachev, *Inside Gorbachev's Kremlin*, 91–94.

59. *Pravda*, March 2, 1989, 2.

❦

CHAPTER FOUR

The Impact of the Congress of Peoples' Deputies: 1989

The elections to the Congress of Peoples' Deputies of the USSR had an extraordinary impact on the entire political system. A significant number of party officials were defeated in the multi-candidate elections for the deputies to the new legislative body in the spring of 1989. This dramatic loss led to an immediate backlash against the general secretary and his program among orthodox party officials in the spring and summer of 1989.

Furthermore, the establishment of the Congress as a genuine legislative body with authority over the executive branch of the government of the USSR made it even more difficult for the leaders of the CPSU to define the responsibilities of party officials. Until 1989, this problem had been relatively simple—to determine the proper relationship between the officials and the Communists who manned the *executive* branch of the government. But the Congress's *legislative* authority over the Council of Ministers made it a direct competitor with the party's full-time officials. What now was to be their proper relationship with the deputies elected to the new legislative body of the USSR?

The leaders of the CPSU divided sharply over this extremely difficult problem. Orthodox leaders concluded that the Politburo, Secretariat, and Central Committee should control and direct the activities of the Communist deputies in the legislature as well as the Communists in the executive branch. In direct contrast, radical Communists such as Yakovlev (and later Boris Yeltsin) wanted to totally eliminate the party officials' "leading role" and to transform the CPSU into a purely parliamentary party operating within the framework of the Congress of Peoples' Deputies.

In 1989 Gorbachev seemed to adopt a typically "centrist" position on this issue. Some public sources suggest that Gorbachev and his closest allies may have hoped to transform the Secretariat and the departments of the Central Committee under its supervision into a "think tank" for the members of the legislature. In fact, two years later Gorbachev did adopt just that position. But his own public comments on the issue in the years between 1989 and 1991 were often ambiguous and hard to interpret.

Buf if his views on this issue were not particularly clear, in the summer of 1989 Gorbachev dramatically shifted his views on local party officials' proper approach to the executive branch of the Soviet state. In a detailed report to a convocation of party officials in July 1989, the general secretary adopted a strikingly eclectic definition of officials' responsibilities. While he reasserted the primacy of their "political work" in very firm terms, he also called on republican and regional officials to "draw up their own plans" for the social and economic development of their respective regions. As usual, the general secretary made no effort to explain his position, in keeping with his long-standing desire to retain the myth of his own infallibility. But the timing of this shift suggests that the emphasis on party officials' economic responsibilities may have been designed to meet his orthodox critics halfway and/or to undermine the authority of such Politburo/secretaries as Sliunkov, who persistently defended the authority of the Central Committee's new commission on social-economic problems.

Whatever his motives, circumstantial evidence suggests that this shift helped to bolster his authority. In August 1989 both the Politburo and the Secretariat endorsed his definitions and his allies in the ideological commission of the Central Committee were able to prepare a strikingly revisionist program on the "nationality question." But just as the general secretary seemed to regain his ascendancy, he was suddenly faced with a series of extraordinary crises both at home and abroad in the fall of 1989. From August to October, the ruling Communist parties in East Europe came under increasingly savage assault from both reformist Communists and anti-Communist political movements. Simultaneously, the growing nationalist movements in the Baltic republics explicitly called for independence from the USSR, and Soviet citizens were confronted with a wave of shortages of basic consumer goods. In the face of these challenges, Gorbachev was obliged to retreat from the revisionist draft program on the nationality issue, and to reassert the Politburo's direct authority over the government's administration of the economy. Unfortunately for the general secretary and his allies, these crises provided his orthodox opponents with an ideal context to press their criticism of his policies in the last months of 1989.

As noted earlier, the leaders of the Secretariat had evidently failed to prepare party officials for the election campaign for the Congress of Peoples' Deputies in early 1989. This proved to have disastrous results. The elections led to the defeat of 32 *oblast* first secretaries (out of 160) with particularly serious setbacks in Leningrad and Moscow and had intensified the existing rifts within the Politburo over the direction of political reform.[1] Gorbachev later reported in his memoirs that he, Medvedev, and Yakovlev were the only members of the Politburo who regarded the outcome as a victory for reform and the progress of democracy. The orthodox majority clearly viewed it as a direct assault on party officials' prerogatives and blamed the defeat of "the party" on those officials responsible for "ideological work" who had ostensibly undermined the CPSU by their loosening of control over the media.

Gorbachev later described the majority's recriminations against the media during a meeting of the Politburo on March 28, 1989. In his memoirs, the general secretary claimed that Vorotnikov had assailed the critical tone of the media, that Ligachev had reminded his colleagues that the "developments" in both Hungary and Czechoslovakia had all begun "from the means of information."[2] Soloviev, the first secretary of the Leningrad *obkom* who had been defeated in the elections, charged that criticism published in both *Pravda* and *Izvestiia* had been particularly subversive, and Zaikov, who had succeeded Yeltsin as the first secretary of the Moscow *gorkom*, called for an end to public criticism of party officials. Chebrikov, a secretary of the Central Committee and head of the newly formed commission of the Central Committee on legal questions, took great umbrage to "insults to the flag." Liukianov condemned the attack on the leadership in the press and its circulation of rumors that the Central Committee had decided to abandon party officials to their own fate at the hands of "demagogues." Gorbachev also claims that Medvedev pledged to counter the promotion of "unhealthy orientations" by the media.[3]

In his own memoirs Medvedev insists that he and Yakovlev had sought to deflect these complaints and had attempted to explain that the media simply reflected public opinion. This conception of the media was anathema to leaders like Ligachev[4] and the majority of the members of the Politburo who were distressed and disoriented by the electoral defeat of party officials, the overt attacks on the regime's economic policies, and the popular support for more thorough democratization.

The leadership of the CPSU seemed to be totally confused about the proper response. This was particularly evident in Medvedev's address in April 1989 marking the anniversary of Lenin's birth. He not only warned party members against "panic," but added that any further "exaggerated claims for success" would deepen the population's alienation from the CPSU.[5] Medvedev attempted to make the case for a reformist orientation, but his efforts to defend the regime's economic policies and to outline the required "new definition of socialism" could hardly have bolstered the faith of party members in their leadership's clarity of purpose. Medvedev's discussion of the mixed economy sought by the leadership was bewildering. His insistence that each level of political authority in the USSR could determine the proper mix of property relations seemed a virtual invitation to administrative chaos and his admission that the leadership had not yet discovered "how to manage the market or to manage with the help of the market" must have discouraged all those who sought coherent direction from the leadership. He repeatedly blurred the differences between "socialist," "bourgeois," and "social democratic" theory and practice, and claimed that socialism in the USSR would triumph over capitalism by incorporating all the "positive" values of the nonsocialist world!

This ideological confusion opened the door for orthodox attacks on Gorbachev and his closest allies in the leadership of the CPSU. When the Central Committee convened in April 1989, Medvedev and Yakovlev were sharply criticized. R. B. Bobovikov, the first secretary of the Vladimir *obkom*, assailed both Medvedev and Yakovlev for their ostensible failure to really defend the regime during the election campaign.[6] I. Polozkov, the first secretary of the Krasnodar *kraikom*, charged that the leadership's abject failure to provide a coherent definition of the renovated socialism it sought to create had confused members of the CPSU and seriously undermined its popular support.

Both officials also sharply attacked Gorbachev's redefinition of officials' priorities. Bobovikov defended the orthodox view that they were responsible for every sphere of activity within their jurisidictions. Polozkov reiterated his earlier charge that local party officials had been badly disoriented by the reform of the apparatus in 1988 and that the leadership had undermined their capacity for "party leadership" by failing to provide adequate guidance.[7]

At the same time some leaders of the Secretariat seemed to adopt an orthodox position on party officials' responsibility for economic development. This became evident at a conference of the directors of the newly formed departments on social and economic questions convened in Moscow immediately after the meeting of the Central Committee. V. V. Sliunkov, the chairman of the new commission on social-economic policy, and V. I. Shimko, the chairman of the department on social-economic questions, did not provide warm support for the general secretary's definitions in their reports to the conference. While they both endorsed the general secretary's stress on the need for "political leadership," in the abstract, they defined the responsibilities of the new departments in broad and inclusive terms. Shimko urged them to focus on the implementation of the reforms adopted in 1987, the solution of immediate problems of food supply, housing, public health, and ecology, the financial health of individual enterprises, and the improvement of labor productivity.

Sliunkov adopted a slightly more orthodox position in his concluding remarks. Most important, he used the term "party leadership of the economy," a phrase that had been traditionally used by orthodox officials to underline officials' economic responsibilities, to describe the activities of the new departments. He did not criticize party officials' continued intervention in economic administration, but characterized it as a legitimate response to the ostensible failure of local state and soviet agencies to take up their new responsibilities. He urged the new departments to focus on the development of small firms based on leasing of facilities from larger enterprises, the struggle against inflation, and insisted that they "work with people" to convince them to adopt new practices.[8]

The ideological commission of the Central Committee also adopted an orthodox position when it convened to deal with the thorny "national question" in May 1989. Medvedev's report on its deliberations refused to recognize the depth of anti-Russian and antisocialist sentiment in the borderlands of the USSR despite the surge of nationalist-separatist movements in the Baltic republics and the conflict between the Armenian and Azerbaijan republics over the fate of the Armenian enclave in Azerbaijan. As a consequence, the report did no more than to belatedly acknowledge that the party's leadership and its social scientists had exaggerated the possibility of a "merger" of the USSR's nationalities and had "underestimated" the growth of support for national self-determination based on greater national self-consciousness. Moreover, its recommendations for action were extraordinarily feeble. The ideological commission called for the development of a "new conception" of the national question based on Lenin's "changing conception" of the problem and an awareness of the changes in the USSR since the 1920s. It also recommended the training of more specialists on the nationality problem, the publication of more non-Russian periodicals, and more conferences.[9]

While the commissions of the Central Committee struggled with these issues, the new Congress of Peoples' Deputies was convened in late May 1989. The general secretary now sought to define the proper relationship between the party officials and the new legislative body. He attempted to solve this problem on a personal level by immediately having himself elected the chairman of the Supreme Soviet of the USSR, the new standing legislature for the USSR. This new position would allow him to play a major role in shaping the agenda for the Supreme Soviet and pressing his legislative priorities. But it did not resolve the fundamental question of the proper relationship between the various commissions and departments of the CC/CPSU, the local party officials, and the new Congress of Peoples' Deputies.

Gorbachev's memoirs and other published sources strongly suggest that the leaders of the CPSU were deeply divided over this issue. Gorbachev reports that many party leaders and members of the Secretariat had wanted to create a disciplined Communist faction within the Congress that would be subordinate to the decisions of the Central Committee.[10] This orientation was expressed in *Partiinaia Zhizn*'s editorial assessment of the first session of the Congress. While it dutifully praised the Congress as a major step toward the democratization of the political system, the editorial repeatedly stressed the influence of the Central Committee, which had met during the first session, on the deliberations of the Congress. The same editorial also stressed the continued role of "the party" in establishing the direction of social-economic policies.[11]

Gorbachev and his allies adopted a different position. He reports in his memoirs that he and the members of his brain trust concluded in the spring of 1989 that the Congress of Peoples' Deputies should replace the Congress of the CPSU as the political forum defining the life of the country! He also asserts that he did not attempt to establish a disciplined Communist faction in the Congress because such "packing" of the legislature threatened to reduce the Council of Ministers, which was constitutionally subordinate to the new Supreme Soviet of the USSR, to an instrument of the Politburo, and to the Secretariat as in the past.[12]

Moreover, some published sources suggest that Gorbachev and his allies may have hoped to subordinate the departments of the Central Committee and local party officials to the Congress of Peoples' Deputies. *Izvestiia TsK KPSS* published a summary of the Central Committee's activity that implied that the departments of the Central Committee and local party officials should henceforth take their cues from the Congress. It explicitly stated that the Politburo had "instructed" the departments of the Central Committee to find "practical solutions" to the problems raised at the Congress and had also urged "party committees" to respond to the criticisms of the activities of the CPSU made at the Congress.[13]

But Gorbachev was unable to win support for such an orientation at this time. In fact, public sources suggest that in the summer of 1989 orthodox leaders of the CPSU sought to limit the general secretary's political independence. This became evident in the Politburo decree of June 6, 1989, elaborating an "action program" designed to fulfill the decisions of the Central Committee plenum of April 1989. The contradictory character of the formulations incorporated into this program suggests that the general secretary and his orthodox opponents had reached an uneasy compromise over the role of the Secretariat, the responsibilities of the departments and commissions of the Central Committee of the CPSU, and local officials. On the one hand, the decree sought to strengthen the authority of the Central Committee and the Secretariat vis-à-vis the Politburo. On the other hand, the decree did endorse some of the general secretary's definitions of officials' priorities.

Most striking, the Politburo's decree granted the Central Committee the right to examine all drafts of documents on important issues before they were discussed in the Politburo and ordered the Secretariat to assure the implementation of all decrees adopted by both the Politburo and the Central Committee.[14] The decree also ordered the members of both the Politburo and the Secretariat to provide direct personal guidance of local party leaders and called for the convocation of a unionwide meeting of first secretaries of all *gorkom* and *raikom* to improve internal communications within the CPSU. Finally, it declared that the commissions of the Central Committee should enjoy "greater influence on the resolution of questions of party leadership of economic and cultural construction," and insisted that the Communists who had leading positions in the government should be held responsible for the fulfillment of the decisions of the Central Committee.

On the other hand, the action program's "balanced" discussion of party officials' priorities seemed to indicate that the general secretary was still sufficiently powerful to assure that some of his formulations were included in the document. First of all, the program did *not* mention Gorbachev's criticism of party officials' "substitution" for state and soviet agencies, urged all local party committees to focus on social and economic problems, and outlined a variety of measures needed to improve the "party's" leadership of the media. However, it did include Gorbachev's insistence that party officials end their "substitution" for their own party committees, called on them to "consolidate healthy forces" around the objectives of perestroika, and to convene their committees to discuss more effective ways to operate in conditions of economic reform and democratization.

In the same spirit, the decree called for the development of new educational courses on the nature of perestroika for local first secretaries, and ordered the departments of ideology and personnel management to convene a conference on "questions of political methods of party leadership." It also ordered the commissions of the Central Committee for ideology, legal affairs, and party construction and cadre policy to convoke a conference to discuss ways to improve the influence of the CPSU on the forthcoming parliamentary elections at the republican and local levels. Finally, it urged the party's ideological workers to develop a "contemporary concept of socialism."

The response of the departments of the Central Committee to the Politburo's action program seemed to reflect the differences within the leadership. The department for social-economic policy seemed to follow the action program's recommendation to broaden the responsibility of its superior commission. In July it issued a report that sharply criticized local party officials for their passivity in dealing with pressing economic issues. It charged that they had failed to provide the necessary "organizational and political work" to assure the implementation of a joint decree of the Central Committee and Council of Ministers in 1987 on the construction of new apartment building, schools, hospitals, and other social-cultural institutions. Most important, on July 13, 1989, the Secretariat issued a decree ordering local party officials to act on the basis of the department's report.[15]

In contrast, the ideological department of the CC/CPSU responded to the action program's call for the development of a "contemporary conception of socialism" in a particularly feeble fashion. In early July, A. Kapto, the head of the department, reported that the Institute of Marxism-Leninism was working on a new assessment of the meaning and scope of the party's ideology, but he was unable to provide any coherent guidance for the party's "ideological workers." While he insisted that the increasingly complex social situation called for improved "ideological-theoretical preparation" of all party members to help them engage in a "dialogue" with those skeptical of the party's program, he did not discuss the content of such preparation. He simply announced that party officials would henceforth receive training in psychology and sociology in order to improve their capacity to guage public opinion.[16]

Kapto's fumbling was one indication of the leadership's inability to provide any coherent direction on critical ideological issues. The leadership's ideological bankruptcy was dramatized with particular force by Secretary Yakovlev's repudiation of Bolshevism in the summer of 1989. Yakovlev had been the director of the propaganda department of the Central Committee and now served as the chairman of its commission on international affairs. In November 1988 he had been named the chairman of the Politburo's commission to investigate past repressions in the CPSU.

By the end of the year he had emerged as an anti-Leninist social democrat defending the extension of individual liberties and the further democratization of the political system as the most important objectives of perestroika. In an address in Perm in December 1988 he had insisted that the CPSU could retain its "vanguard position" only by further democratization, attacked those who feared the growing pluralism of opinion, and portrayed "freedom of thought" as a paramount human value to be defended and extended in the USSR.[17]

Yakovlev became increasingly critical of the CPSU after his election to the Congress of Peoples' Deputies in May 1989. In his public comments Yakovlev implied that the Congress of Peoples' Deputies should replace the CPSU as the major instrument to reform the political system.[18] He praised the formation of the Congress as a massive step toward the democratization of the political system and as a bulwark against the return to authoritarianism, ignored the CPSU, and called for the cultivation of social attitudes and the creation of state institutions that would advance and protect individual freedom in a more humane socialist system.[19] In mid-June he had stressed the development of a sense of social responsibility to assure that the USSR made a succesful transition from an "autocratic and authoritarian" to "civic society."[20] Later that month he had praised the Congress for effectively overcoming the previous "psychology of self-disparagement" that had slowed reform and applauded the deputies for their "honest and courageous" appraisal of the country's problems. He also maintained that the creation of the Congress had established "mutual ties" between the society and the regime that had been lacking previously.[21]

Yakovlev's growing disdain for the CPSU was most dramatically reflected in his extraordinary address marking the 200th anniversary of the French Revolution in July 1989. Yakovlev now urged the leadership of the USSR to adopt the concept of separation of powers between legislative, executive, and judicial branches of government, to establish an economy based on individual initiative rather than governmental action, and to rebuild the legal system based on the presumption of innocence. These changes, concluded Yakovlev, would assure Soviet citizens the "natural and inviolable rights of man" outlined in the Declaration of the Rights of Man and the Citizen.[22]

Furthermore, Yakovlev used his discussion of the role of violence in the French Revolution to assail the Bolsheviks' use of terror during the civil war and its subsequent impact on the entire system. While he claimed that Lenin had been aware of the dangers of using "unjust means to achieve just ends," he concluded that the Bolsheviks' romanticization of violence had laid the basis for Stalin's despotism, and he now declared that the concept of violence as the "mid-wife" of positive social change had completely discredited itself.

Yakovlev's brief discussion of the current situation in the USSR was extraordinarily frank. He not only recognized that many had lost their faith in socialism, but regarded this as a legitimate response to the "dogmatism, statism, and indifference" of previous regimes. He concluded that only a "revolution in consciousness" could restore the system's vitality, implied that the CPSU had become too moribund to play a positive role in this process, and declared that the new Congress of Peoples' Deputies "may and must become a fundamental turning point" in the transformation of the political system."[23]

Yakovlev's virtual repudiation of the CPSU and his enthusiasm for the Congress of Peoples' Deputies contrasted sharply with the general secretary's strained and confusing effort to define the overall relationship between the party and the new legislative body. In his report to an assembly of party officials in July 1989, he adopted a contradictory position on this issue. On the one hand, he asserted that the CPSU remained the "political vanguard" of the society and denounced the view, which evidently had been expressed at the Congress of Peoples' Deputies, that the Congress was somehow "higher" than the CPSU. On the other hand, he insisted that it was impossible to determine the relative importance of the two institutions, because the Congress was a state institution and the CPSU was a "social-political organization" operating on a "different plane."[24]

The general secretary's discussion of the role of Communist deputies was equally incoherent. He claimed that they had obligations to both the party as a whole and to their constituents, but he was unable to define how these responsibilities were to be combined and/or resolved. He insisted that deputies were obliged to support the "fundamental positions" of the CPSU (which he was clearly unable to identify) but were free to follow their own consciences in "everything else." Despite this confusion Gorbachev was now clearly deeply concerned about the outcome of the forthcoming elections for republican and local legislative bodies scheduled for the following year. He assailed local party officials for having remained "on the sidelines" during the 1989 elections and insisted that they develop effective local programs, select candidates for the election with great care, and study local public opinion thoroughly in preparation for the campaigns.[25]

While Gorbachev found it difficult to define officials' orientation toward the legislature, he now adopted a strikingly eclectic definition of their responsibilties toward the executive branch. He reiterated his emphasis on party officials' political work in no uncertain terms, and gave particular stress to the overriding importance of their "ideological work." But he now seemed to give equal attention to officials "economic work" and explicitly declared that republican and *oblast* leaders should develop "their own plans" for the social-economic development of their respective regions. This dramatic shift in definition provided an immense opening for the proponents of local officials' "economic work."

Gorbachev told the assembled officials that in the past "the party was elevated over everything and it controlled all the processes of state, economic, and ideological life, supplanting and crushing everything without exception, issuing incontestible directives and commands to state and economic agencies and public organizations."[26] He now declared that it was necessary to "reconceptualize" the role of the party, urged party officials to limit their interference in soviet and state bodies, and to focus on organizational and ideological work and personnel management. He insisted that the liberation of party bodies from "inappropriate functions" would now "allow us at long last to make ideological work the paramount area of the party's activity."

But Gorbachev was unable to define the nature and scope of "ideological work." He recognized that the massive changes in the political and economic systems had created an "ideological vacuum" and that it was therefore essential to "sort out general questions of theory" in order to prevent errors and miscalculations in the future. But he could not elaborate the "new conception of socialism," which he had deemed essential for the future, and his own definition of the role of ideology in the CPSU's activities could not have provided guidance for anyone. He declared that "the party" worked out its policy "on a scientific Marxist-Leninist basis, with consideration for the urgent requirements of social development and the interests and sentiments of the masses."

In contrast to these platitudes, Gorbachev's discussion of party officials' responsibility for economic affairs was far more coherent. He declared that "the party" should never retreat from its responsibility for economic development, that the country's economic policy was no longer made at the "center," and praised those republican and *oblast* party leaders that had worked out their own plans for social and economic development in accord with local conditions. In this context he urged party officials to foster the development of "diverse forms of social property" and to establish a regulated market economy in accordance with the specific needs of their own region.

Gorbachev now defined party officials' proper relationship with local soviet institutions in the same way. He called for the establishment of a new "mechanism of interaction" at the local level that would oblige party agencies "to implement policy decisions in bodies of peoples rule only through persuasion, recommendations and democratic agreements, through Communists working in the Soviets and their executive agencies."

Gorbachev's orthodox critics responded to his formulations in a highly selective fashion. They continued to attack his emphasis on party officials' "political leadership" and his formulations on "ideological" questions and tended to ignore his support for the autonomy of local officials in dealing with economic questions. For example, S. G. Arutyunyan, the first secretary of the Armenian Communist Party, complained that the leadership had failed to provide a coherent definition of the role of the "party" and its relationship with the soviets. He warned that the resurrection of the slogan "all power to the soviets" had provided the party's opponents with a firm grounding for challenging its leading role.

L. N. Zaikov, a Politburo/secretary and the first secretary of the Moscow *gorkom*, complained that party officials had not even begun to master "political methods of leadership" because the soviets were unable to cope with their new responsibilities. He also complained bitterly about the party's loss of control over the press. The first secretary of the Uzbek Communist Party chided the leadership for its ostensible failure to define contemporary "party-political work."[27]

L. F. Bobykin, the first secretary of the Sverdlovsk *obkom*, was particularly outspoken. He charged that the "premature" abolition of the industrial branch departments of the Central Committee had undermined "party influence" on economic questions, and expressed the hope that the new departments for social-economic policy would restore it and help to create appropriate state legislation. He complained that the leadership's inability to provide local officials with documentary materials explaining the "ideology, policy and practise of perestroika" had so disoriented local ideological workers that they had been unable to counter "hostile propaganda against the party and the soviet system." He not only argued that the Secretariat itself had been "recently weakened," but called for the restoration of the position of "second secretary" (which Ligachev had held from 1985 until the fall of 1988.)[28]

Politburo/Secretary Ligachev devoted most of his own address to the agricultural sector and its problems, but he explicitly opposed the reform of the apparatus and the extension of the authority of the soviets at the expense of party officials. He sharply criticized "party committees" who had ostensibly withdrawn from the solution of social and economic questions, and vigorously opposed any attempt to subordinate party bodies to the soviets, insisting that their role could be broadened only if the party and its discipline were strengthened. He also assailed the loss of party officials' control over the press, insisted that it be used to shape and direct public opinion, and criticized those who had argued that the press merely reflected the complexities of Soviet life. In the same vein, he reiterated his early assaults on those who were providing a "one sided" view of the USSR's past and warned that such activities threatened to subvert the entire system. Most striking, he warned that the introduction of a multiparty system in the USSR's federal structure would lead to the disintegration of the USSR.[29]

V. Medvedev, the Politburo/secretary who headed the commission on ideology of the Central Committee, sought to respond to the concerted assault on his own activities. While he recognized the legitimacy of this criticism, he repeatedly complained that the immense complexity of the existing situation had made ideological work extraordinarily difficult and insisted that he and his colleagues had actually provided a "firm line." While he pledged to restore party officials' control over the media, he seconded Gorbachev's conclusion that party officials now had to share authority with newly elected soviet bodies. Medvedev assserted that the role of the media would henceforth be determined by a new law on the press to be submitted to the Supreme Soviet of the USSR rather than by his commission on ideology and subordinate specialists in "ideological work."[30]

N. I. Ryzhkov, the chairman of the Council of Ministers of the USSR, did not mince words in his criticism of Gorbachev's position. Ryzhkov charged that the media's concerted assault on the CPSU and its policies had seriously undermined its authority and that the policies adopted by the secretaries of the Central Committee responsible for "ideological work" were leading inexorably to the "deideologization" of the society.

Ryzhkov was particularly concerned about the general secretary's failure to define the proper relationship between the Central Committee of the CPSU, the Supreme Soviet of the USSR, and the USSR Council of Ministers. He was extraordinarily blunt—he charged that the establishment of the Supreme Soviet as the country's standing legislature had so blurred the role of the Politburo and the Central Committee in the development of the country's policies that it threatened the continued "influence of the CPSU on the state." Moreover, he expressed the fear that the leadership's continued failure to define the proper relationship between the leading party and state institutions would have disastrous results for the proper governance of the republics and regions of the USSR.

Ryzhkov was evidently particularly enraged by Gorbachev's declaration that economic policy was no longer made at the center but by local party and state authority. The chairman regarded this as a massive threat to the role of the Council of Ministers in the development of economic policy, and he explicitly declared that the "new government" approved by the Supreme Soviet of the USSR was the source of economic policy. He concluded his remarks by urging the general secretary to stop interfering in the development of state economic policy and focus on his major task of perestroika within the CPSU.[31]

Ryzhkov's assault on Gorbachev had important political repercussions. Ryzhkov subsequently reported in his memoirs that the Politburo split irrevocably into two warring camps after this conference of party officials in July 1989. According to Ryzhkov, Gorbachev was supported by Medvedev, Yakovlev, and Shevardnadze, and opposed by Ryzhkov, Ligachev, Vorotnikov, Sliunkov, and Zaikov, with other members remaining in "the swamp" between them.[32] (In his own memoirs, Gorbachev claims that Ligachev and

Ryzhkov first joined forces against him at the Politburo meeting of June 16, 1989.)[33] At the same time, Ryzhkov admits that his colleagues were unable to form a united front against the general secretary because of the personal and bureaucratic differences among them.

This failure to form a coherent united front may help to explain why the Secretariat and Politburo explicitly endorsed Gorbachev's views on the importance of party officials' "political methods of leadership" despite the widespread criticism of his views. On July 29, 1989, the Secretariat endorsed the general secretary's position in an important decree dealing with the reform and function of the party's press. In defining the function of the party's major publications, the decree declared that *Partiinaia Zhizn'* was now obliged to educate party workers of a "new type" who would be able to "master the political forms and methods of work."[34]

Partiinaia Zhizn' immediately followed suit. Its lead editorial on August 1, 1989, recognized that it was difficult for party officials to master the "complex science of political leadership" but urged them to become "commissars of perestroika" able to replace the old command style with a sympathetic orientation toward the immediate needs and aspirations of Soviet citizens. *Partiinaia Zhizn'* concluded that effective "political and organizational work" would allow officials to understand the mood and aspirations of the citizens, to improve their standard of living, and to deal with economic issues "in an exclusively political manner" by working out the "correct line," and by focusing on personnel management and the verification of implementation. Such a reorientation, concluded the journal, could restore the people's faith in the CPSU.[35]

The same issue also included an essay by V. Novikov, a secretary with the Moscow *obkom*, that indicated that some local party officials responded with alacrity to Gorbachev's renewed emphasis on local officials' autonomy in the development of social and economic programs. Novikov asserted that the reform of the apparatus in 1988 and the extension of the authority of the Soviets had now created a genuine basis for a shift to "political methods of leadership," which he defined as directing social development "through the toilers and for them."[36]

Following Gorbachev's lead, Novikov urged local party officials to develop economic policies in accordance with local needs and to help the primary party organizations in industrial enterprises to protect the workers from excessive intervention by ministerial authorities! Most important, Novikov indicated that the Moscow *obkom* had developed new institutional structures to deal with social and economic policies. He reported that it had established new commissions to deal with the introduction of full self-financing by enterprises and conglomerates, the development of a local financial plan, the introduction of leasing and other new economic methods, the production of food and other consumer goods, the construction of adequate housing, and all other issues related to the standard of living of Soviet citizens. These oblast level commissions were to monitor the activity of similarly organized commissions at subordinate party organizations.[37]

Shortly afterwards, the Politburo also seemed to endorse the general secretary's definitions; on August 15, 1989, it ordered party officials to develop "political methods of leadership of genuine practicality."[38] While the caveat about "genuine practicality" may have been designed to meet orthodox objections, the Politburo's enumeration of priorities for the commissions and departments of the Central Committee responsible for the main elements of "political work" reflected the general secretary's definitions.

The Politburo ordered the commissions on party construction and cadre policy, ideology, and legal matters to convene a conference of party secretaries and the directors of these departments in order to improve party officials' participation in the forthcoming elections to republican and local soviets. The commission on party construction was told to find "new ways" to foster the democratization of personnel management, and to improve the education of party officials at the Central Committee's Academy of Social Sciences, its higher party school, and local party educational institutions. The Politburo ordered the ideological commission to work out "a new conception of ideological activity for the party" responsive to changing social conditions.

The Politburo also outlined priorities for the departments of the CC/CPSU. It instructed the department of ideology in the Central Committee to convoke a series of conferences designed to improve the various levels of theoretical work and education. In addition, the Politburo ordered the state and legal department of the Central Committee to work out a more effective program for dealing with crime and strengthening law and order and legal education. The departments for ideology, party construction and cadres, and state and legal affairs were instructed to prepare recommendations for the Central Committee on the improvement of relations between party organs and independent social organizations. The departments of party construction and cadres, ideology, and the general department of the Central Committee were told to prepare suggestions for improving the interactions between the Politburo, the commissions of the Central Committee, and local party organizations.

Finally, the Politburo insisted that Communists working in both the Supreme Soviet and the Council of Ministers and other state agencies as well as local party committees examine the materials provided by the conference of party officials in July to improve their own work. The decree gave particular stress to the revival of the primary party organizations as the major instrument of party influence, and concluded by urging Communists at all levels to focus on problems of food supplies and other immediate social and economic problems, and to be more responsive to the complaints of citizens.[39]

The departments of the Central Committee followed the Politburo's lead in a variety of ways. In late August the department on social and economic questions and the department of party construction and cadres issued a joint report on the "national question" that charged that the ethnic conflicts in the republics in Central Asia and the Caucasus had been fostered by excessively high levels of unemployment in these regions. The report upbraided both party and state officials for their failure to deal with this problem and outlined specific proposals for action. On August 31 the Secretariat sharply ordered both party agencies and particular ministries to follow these guidelines.[40]

The ideological commission of the Central Committee also focused on the "national question" but in a totally unorthodox fashion. On August 17, 1989, it provided the long awaited "new conception" of this issue in the form of a draft program that repudiated the long-standing orthodox formulations about the nature of the USSR's federation. It not only assailed the Stalinist system for limiting the sovereignty of the member republics of the USSR, but also explicitly recognized that the system of centralized planning had damaged both the economies and ecologies of all of the republics. Most remarkable, the draft explicitly recognized that non-Russian citizens' fears about the impact of Russian immigration on their own sense of national identity had proved to be completely legitimate!

The draft recommended the negotiation of a new federal treaty that would grant vast autonomy to both the union republics and the autonomous republics within them. It defined the republics as sovereign socialist states (as did the existing constitution) with the right to develop their own economic programs and methods, and portrayed the government of the USSR as the coordinator rather than the director of the economy. It also called for a broadening of the independence of the Communist parties in all of the non-Russian republics and the establishment of institutions within the RSFSR that would give Russian Communists a much larger role in the development of policy. In particular, the draft called for the creation of a special Bureau for the RSFSR in the Central Committee and the regular convocation of Communists within the RSFSR to deal with their own special concerns.[41]

But the publication of this extraordinarily revisionist document was immediately overshadowed by dramatic political developments in the Baltic republics. By this time, the leaders of the Communist parties in the Baltic republics were no longer able to control the decisions of the nationalist deputies who dominated the republican legislative bodies. On August 22, 1989, a special commission of the Supreme Soviet of Lithuania unilaterally declared that both the Nazi-Soviet pact of 1939 and the Lithuanian Supreme Soviet's declaration of entry into the USSR in 1940 were invalid. The following day nationalist groups in all three Baltic republics held simultaneous demonstrations calling for their independence from the USSR.

These actions clearly enraged the leadership of the CPSU. On August 27, 1989, the Central Committee of the CPSU branded the Baltic nationalists as "anti-socialist, and anti-Soviet" agents of unnamed foreign powers and called on the citizens in the region to resist the nationalist "extremists."[42]

In this context, the general secretary evidently felt obliged to distance himself from the revisionist formulations of the draft platform on the national question. In his report to the Central Committee in September 1989 the general secretary endorsed more orthodox definitions of the national question. In particular, he now balanced the draft's criticism of Stalin's policies with a positive portrayal of the political and economic benefits of membership in the USSR, muted his attack on the Nazi-Soviet pact, and claimed that the Baltic states had joined the USSR voluntarily! He now asserted that republican leaders themselves had helped to create "distortions" in their respective economies and bracketed the draft's endorsement of economic autonomy for the republics with renewed emphasis on the importance of centrally defined economic policies and the autonomy of individual enterprises. He qualified his references to greater independence for the Communist parties in the republics with a sharp attack on any "federalization" of the CPSU and a vigorous defense of the Russian language as the common means of communication for all citizens of the USSR.[43]

The platform adopted by the Central Committee reflected Gorbachev's reversion to orthodox formulations. It reasserted the "internationalist" stance of the CPSU, openly condemned the concept of a federalized CPSU, and muted its support for greater independence for each republican Communist party. However, the platform did call for a significant change in the institutions responsible for the development of the leadership's position on the "national question." In particular, the platform recommended the formation of specialized commissions on nationality policy for the Central Committee, the republican party organizations, and the *obkom* and *kraikom* when necessary.[44]

In the midst of these difficulties the leadership was obliged to respond to an extremely serious economic crisis. By the fall of 1989 serious shortages of basic necessities had developed throughout the USSR and Soviet citizens increasingly blamed the regime for these problems. On September 9, 1989, the

Politburo issued a decree on the proper response to these problems that brushed aside the general secretary's formulations about the primacy of party officials' political work and reasserted the Politburo's control over the state's administration of industry in particularly dramatic fashion. The decree sharply attacked Gosplan and a variety of ministries for their failure to produce adequate supplies of such basic consumer items as soap, school notebooks, pencils, toothpaste, shoes, and batteries, and lashed out sharply at the alleged failure of the party units within ministries to monitor the performance of the "Communist leaders" (i.e., the ministers.) The Politburo summarily fired the deputy chairman of Gosplan, called on the party control commission to examine the records of ministerial personnel deemed responsible for the shortfalls in production, and demanded that all party bodies henceforth monitor the performance of "Communist leaders" more closely and effectively.[45]

The Politburo's dramatic criticism of individual members of the Council of Ministers and its call for more effective oversight of "Communist leaders" prompted a surge of published support for a more orthodox definition of officials' priorities. In mid-September 1989, *Partiinaia Zhizn'* once again stressed the need to strengthen "party influence" in the economy and cited Lenin's dictum about the overriding importance of economic policy in support of its position. While the journal did stress that "party influence" had to be conducted through "political means" and condemned party officials who continued to act in the "old way," it gave massive emphasis to the role of primary party organizations in enterprises raising labor productivity and assuring the efficient use of reserves and resources.[46]

At this juncture, Ligachev resumed his criticism of the general secretary with a vengeance. In the spring and summer of 1989, he had been hobbled by the accusations made by N. V. Ivanov, a vigorous and outspoken investigator for the USSR's Procurator's office, that Ligachev had taken bribes while serving as the Central Committee's emissary to the Uzbek Communist Party in the 1980s. Ligachev had immediately called for investigations by both the Procurator's office and the Politburo to clear his name, and the Congress of Peoples' Deputies had created its own special commission to investigate the charges against both Ligachev and the state prosecutors.[47]

In the midst of these investigations he resumed his trips to the major agricultural regions of the USSR in August 1989 as the chairman of the Central Committee's commission on agriculture. During his tour he repeatedly lashed out against those who sought to restore private property, a market economy, and a multiparty system, and called for the restoration of the ideological and organizational unity of the CPSU.[48] After his vindication by the Procurator in September 1989, he intensified his critique of those who had sought to limit the authority of party officials. In his remarks to the Central Committee in September, he insisted that the accusations against him were part of a broader and well-organized effort to discredit the Politburo and to set the rank-and-file Communists against the party's full-time officials.[49]

In a subsequent interview (which was not published until the following month) he sharply attacked those who argued that there were "two parties"—the apparatus of full time officials and the CPSU composed of its rank and file. "We do not have two parties: the apparatus is also made up of party members. If the wrong people end up in the apparatus, they should be fired and we should augment party committees with different communists by different means. Pay attention to the fact that all attacks on the CPSU have always begun with attacks on the party apparatus."[50]

Ligachev linked this defense of the apparat with sharpened criticism of the general secretary and his closest allies. While he praised perestroika for allowing greater freedom of expression, broadened popular participation in administration and the construction of schools, housing and health care facilities, he assailed the leadership for its growing and uncritical enthusiasm for nonsocialist institutions and practices. He recognized the need to use Western technology, but he derided the conclusion that the development of public ownership in the USSR had so alienated the working class that the restoration of private ownership of the means of production had become essential for economic revival. He warned that such restoration would only produce unemployment, class stratification, and instability.

As Ligachev pressed his attack on the general secretary, the various commissions and departments of the Central Committee seemed to become more assertive in dealing with both the "political" and economic responsibilities of party officials. In October 1989, a conference of the commissions of the Central Committee for party construction and cadre policy, legal affairs, and ideology was convened to develop an appropriate strategy for the forthcoming elections for legislative bodies in the republics of the USSR and all lower levels of the political system. Both Secretary Medvedev and Secretary Razumovsky addressed the conference. The published report on its deliberations indicated that the leadership now wanted the local party officials to play a more direct role in the electoral process than in the previous year. It condemned their passivity during the elections for the Congress of Peoples' Deputies of the USSR in 1989 and ordered them to respond to the voters' concern with problems of adequate supply of goods and social services.[51]

At the same time, the Politburo's dramatic intervention in economic administration seemed to encourage the Central Committee's department for social-economic problems to become more aggressive. Sometime in late October, it issued a report that assailed both the Council of Ministers and local soviet agencies for their failure to cope with the massive scarcity of medicines throughout the USSR. In response, the Politburo issued a decree on November 3, 1989, that attacked the chemical industry's abject failure to produce sufficient and appropriate medicines for the general public and medical institutions and demanded that the Council of Ministers of the USSR take appropriate action.[52] The department also issued a report calling for the development of more small and medium-sized enterprises to meet the pressing needs for consumer goods. On November 10, 1989, the Secretariat issued a decree urging the Council of Ministers to play a more aggressive role in fostering these enterprises.[53]

Notes

1. Medvedev, *V komande*, 85.

2. Gorbachev, *Zhizn'*, vol. 1, 428.

3. Ibid., 428–429.

4. Medvedev, *V komande*, 86–87.

5. *Pravda*, April 22, 1989, 2.

6. *Pravda*, April 27, 1989, l.

7. Ibid.

8. Shimko's and Sliunkov's reports were published together in *Pravda*, April 28, 1989, 2–3.

9. *Izvestiia TsK KPSS*, no. 6 (1989), 77, 88–89.

10. Gorbachev, *Zhizn'*, vol. 1, 437.

11. "Vazhnyi etap perestroikei. K itogam s'ezd narodnykh deputatov sssr," *Partiinaia Zhizn'*, no. 13 (1989), 3–4. Approved for publication June 20, 1989.

12. Gorbachev, *Zhizn'*, vol. 1, 438.

13. "O rabote tsentral'nogo komiteta KPSS," *Izvestiia TsK KPSS*, no. 7 (1989), 3–4.

14. For the entire text, see *Spravochnik partiinogo rabotnika* (1990), 102–110.

15. See *Spravochnik partiinogo rabotnika* (1990), 208–211.

16. A. Kapto, "Ideologiia I praktika obnovleniia," *Partiinaia Zhizn'*, no. 14 (1989), 3–11. Approved for publication July 4, 1989.

17. *Pravda*, December 17, 1988, 2.

18. See Julia Wishnevsky, "Aleksandr Yakovlev to Regain the Ideology Portfolio?" *Report on the USSR*, July 29, 1989, 9–11.

19. *Pravda*, May 13, 1989, 4.

20. *New Times*, no. 24 (June 13–19, 1989), 6.

21. *Pravda*, June 28, 1989, 3.

22. *Sovetskaia Kultura*, July 15, 1989, 3.

23. Ibid., 4.

24. Gorbachev stressed this point in his own discussion of his report in his memoirs, see Gorbachev, *Zhizn'*, vol. 1, 453.

25. *Pravda*, July 19, 1989, 4.

26. Ibid., 1.

27. *Pravda*, July 21, 1989, 1–2.

28. Ibid., 2.

29. Ibid.

30. Ibid., 4.

31. Ibid., 3–4.

32. Ryzhkov, *Desiat*, 134.

33. See Gorbachev, *Zhizn'*, vol. 1, 450.

34. The text of the decree is in *Spravochnik partiinogo rabotnika* (1990), 162–164.

35. "Avtoritet partiinogo rabotnika uverzhaetsiia delom," *Partiinaia Zhizn'*, no. 16 (1989), 3–8. Approved for publication August 1, 1989.

36. V. Novikov, "Ovladevta politicheskimy metodamy," *Partiinaia Zhizn'*, no. 16 (1989), 26.

37. Ibid., 29–31. For a detailed discussion of these commissions at the *raikom* level, see V. Efimov and A. Losik, "Kak perestraivat partiinuiu rabotu," *Partiinaia Zhizn'*, no. 17 (1989), 38–43. Approved for publication August 22, 1989.

38. The decree was published in *Izvestiia TsK KPSS*, no. 9 (1989), 3–4.

39. Ibid., 10–11.

40. See the decree of the Secretariat in *Spravochnik partiinogo rabotnika*, 1990, 220–224.

41. *Pravda*, August 17, 1989, 4.

42. *Pravda*, August 27, 1989, 1.

43. *Pravda*, September 20, 1989, 1.

44. The text of the platform is in *Spravochnik partiinogo rabotnika* (1990), 46–64.

45. The text is in *Spravochnik partiinogo rabotnika* (1990), 235–236.

46. "Ekonomicheskaia reforma I partiinyi komitet," *Partiinaia Zhizn'*, no. 19 (1989), 3–8.

47. *Pravda*, May 19, 1989, 3; May 23, 1989, 2; June 2, 1989, 5.

48. *Pravda*, August 8, 1989, 2; September 9, 1989, 2.

49. *Pravda*, September 22, 1989, 7.

50. *Argumenty i fakty*, no. 42 (October 21–27, 1989), 3.

51. *Pravda*, October 13, 1989.

52. *Spravochnik partiinogo rabotnika* (1990), 238–242.

53. Ibid., 243–246.

CHAPTER FIVE

◁≋▷

Gorbachev's Growing Revisionism: 1989–1990

In the last months of 1989, as the Communist parties in Eastern Europe tumbled from power, the nationalists in the borderlands of the USSR intensified their demands for independence, and Soviet consumers complained bitterly about their plight. In this increasingly threatening situation, General Secretary Gorbachev found it difficult to assert his own authority over the major components of the political system in the USSR. The decentralization of authority that he had fostered during the mid- and late 1980s now began to undermine his own capacity to direct both party and state institutions. At the 19th Conference of the CPSU in mid-1988, he had championed the expansion of the relative authority of both the executive and legislative branches of the Soviet state. But in the following year he discovered that the leaders of these bodies had their own views and did not automatically endorse Gorbachev's preferences.

The general secretary was faced with analagous problems with the CPSU. His support for the decentralization of authority within the party now made it extremely difficult for him to impose his own conception of officials' priorities on his subordinates. The response of party officials became increasingly diverse. On the one hand, orthodox leaders, including the directors of some of the commissions of the Central Committee, questioned his views with increasing bravado. On the other hand, local party officials responded to his support for their autonomy by sharing power with local state and soviet agencies in the development of economic policy.

In late 1989 and the first months of 1990, Gorbachev sought to shore up his authority in a variety of ways. In late 1989, he sought to undermine the remaining ideological basis for party officials' leadership by revising the official ideology in a fundamental fashion. His ideological revisionism sparked a fierce counterattack by orthodox officials, but he remained sufficiently powerful to persuade the members of the Central Committee to end the constitutional guarantee of the CPSU's monopoly of power in February 1990. This decision opened the way for the development of a multiparty system in the following months.

In March and April 1990, he moved to strengthen his power over the Soviet state by establishing a totally new executive position—the president of the USSR. The establishment of the presidency implicitly repudiated the entire concept of "party leadership of the soviet state" and was thus the ultimate "revisionist" act. While his spokesmen claimed that a president was needed to bring necessary changes in the CPSU, his orthodox opponents assailed Gorbachev for repudiating the concept of "party leadership."

Gorbachev's decision to become the president of the USSR did not mean that he had foresworn his authority as general secretary. In the spring of 1990 Gorbachev sought to protect his authority over the CPSU by suddenly reviving the authority of the Secretariat. This decision seemed to please Ligachev and other orthodox critics and helped to reduce the level of internal conflict within the CPSU in the last months before its 28th Congress.

As noted above, in 1989 Gorbachev had sought to use his new position as chairman of the Supreme Soviet to convince the Council of Ministers of the USSR to introduce a "socialist market economy" and to replace the existing specialized industrial ministries with a totally decentralized system of economic administration. Gorbachev adopted this approach on the grounds that the "market" had proved to be the most effective and democratic means of economic management.[1] In his first report as chairman of the Supreme Soviet to the Congress of Peoples' Deputies in May 1989, he had insisted that the full implementation of the program of administrative decentralization adopted in mid-1987 would eliminate the central ministries and establish an administrative system based on a voluntary union of self-sufficient and self-financing enterprises. In the process, he claimed that those who regarded these reforms as a threat to the state's role in industrial management had mistakenly "confused the branch ministries with the state."[2] (In his report Gorbachev made no reference to the role of party officials in the administration of the economy.)

But Chairman Gorbachev quickly discovered that he could not simply impose his own views on Chairman Ryzhkov and his allies in the Council of

Ministers of the USSR. In July 1989 the Council had established a state commission on economic reform headed by Abalkin, who was named deputy prime minister, to work out the government's program. The commission did not endorse Gorbachev's conclusion that the branch ministerial system should be eliminated. After months of debate over a wide variety of alternatives, the commission finally recommended a "radical moderate" program that sought to combine some elements of a market economy with continued state regulation of prices, levels of incomes, and inflation, and a program of social welfare for the poorest segment of society.[3] In November 1989 the commission presented its program to a huge conference of more than a thousand economists, enterprise directors, party and state officials, and members of the top leadership.

Abalkin's commission had not discussed the role of party officials in the implementation of this program. But the proceedings of the conference revealed that some leaders believed that the state's economic agencies should not be allowed to proceed without the supervision of the secretaries of the Central Committee. In particular, N. N. Sliunkov, the chairman of the Central Committee's commission on social-economic policy, maintained that it not only had the right to make suggestions to improve the government's program, but also was obliged to monitor its actual implementation. In his closing address to this conference, he urged the Abalkin commission and other state agencies (Gosplan, the State Committee for Science and Technology, the Ministry of Finance, the state Committee on Construction, the Academy of Sciences, and other agencies) to "clarify" the various proposals. He also argued that the commission had the right to examine "the progress of economic reform" in the near future.[4] In fact, in the following month, Sliunkov and his commission adopted a far more critical stance toward the government's reform program.

At the same time, the general secretary made a concerted effort to change fundamental elements in official ideology. In late November 1989, *Pravda* published a lengthy summary of his most recent public pronouncements that was revisionist from beginning to end. In this essay he claimed that the leaders of the CPSU continued to act on the basis of Marxist and Leninist ideas, but his interpretation of these ideas repeatedly blurred the differences between socialist and nonsocialist ideologies. For example, he criticized Marx (and by implication his successors) for their failure to appreciate the capacity of capitalism to democratize its political system and to improve the workers' standard of living. He also represented Lenin's adoption of the NEP and his support for cooperatives as the essence of Leninist theory on the construction of socialism. In addition, he insisted that the "idea of freedom" was central to socialist thinking and represented the "values of world civilization" as an important source of orientation for the CPSU. In this context, he stressed the importance of social democratic theory and practice for the future development of the USSR, and he explicitly endorsed the introduction of representative parliamentary democracy (with a clear separation between legislative, executive, and judicial branches in the USSR) as a major step toward the establishment of "democratic socialism."

Gorbachev also overtly discarded the orthodox view that the "party's" knowledge of Marxism-Leninism was the basis for its leadership. He now defined it as but one source of guidance coequal with the "analysis of the country's existing reality and world experience." In similar fashion, Gorbachev also implicitly discarded the orthodox view that the unity of the party was essential to its "leadership" by explicitly declaring that the CPSU itself was encouraging competing opinions and promoting pluralism. At this juncture, Gorbachev hinted at the need for additional reforms within the apparatus but provided no details.[5]

Most important, Gorbachev's comments on the role of "the party" threatened to destroy the ideological rationale for party officials' "leadership" of the Communists who manned soviet and state institutions. He now implied that the conclusions reached by party officials had no binding force but were to be considered "recommendations" that could be accepted or rejected by soviet and state bodies! Gorbachev insisted that the CPSU was the "political vanguard" of the society, and was "ridding itself" of its operational, executive, and managerial functions in order to prepare political and ideological platforms that would be "recommended" to the society and state through its elected organs. He insisted that the influence of the CPSU would be transmitted by its members without "issuing commands" to soviet and state agencies.

But important regional party officials openly challenged Gorbachev's revisionism. Two days after the publication of Gorbachev's lengthy essay on perestroika, *Pravda* published an interview with B. V. Gidaspov, who had recently been elected first secretary of both the Leningrad *gorkom* and *obkom*. Gidaspov argued that the general secretary had failed to provide a coherent sense of direction and purpose for both party officials and rank-and-file members. He declared that "today we lack the things that were always the Bolsheviks' strengths—clarity of long term aims and the skill of showing people clear prospects for the future. Yet it was on this basis that the party's ideological commitment and authority, its real, not merely stated leadership role were formed."[6] Gidaspov called for a restoration of greater discipline in "party work" and greater centralism in the relationship between higher and lower party units.

Gorbachev seemed to respond in part to such criticisms in his report to the Central Committee in December 1989, which had been convened to discuss the forthcoming session of the Congress of Peoples' Deputies of the USSR, the coming elections to soviets at the republican and local levels scheduled for early 1990, and the possible formation of an autonomous Communist Party for the RSFSR.

In his discussion of the forthcoming session of the Congress of Peoples' Deputies, Gorbachev once again gave priority to party officials' "political" responsibilities. He now gave particular attention to their role in the forthcoming elections to the soviets in the republics and regions and insisted that the mastery of electoral politics was one of the "main areas" of party work. He urged officials to assure the nomination of effective candidates, to help to prepare electoral programs in tune with local conditions, and to develop new approaches to agitprop work in support of the party's candidates.

In his discussion of officials' "economic work," Gorbachev now seemed to draw a clear distinction between their responsibilities for agriculture and for industry. First of all, he implied that party officials continued to retain full responsibility for agriculture; he warmly approved the Central Committee's convocation of a meeting of the *oblast* first secretaries in the RSFSR to respond to the severe shortages of agricultural products in major Soviet cities.[7] But he did not refer to the role of the Central Committee and its commissions in the development of industry or of the country's overall economic plan. This omission seemed to imply they did not have a significant role in this sector.

The response to Gorbachev's definitions was diverse. First of all, the Politburo endorsed his views on officials' responsibility for the agricultural sector. Shortly after the meeting of the Central Committee, the Politburo issued a stern decree castigating both local party officials and the ministries responsible for agriculture for their failure to cope with the shortages with sufficient speed. This decree was based on a report filed on December 1, 1989, signed by Ligachev, Stroev (the secretary of the Central Committee responsible for agriculture), and Skiba.[8]

But some leading officials seemed to challenge Gorbachev's views on the role of the Central Committee and its commissions in the development of industry. Once again, V. V. Sliunkov, the chairman of the Central Committee's commission on social-economic policy, strongly defended its role in the supervision of the government's economic policy. On the eve of the meeting of the Central Committee, his commission had not only discussed the program of the Council of Ministers, but also had made a number of recommendations to the Council about its plans.[9] Immediately after the meeting of the Central Committee, Sliunkov reported that it had adopted the commission's recommendations as well as the government's program.[10]

Despite these important reservations, the Central Committee did support Gorbachev's views on the centrality of electoral politics.[11] In fact, the Central Committee's election manifesto, which was issued at the end of its meeting in December 1989, proved to be an extraordinarily revisionist document. It did not define the CPSU as a "political vanguard," implied that it had become a purely parliamentary party, and portrayed the transformation of the soviets into genuine legislative bodies as a major contribution of perestroika. The manifesto declared that this reform had closed the breach between the regime and the society, and repeatedly emphasized that the new legislative bodies would be responsible for social and economic development within their respective jurisdictions. The manifesto also stressed the CPSU's awareness of the difficulties of Soviet life and its deep commitment to the improvement of social and economic conditions, but implied that it would act only within the framework of the rejuvenated system of soviets.[12]

As Gorbachev pressed party officials to focus on the CPSU's parliamentary path, he was forced to respond to two fundamental threats to the integrity of the CPSU from powerful regional and republican party officials. Orthodox regional party officials within the RSFSR were demanding the formation of an autonomous Communist Party for the RSFSR, while nationalist party officials at the head of the Communist Party of Lithuania sought to establish an independent Communist Party.

Gorbachev had attempted to deal with the question of the formation of a Communist Party for the RSFSR in a separate report to the Central Committee in December 1989. After a lengthy and rambling tribute to the Russian people and their contributions to the USSR, Gorbachev had reluctantly agreed to the formation of a Bureau for the RSFSR in the Central Committee (without a separate apparatus of its own) with himself as chairman. Gorbachev was not very enthusiastic about the formation of the Bureau. He repeatedly warned about the dangers inherent in the move toward the "federalization" of the CPSU, and his brief outline of the new Bureau's agenda gave more attention to administrative reform of the RSFSR than to internal party matters.[13]

Nor could he have been very pleased with the composition of the Bureau—it included powerful secretaries of the Central Committee (Iu. A. Manaenkov and G. I. Usmanov) and first secretaries of important party organizations (B. V. Gidaspov, the first secretary of the Leningrad *obkom* and *gorkom*, Iu. A. Prokofiev, first secretary of the Moscow *gorkom*, O. S. Shenin, first secretary of the Krasnoiarsk *kraikom*, and others) who had no enthusiasm for Gorbachev's program and ideology. Gorbachev later admitted that he had established the Bureau because he could not think of any alternative at the time and that he had not convened it very often because of the press of other business.[14] The general secretary's reluctance to provide leadership to the bureau probably contributed to the subsequent and ultimately successful effort to form the CP/RSFSR during the following year.

While Gorbachev had reluctantly compromised with the orthodox party officials in the RSFSR, he clearly had no patience with the nationalist officials at the head of the Lithuanian Communist Party. During the last months of 1989 the Communist Party of Lithuania had moved closer to a full declaration of independence from the CPSU. The general secretary could not conjure up any new approach to this problem—he simply dispatched V. Medvedev to Lithuania in a last-ditch effort to convince the leadership of the Communist Party not to break with the CPSU. Medvedev's published comments revealed that he had no sympathy for the grievances of the Lithuanian Communists. He insisted that their objectives could be fully achieved within the framework of the federation of "sovereign" states being formed in the USSR and warned that the proposed withdrawal from the CPSU seriously threatened the future of perestroika.[15] Medvedev's efforts were to no avail. On December 20, 1989, the Lithuanian Communist Party broke with the CPSU and on December 25–26, 1989, the Central Committee of the CPSU was reconvened into a special session to decide how to respond.

The hard-pressed Medvedev was named the chairman of the special commission appointed to formulate the proper response. The commission condemned the decision to leave the CPSU in particularly harsh terms, and called for the dispatch of a high-level delegation of party leaders to visit Lithuania to reason with their comrades.[16] Medvedev's comments at the end of the meeting of the Central Committee reflected the rigidity of the leadership's position. He assailed the Lithuanian Communists for their "preoccupation" with the events of 1939–1940, their focus on the "negative features" of membership in the USSR, their ostensible capitulation to the "nationalist forces" in the republic, and their "double dealing" with the Politburo.[17] In accordance with the Central Committee's resolution, in early January the general secretary led a delegation to Lithuania for extensive discussions with party leaders.

At approximately the same time, the general secretary was faced with a totally different set of challenges in the Caucasus. While the problems in the RSFSR and the Baltic had been caused by the vigorous action of party officials, the difficulties in the republics of Armenia and Azerbaijan were caused by the near total breakdown of local party officials' authority. The leaders of the Communist parties in both republics had proved unwilling or unable to resolve the conflict over the status of Nagorno-Kharabakh and armed conflict had flared anew. Shortly thereafter, the party officials at the head of the party in Azerbaijan lost control over the stormy events in their republic. Soviet armed forces were dispatched to Baku to repress nationalist demonstrations against the Communist Party.

These dramatic developments in the RSFSR and the border republics of the USSR demonstrated that the decentralization of authority fostered by the general secretary was threatening the very integrity of the USSR's political system. Nevertheless, the leadership's discussion of party officials' responsibilities continued to stress the need for independent action at the regional and local levels. In January 1990, when *Partiinaia Zhizn'* resumed its discussion of "political methods of leadership," it insisted that individual Communists and primary party organizations should no longer wait for "commands from above" but instead demonstrate "political will" by taking the intitiative in responding to local problems. The journal now defined the primary party organizations as "the political core, the source of direction, and the consolidating force" in work collectives and held them responsible for the fulfillment of a wide range of both traditional and reformist objectives. The PPO were told to improve labor discipline and labor productivity, and assure the introduction of technology, economic reforms, "new economic mechanisms," and new types of leasing arrangements for individual enterprises.[18]

In the first months of 1990, *Partiinaia Zhizn'* also published a series of articles by local party officials that underlined their capacity to work with local soviet and state agencies in the development and implementation of social-economic programs. These essays indicated that although the exact division of labor varied from region to region, the party officials consistently helped to define the objectives of state and soviet agencies and attempted to coordinate and supervise their activities. These essays also revealed that the renewed stress on the role of primary party organizations in mobilizing work collectives to fulfill both traditional and reformist objectives may have helped to bolster the authority of their own secretaries and their immediate supervisors at the *raikom* level.

For example, G. Kobelev, the first secretary of the Moscow *raikom* in Kazan, lauded *raikom* and PPO leaders who had learned how to use "persuasion" rather than administrative pressures to convince the workers of the superiority of self-financing and leasing arrangements. Kobelev insisted that the introduction of these reforms had made it possible for enterprises to help finance new schools, hospitals, etc. He also praised the leadership of the *raikom* for persuading the Communists in local soviet organs to respond to the social needs of the workers. Kobelev admitted that many party officials were not really ready for this approach, but he also congratulated those who had managed to stop issuing commands to state agencies and who had learned to "work with people" to determine their moods and aspirations.[19]

In the same spirit, a party secretary from the Altai *kraikom* praised local party leaders who had shifted their focus from "operational questions" to such long-term objectives as the economic education of workers, the cultivation of leasing contracts, the introduction of progressive technology, and the implementation of economic reform.[20] While this official acknowledged that many party organizations still focused exclusively on problems of production, he concluded that a new system of internal education for party secretaries would help them to give due attention to cadre management, internal democratization, and glasnost. In this context, he argued that it was necessary to clarify the responsibilities of the secretaries of primary party organizations in order to free them from their dependence on enterprise directors and allow them to fight for greater labor discipline and against "bureaucratic tendencies" at the workplace.

Finally, *Partiinaia Zhizn'* published an essay by a A. Agaponov, a party official studying at the Central Committee's Academy of Social Sciences, insisting that the success of party officials' "political leadership" was now dependent on their development of an effective social policy. The author assailed party officials for their traditional indifference to the needs of schools, museums, libraries, etc., and their failure to denounce the profiteering which had led to shortages of important consumer goods.[21] He concluded that local party leaders should act independently to develop regional social-economic plans based on consultation with the local population. He praised the bureau of the *kraikom* in Krasnodar for organizing citizens' discussion of these plans before their submission to the local soviet and for its assumption of "kontrol" over the soviet's activities in the areas of consumer goods, housing, and food supplies. The author urged other party officials to follow the example of their colleagues in Krasnodar.

Partiinaia Zhizn' published materials by "ideological workers" which also emphasized the need for independent activity based on local conditions. E. Bystrov, the director of the ideological department in the Novgorod *obkom*, argued that "ideological work" could no longer be designed to build local support for decisions imposed from above but should be reformed to assure that party officials considered local public opinion in their decision making. Bystrov reported that his department had used sociological research to determine citizens' immediate needs and objectives and had forwarded the results to both the bureau of the *obkom* and the *ispolkom* of the local soviet, which proceeded to establish new cultural institutions. He also reported that his department would engage in sociological research in order to make its political and economic educational programs more responsive to citizens needs.[22]

While local party officials were working toward a variety of power-sharing arrangements with local soviets, the leadership turned its attention to a critical ideological problem—the preparation of a draft platform for the forthcoming 28th Congress of the CPSU. Sometime in early 1990, Medvedev's commission on ideological questions of the Central Committee had begun to formulate this platform. At the time, he had told the commission that the draft to be presented to the Central Committee in February would reflect the leadership's "creative approach to Leninism."[23] However, he later revealed in his memoirs that the deep ideological divisions within Gorbachev's inner circle had made it impossible to reach agreement over both the tone and content of the draft. Medvedev reports that in the end the general secretary accepted a compromise document worked out by Boldin with reluctant cooperation from Medvedev.[24]

In early February the Central Committee was convened to hear Gorbachev's report on the draft (which was not published until after the meeting, in amended form). At this juncture, he called for a number of dramatic reforms of the state structure that would limit the authority of both the leading organs of the CPSU and local party officials. First of all, he explicitly called for the establishment of a president of the USSR to assure a more decisive response to the country's ever growing list of problems. At the same time, despite some ambiguities in formulation, he now defined the CPSU as a purely parliamentary party. He declared that it could fulfill its "vanguard role" only as a "democratically acknowledged force" that would renounce all legal and political advantages in its "fight to be a ruling party" within a democratic process, and would cooperate with other organizations. Gorbachev reiterated his call for increased internal democratization within the CPSU, insisted that party officials act as the agents of elected party committees, and praised local party units for developing their own programs. He also hinted at the possible reduction in the size of the Central Committee and some future reform of the apparatus.[25]

The debate on the draft platform in the Central Committee revealed that only his closest allies were willing to endorse his position. Shevardnadze supported the draft program in its entirety, and Yakovlev praised its emphasis on human freedom, on the need for a wide range of property relations, and insisted that it could serve as a rallying ground for the "healthy political center" of the CPSU.[26]

While Medvedev supported the draft platform, his remarks provided an inadvertent indictment of the Gorbachev regime. He openly acknowledged that the Gorbachev leadership had dismantled many aspects of the old regime without establishing effective new "mechanisms" for the reform of both the economy and the political system, and had not yet found a way to provide ideological leadership. He also implied that party officials had proved unable to work out a coherent way to control the media and that henceforth it would be regulated not by the ideological specialists in the apparatus, but by the Supreme Soviet's legislation on the press.[27]

Boris Yeltsin used the debate to denounce the party apparatus in no uncertain terms. He called for the renunciation of the principle of democratic centralism, the abolition of the apparatus as an "instrument of power," the decentralization of the CPSU based on a system of self-management for every unit of the party, and the revocation of Article 6 of the Constitution. He explicitly endorsed the establishment of a multiparty system.[28]

But the local party officials who spoke at the meeting denounced both the draft platform and the general secretary. A. I. Koriyenko, the first secretary of the Kiev *gorkom*, complained bitterly about the leadership's failure to respond effectively to the growing wave of anti-Communism. He faulted the draft platform for its vague references to internal reforms within the CPSU, for its obscure discussion of sharing power with other political organizations, and its failure to discuss the "ideological and educational role" of the CPSU or provide "any integral ideological platform."[29]

The first secretary of the Moscow *obkom*, V. K. Mesyats, adopted a similar position and pointedly noted that his party organization had adopted its own program giving "due attention" to Marxism-Leninism and the importance of the CPSU's leading role. He declared that the failure of the platform to provide a more coherent definition of the "vanguard role" for the CPSU would disorient many party members and push the CPSU to "the sidelines." Prokofiev, the first secretary of the Moscow *gorkom*, criticized the draft for its inability to define the ideological orientation of a renewed party and clearly lamented the loss of ideological unity.[30]

Ligachev did not support the draft platform in any fashion. He explicitly declared that its provisions would transform the CPSU into an "amorphous political club," and implied that party officials should be more actively involved in the solution of economic issues in a variety of ways. He praised the Politburo's resolution holding Communist leaders responsible for agricultural production and criticized Gorbachev for failing to consult with the first secretaries of local party organs about the reform of the apparatus in 1988. He said nothing about the fate of Article 6 of the Constitution.[31]

V. A. Ivashko, the first secretary of the Communist Party of the Ukraine and member of the Politburo, gave little support to the draft platform in his remarks to the Central Committee. He did not even refer to Gorbachev's conception of the role of "the party," which probably indicated that he did not share the general secretary's views. His only reference to the draft platform was his comment that it would take time to implement. Ivashko focused on the need for immediate action by the government to stabilize the economic situation.[32]

Chairman Ryzhkov provided the most explicit discussion of the role of party officials in his remarks to the Central Committee. After criticizing the leadership's immense ideological confusion over "the role of the party," he argued that its failure to define "how the party should act as a political leader" had made it impossible to work out a coherent division of functions between "the party, the soviets, and economic management." Ryzhkov directly criticized the entire "ideology" of reform advocated by the general secretary—that the "party" should give up its operational-economic functions to focus on the elaboration of programs for the country's development. Ryzhkov concluded that this might be possible at the republican level, but was unworkable at the lower level where the local committees and their officials continued to work on economic issues and to "supplant and duplicate" the activities of local soviet and economic agencies.[33]

Politburo/Secretary N. N. Sliunkov used the debate to emphasize the continued responsibility of the Central Committee's department and commission for social economic policy for the development of the country's economic policy. Sliunkov insisted that the two organs would work with appropriate ministries to develop specific proposals for approval by the Politburo. While he recognized that these agencies of the Central Committee shared responsibility with the government for the failures in economic policy, he also implied that they would act to assure more "resolute and effective measures" than those outlined by the Council of Ministers of the USSR.[34]

While Sliunkov gave little real attention to the draft, other speakers sharply assailed its failure to provide useful definitions. S. S. Shatalin of the Academy of Sciences assailed its inability to provide an adequate conception of socialism or to present an honest appraisal of social democracy.[35] V. V. Nikitin, the first deputy chairman of the USSR Council of Ministers, asserted that draft's definition of "humane democratic socialism" was so broad that it could be an appropriate objective for a nonsocialist society![36]

The widespread criticism of the draft led Gorbachev to establish a commission of seventy members under his chairmanship to produce a final version of the platform. Medvedev reports that the general secretary took on the primary responsibility for the revision of the text.[37] The text of the revised platform (which was published about a week after the meeting of the Cen-tral Committee) revealed that Gorbachev was once again obliged to pay heed to the views of his orthodox opponents to a certain extent. The revised platform for the Congress did include a number of orthodox formulations. It emphasized the importance of Marxism-Leninism for the party's educational work, stressed the role of the Central Committee as the collective leader of the CPSU, did not mention the need for another reform of the apparat, and retained the traditional ban on organized factions within the CPSU.

But the overall thrust of the platform was revisionist. It represented Marxism-Leninism as but one of many sources of the CPSU's guidance and de-fined the CPSU as a parliamentary party willing to share power with others. It declared that the CPSU "like other social-political organizations and mass movements participates (*uchastvuet*) in the administration of state and social affairs, nominates its representatives to the Congress of Peoples Deputies and other state organs. The party does not take upon itself any powers of state au-thority."[38] Finally, the draft platform redefined the party's "vanguard" role in dramatic fashion. The platform declared that the CPSU would henceforth concentrate on "the elaboration of theory and action programs," on organiza-tional and educational work, the implementation of its cadre policy, and en-gage in both debate and cooperation with other social-political organizations.[39]

Finally, the platform's description of the internal organizational structure of the CPSU repeatedly emphasized the decentralization of authority to lo-cal party units. It repeatedly stressed the importance of internal democrati-zation, based on the principle of election of leadership at all levels, recog-nized the autonomy of the Communist parties in the republics, granted the Russian Communists the right to convene a republican congress before the 28th Congress, and proposed that the first secretaries of republican parties be named to the proposed new leadership organ of the Central Committee, which was to be named the Presidium, and that the Central Committee would elect its own chairman. (These proposed changes in the names of the Politburo and the general secretary were not adopted at the 28th Congress of the CPSU.) The platform also called for the expansion of the rights of all lower party bodies and insisted that their activities be based on the needs and interests of the primary party organizations.[40]

In the first months of 1990, the general secretary mobilized the leading or-gans of the CPSU around the propagation of the draft platform for the 28th Congress. In February 1990, the Secretariat met to discuss the use of televi-sion "roundtables" to stimulate interest in both the draft platform and the Congress, while the Politburo declared that discussion of the proposed plat-form was the most immediate objective of all "political and organizational work." The Central Committee sponsored a conference for propaganda groups to mobilize discussion of the draft program among rank-and-file Communists. At the same time, its commission on questions of party construction and cadre policy examined the proposed changes of the party's rules to be submitted to the Congress as well as the regulations for the selection of delegates to the meeting.[41]

The focus on the platform led to a considerable lull in the public discussion of party officials' responsibilities and priorities. In particular, party officials no longer presented their views in *Partiinaia Zhizn'* and the academic specialists who took their place did little more than provide a gloss on the formulations incorporated into the draft program.[42]

But the preparations for the forthcoming Congress were suddenly disrupted in March 1990. Gorbachev reconvened the Central Committee into a special session and abruptly urged it to ask the Congress of Peoples' Deputies to eliminate Article 6 in the Constitution that had legitimized the leading role of the CPSU. This issue had been discussed during the debate on the draft platform in the Central Committee in February 1990, but the Central Committee had not issued a resolution on the subject. Gorbachev now simply distributed his proposed text during a break in the first session, which prompted bitter complaints from some leading party officials.[43] After considerable discussion the Central Committee agreed to modify the wording of Article 6 of the Constitution rather than to simply discard it. The revised article was worded ambiguously, but it clearly seemed to place the CPSU on equal footing with other parties in the development and implementation of state policy.[44]

The elimination of the constitutional guarantee of the "leading role" of the CPSU had immense implications for the distribution of authority in the political system. It not only threatened to destroy the rational for party officials' "leadership" of the Communists in soviet and state bodies, but also indirectly challenged the legitimacy of the general secretary's own extensive powers. His leadership of party officials had been portrayed as essential to the maintenace of their own leadership of Communists in state agencies. The general secretary's declaration that this leadership now had to be "won" in an electoral contest with other parties or organizations implied that he had no legitimate claim to be the "leader" of the USSR, except on an electoral basis.

The general secretary seemed to be fully aware of this problem. During the first months of 1990 he sought to create a new institutional base for his leadership of the USSR—the president of the USSR. Gorbachev had mentioned the need for a president of the USSR in his report on the draft platform for the 28th Congress to the Central Committee in February 1990 and his closest supporters had portrayed the establishment of the presidency as the solution for all of the USSR's many problems. For example, Medvedev had told the Central Committee that the establishment of the presidency was the only way to allow the CPSU to create the "real social, political, and economic mechanisms of democratic socialism" and to prevent the population from falling under the influences of "demagogues."[45]

But this declaration that the reform of the CPSU was dependent upon the establishment of a new powerful chief executive for the Soviet state implied that the definition of the CPSU as the "vanguard" of the political system had become obsolete. Yakovlev was the only member of the leadership willing to adopt this position in public. In late February 1990 he declared that the new presidency would restore law and order, provide "a symbol of unity, a guarantee of democracy and confidence in life," and serve as a custodian of the constitutional foundations of the political system. He did not even bother to refer to the CPSU.[46]

In March 1990 when the Central Committee was reconvened, it nominated Gorbachev to be the first president of the USSR. Ryzhkov, the chairman of the Council of Ministers nominated Gorbachev for the position and the Central Committee approved the nomination by unanimous vote.[47] When the Congress of Peoples' Deputies convened to discuss the nomination, Medvedev ruefully admitted that the presidency was designed to replace the CPSU as the ruler of the country! He reported that the leadership of the CPSU had been so absorbed with the establishment of new legislative bodies and the transformation of the CPSU from the "kernel" of the administration into a "social political organization," that it had "underestimated" the need for a powerful executive. Medvedev concluded that once the Central Committee had agreed to give up the CPSU's monopoly of political power, the establishment of the presidency was the only means to prevent anarchy and chaos in the face of unprecedented economic problems and nationalist threats to the integrity of the USSR.[48]

But this argument that the CPSU had been replaced by the presidency of the USSR provided Gorbachev's various opponents with an excellent rationale to demand that he give up his position as the general secretary. During the first stage of the discussion of Gorbachev's nomination in the Congress of Peoples' Deputies his opponents proved sufficiently powerful to persuade the deputies to consider a constitutional amendment to prevent him from holding the positions of general secretary and president at the same time. Medvedev reports that this amendment was supported by a coalition of radical democrats who sought to limit Gorbachev's authority and orthodox Communists who sought to replace him with a more orthodox general secretary.[49] The proposed amendment was supported by 1,303 deputies and opposed by 607. While this fell short of the necessary majority of two-thirds of the house, it revealed that support for Gorbachev had diminished sharply. He was elected as president of the USSR by a vote of 1,329 to 495.

After the Congress of Peoples' Deputies had elected Gorbachev as president of the USSR, the Central Committee continued its session. Ligachev used the occasion to express his grave reservations about the political implications of this basic institutional reform. Although he endorsed Gorbachev's election, Ligachev clearly did not regard the establishment of the presidency as the cure-all for the massive problems of governance faced by the USSR. He insisted that "presidential power as such will not lead the country out of the complex situation," and that only the party and the soviets could achieve that goal.[50]

He warned the Central Committee that the country was on the edge of political and economic chaos, that antisocialist elements sought to transform the CPSU into a social democratic party and to restore capitalism as had already been done in Eastern Europe. He concluded that the major source of the country's difficulties was the organizational and ideological weakness of the CPSU, and he endorsed a purge of oppositionist and anti-socialist elements to restore the party discipline essential to operate effectively in the emerging multiparty system. He did not endorse Gorbachev's view that the CPSU had to compete with others to attain its "vanguard" role, reasserted his orthodox view that the CPSU was the "ruling party" responsible for "all the country's affairs, including and primarily the economy," and sharply condemned those party officials who had been unwilling to take on the responsibility for economic policy for fear of being charged with "interference" in economic affairs.[51]

Ligachev not only vigorously supported orthodox views of party officials' priorities, but also sought to defend the CPSU against organized efforts to limit internal party discipline and to transform it into a "purely" parliamentary party. In the spring of 1990 he led the charge against the Democratic Platform, a reformist faction within the CPSU that had seized upon the general secretary's own revisionism to call for a repudiation of "democratic centralism," and the transformation of the CPSU into a purely parliamentary party.

The Politburo was deeply divided over the proper approach to the Democratic Platform. Medvedev reports that Ligachev and like-minded members of the Politburo wanted the Central Committee to condemn the Democratic Platform as factionalist and expel its members from the CPSU, while Medvedev and others adopted a more conciliatory approach to the issue. After considerable debate, on April 1, 1990, the Politburo agreed to publish an "open letter" that appealed for the restoration of the ideological and organizational unity of the CPSU and warned against the dangers of "factionalism" within the CPSU without openly condemning the Democratic Platform.

Medvedev reports that this "open letter" only deepened the ideological confusion within the leadership of the CPSU.[52] This became particularly evident at a conference of ideological secretaries convened by the Central Committee on April 23–24, 1990, under the direction of Medvedev and Kapto, the chief of the ideological department of the Central Committee. *Pravda's* report on the conference clearly indicated that these officials had been completely disoriented by the establishment of the presidency of the USSR, the general secretary's repudiation of orthodoxy, and his declaration that the CPSU was a parliamentary party.

While the assembled secretaries for ideology reportedly agreed on the need for "fundamentally new conceptual approaches" to ideological work, they were themselves unable to define them. They reportedly concluded that the new draft platform would help in the "renewal of ideology" and in the struggle against "political renegades, new pseudo-revolutionary leaders, dogmatists, conservatives, and separatists." They also reportedly agreed that the "new model" for ideological work would be based on "historical knowledge, modern theory and practice, and the priority of values common to all mankind."[53]

While the secretaries for ideology fumbled over these definitions, the Politburo, the Secretariat, the Russian Bureau, and the various commissions of the Central Committee were all focusing on the "complex organizational questions" related to the forthcoming Congress.[54] Most important, at this juncture, the general secretary now suddenly decided to revive the Secretariat of the Central Committee of the CPSU. While Gorbachev does not discuss this critical decision in his memoirs, Medvedev later revealed that in April 1990 the general secretary had ordered him to reactivate the Secretariat and to act as its chairman in order to protect Gorbachev's control over the CPSU! Medvedev claims that he immediately restored regular meetings of the Secretariat in order to overcome the "defeatest mood" of many of its officials.[55]

The revival of the Secretariat, which Ligachev had called for earlier, may help to explain his decision to suddenly curtail his criticism of the general secretary and his views. In May, Ligachev praised the process of democratization, made no reference to impending crisis and chaos, and asserted that failures in policy reflected problems of implementation rather than misguided strategy. Ligachev now insisted that he was not a "conservative" but a "realist" who sought gradual change based on more frequent consultation between the leadership and all appropriate groups and organizations.[56]

Notes

1. *Pravda*, May 31, 1989, 2.

2. Gorbachev gave this point particular stress in his memoirs. Gorbachev, *Zhizn'*, 442.

3. Ibid., 566–567.

4. *Pravda*, November 16, 1989, 3.

5. *Pravda*, November 26, 1989, 1–4.

6. *Pravda*, November 28, 1989, 2.

7. *Pravda*, December 10, 1989, 2.

8. See *Spravochnik partiinogo rabotnika*, 1990, 305–308.

9. See *Spravochnik partiinogo rabotnika*, 1990, 246–253.

10. Moscow TV Service, December 10, 1989, in *FBIS-SOV-89-236* (December 11, 1989), 63–66.

11. *Pravda, op. cit.*, 1.

12. For the text of the appeal, see *Spravochnik partiinogo rabotnika* 1990, 68–69.

13. *Pravda*, December 10, 1989, 3.

14. Gorbachev, *Zhizn'*, 531–532.

15. *Pravda*, December 2, 1989, 4.

16. *Spravochnik partiinogo rabotnika* (1990), 75–77.

17. *Pravda*, December 27, 1989, 2. For the stenographic record of the discussion, see *Izvestiia TsK KPSS*, no. 6 (1990).

18. "Proiavliat' politicheskuiu voliiu," *Partiinaia Zhizn'*, no. 2 (1990), 55–56. Approved for publication January 9, 1990.

19. G. Kobelev, "Ubezhdat I deistvovat," *Partiinaia Zhizn'*, no. 2 (1990), 60–63.

20. Iu Zhil'tsov, "Otrkrytost, glasnost, uchet mnenii kommunistov," *Partiinaia Zhizn'*, no. 3 (1990), 46–47. Approved for publication January 23, 1990.

21. A. Agaponov, "Blizhe k liudiam, bol'she zaboty o nikh," *Partiinaia Zhizn'*, no. 3 (1990), 48–51.

22. E. Bystrov, "Nekomandovat a sovetovatsiia," *Partiinaia Zhizn'*, no. 3 (1990), 52–53.

23. *Pravda*, January 27, 1990, 2.

24. Medvedev, *V komande*, 123–124.

25. *Pravda*, February 6, 1990, 1.

26. *Pravda*, February 8, 1990, 5.

27. *Pravda*, February 8, 1990, 4.

28. *Pravda*, February 6, 1990, 5.

29. *Pravda*, February 6, 1990, 2.

30. *Pravda*, February 6, 1990, 3.

31. *Pravda*, February 7, 1990, 6.

32. *Pravda*, February 8, 1990, 2.

33. *Pravda*, February 7, 1990, 4.

34. *Pravda*, February 8, 1990, 4–5.

35. *Pravda*, February 8, 1990, 6.

36. *Pravda*, February 8, 1990, 3.

37. Medvedev, *V komande*, 125–126.

38. *Partiinaia Zhizn'*, no. 5 (1990), 16.

39. Ibid.

40. Ibid., 17–19.

41. See the survey of the activities of the Central Committee for February 1990 in *Izvestiia TsK KPSS*, no. 3 (1990), 3–6.

42. See the contributions to the symposium "Osvobozhdaias ot komandnykh funkstii," *Partiinaia Zhizn'*, no. 5 (1990), approved for publication February 20, 1990.

43. *Materialyi plenuma tsentral'nogo komiteta kpss* (Moscow: Politizdat, 1990) vol. 2, March 14–16, 1990, 9, 23–24.

44. See the amended article as quoted in Gorbachev, *Zhizn'*, 483.

45. *Pravda*, February 8, 1990, 1–2.

46. *Izvestiia*, February 24, 1990, 3.

47. *Materialy*, vol. 2, March 14–16, 1990, 73–74.

48. *Izvestiia*, March 14, 1990, 3–4.

49. Medvedev, *V komande*, 111–112.

50. *Pravda*, March 18, 1990, 3.

51. Ibid.

52. Medvedev, *V komande*, 129–130.

53. *Pravda*, April 25, 1990, 2.

54. *Izvestiia TsK KPSS*, no. 6 (1990), 3.

55. Medvedev, *V komande*, 133.

56. Moscow TV, May 7, 1990. FBIS SOV90–089 (May 8, 1990), 33–34. See also *Pravda*, May 12, 1990, 3.

CHAPTER SIX

⬯

Toward the 28th Congress of the CPSU: 1990

The establishment of the position of the president of the USSR indicated that Gorbachev had sufficient authority to create totally new institutions. But in the spring of 1990 he quickly discovered that his new position as president did not provide him with the leverage needed to lead a political system that was crumbling into its component parts. First of all, he found that as president he could not impose his views about the proper administration of the economy on the newly empowered executive and legislative organs of the USSR. Second, he also discovered that as president he was unable to prevent the newly elected Congress of Peoples' Deputies of the RSFSR from electing Boris Yeltsin as the chairman of the RSFSR's Supreme Soviet.

At the same time Gorbachev discovered that he had seriously undermined his own authority as general secretary by his strong support for the decentralization of authority within the CPSU. His support for the autonomy of party organs and for their right to elect their own leaders made it virtually impossible for him to prevent the orthodox officials in the RSFSR from establishing an "autonomous" Communist Party for the RSFSR, and electing one of their own (I. K. Polozkov) as its first secretary in June 1990.

The election of Yeltsin and Polozkov to the leading positions in the RSFSR created an institutional base for both the radical and orthodox wings of the growing opposition to President/General Secretary Gorbachev. In response to these dramatic challenges to his authority and program, Gorbachev adopted a conciliatory position. This was particularly evident in his public comments to the 28th Congress of the CPSU that was convened in the summer of 1990.

Gorbachev now sought to preserve the unity of both the USSR and CPSU. He made no public attacks on either Yeltsin or Polozkov and they responded in kind. The desire of the delegates to the Congress to preserve the unity of both the USSR and CPSU evidently helped him to win their support for his ideological formulations and his proposals to reform the party's leading organs. Despite sharp criticism of his program and policies at the Congress it accepted his revisionist platform, his proposals for fundamental changes in the party's rules, and for a radical reform of the composition of both the Central Committee and Politburo.

With the Secretariat under the leadership of the loyal Medvedev and party officials deeply involved in the preparations for the Congress of the CPSU, Gorbachev attempted in early 1990 to use his new position as president of the USSR to shape the development of the country's economic policy. He quickly discovered that the explicit repudiation of the "leading role" of the CPSU and the stress on the autonomy of governmental institutions made it extremely difficult for him to lead the members of the Council of Ministers and the deputies in the Congress of Peoples' Deputies. Both groups were bent on playing an important role in the formulation of the government's economic program.

In April 1990 the president sought to use two newly created state institutions to provide direction for governmental policies—the Council of the Federation, which included the state leaders of all of the member republics of the USSR and the Presidential Council, an appointive advisory body. In mid-April Gorbachev convened the two bodies in joint session under his leadership to review the latest proposal for economic policy of the Council of Ministers. But the president's intervention seemed to intensify rather than resolve the deep disagreements within the leadership over the nature of the "regulated market economy" to be established in the USSR.

After a "stormy discussion," the two councils rejected the Council of Ministers' program as too general and demanded that the government submit a new proposal by the following month. The government complied. On May 22, 1990, the two councils discussed the new program, but they were too divided to approve it and ordered Chairman Ryzhkov to submit it directly to the Supreme Soviet of the USSR. When Ryzhkov submitted the program, he explicitly recognized the need for increases in prices and this evidently prompted a wave of panic buying throughout the USSR. This in turn led the Supreme Soviet to order the Council of Ministers to submit a revised program by September 1, 1990.[1]

While the president and the Council of Ministers floundered over the development of a coherent economic policy, the political system in the USSR was transformed by a series of dramatic political changes in the Russian republic. In the spring and summer of 1990 both the orthodox and radical oppositions to the general secretary/president gained an institutional base for their assaults on Gorbachev's policies. In May 1990 Boris Yeltsin was elected to the position of chairman of the Supreme Soviet of the RSFSR. Under his leadership, in June 1990 the Supreme Soviet of the RSFSR declared that its legislation took precedence over the legislation of the USSR. Henceforth, Chairman Yeltsin and his supporters were able to use the newly elected parliament of the RSFSR as a battering ram against the president of the USSR.

In June, the Communist Party of the RSFSR was established as an autonomous Communist Party within the CPSU and elected Polozkov as its first secretary. This gave orthodox Communists an institutional base for an assault on the prerogatives and policies of the general secretary. Gorbachev later recognized that the establishment of the Communist Party of the RSFSR had undermined his authority in the CPSU in the same way that the declaration of sovereignty by the Yeltsin regime had weakened the authority of the president and the government of the USSR.[2]

Gorbachev had sufficient authority to impose institutional changes from above to create the new presidency and other new state agencies. But his support for the democratization of both party and state bodies and the decentralization of authority within the CPSU had deprived him of effective leverage to deal with these challenges to his authority as general secretary/ president. In retrospect, it seems clear that Gorbachev's insistence that party officials share authority with the newly established legislatures and his acceptance of elections as the only source of legitimacy deprived him of leverage against the use of the new electoral machinery by the "radical democrats." The insistence that the CPSU was now a parliamentary party, the acceptance of the Congress of Peoples' Deputies for the RSFSR as the legitimate legislative body for the republic, and the introduction of genuine elections for both the deputies to that body and of its officers made it very difficult to prevent the election of Yeltsin. In this new framework, Gorbachev could do no more than denounce him and try to find an attractive alternative candidate.

Gorbachev insists in his memoirs that he had understood the importance of the "Russian problem" in the spring and summer of 1990. He also acknowledged that he had been unable to prevent Yeltsin's election as chairman of the Supreme Soviet of the RSFSR because of his commitment to the "democratization" of the USSR's political system. But Medvedev reveals that the general secretary proved to be no more effective in dealing with the new world of electoral politics than many of his colleagues. According to

Medvedev, Gorbachev actually adopted a passive attitude toward the elections in the Russian republic and confused his colleagues in the Poliburo by his lack of attention to the issue.

The Politburo had initially supported A. V. Vlasov, the chairman of the Council of Ministers of the RSFSR, to run against Yeltsin. But Vlasov's report on his government's policies to the Congress of Peoples' Deputies had proved to be so banal and pedestrian that it had alienated many of the deputies. The Politburo searched for an alternative and then unaccountably endorsed Polozkov, the orthodox first secretary of the *kraikom* in Krasnodar, to run against Yeltsin. Polozkov won sufficient support from the deputies in the first two rounds of the election to prevent Yeltsin from winning a majority. But once it became clear that Polozkov could not win a majority, the Politburo shifted its support back to Vlasov, who lost to Yeltsin on the third ballot by a tiny margin.[3]

Gorbachev faced strikingly similar problems when dealing with the foundation of the Communist Party of the RSFSR. In this instance, his previous recognition of the autonomy of republican Communist parties and his support for the election of party officials by their respective committees made it extremely difficult for him to prevent the formation of an autonomous Communist Party for the RSFSR. Gorbachev subsequently asserted in his memoirs that in 1989 his conservative opponents had been so deeply impressed by the effective use of nationalist slogans by the "radical democrats" in the RSFSR that they had decided to "play the Russian card" by launching a campaign to create an autonomous Communist Party for the Russian republic. Gorbachev ruefully acknowledged that it had proved impossible to stop this campaign because the Russian republic was the only one in the USSR that did not have its own Communist Party. As a result, many Russian members of the CPSU who did not necessarily support the general secretary's conservative opponents were willing to endorse their efforts to create an autonomous Communist Party.

Gorbachev temporized in the face of this challenge. He later confessed that he had realized that the formation of an autonomous Communist Party for the RSFSR not only threatened to split the CPSU, but also could be used by his conservative opponents against him and his supporters. But he also admitted that he had regarded the formation of the Communist Party for the RSFSR as "becoming objectively unavoidable," and had done very little to prevent its formation. He did not attempt to use the Bureau for the RSFSR, which had been established under his chairmanship in late 1989, to block the formation of the new party. In fact, Gorbachev subsequently admitted that the entire issue had been "allowed to drift," leaving the "Russian movement" in the hands of his various opponents.[4] In early April 1990 the Bureau for the RSFSR met with the preparatory committee that had been established to convene an all-Russian conference and agreed to convoke it on June 19, 1990.[5]

The general secretary's apparent inability to block the foundation of the Communist Party of the Russian republic clearly undermined his authority as the "leader" of the CPSU. This became painfully obvious at the founding conference for the Communist Party of the RSFSR in June 1990, where he was not treated with the usual deference due the general secretary. The delegates immediately transformed the conference into a founding Congress for the Communist Party of the RSFSR without asking for his approval, and he was allowed to present his report only after the delegates had finished their own debate on the agenda. Most remarkable, his opponents were evidently so sure of their strength that they had prepared an alternative report for distribution at the conference. Gorbachev was able to prevent the circulation of this report at the last minute.[6]

In his report to the founding Congress Gorbachev warned the delegates of the grave dangers of setting the Russian republic against the USSR and the Communist Party of the RSFSR against the CPSU. He openly assailed the continued legacy of Stalinism in the political system and vigorously defended his efforts to reform it and to establish a "socially oriented market economy," but he was unable to set the tone of the meeting as he had done so often in the past. Although Ligachev muted his criticism of the Gorbachev regime and actually praised the general secretary for his leadership in his own remarks to the Congress,[7] local party officials sharply attacked the Gorbachev regime. For example, A. G. Melnikov, the first secretary of the Kemerovskii *obkom*, announced that his party organization had passed a resolution of no-confidence in the Central Committee and Politburo and demanded their resignation.[8] Such expressions of independence by regional party officials became increasingly common during the following year.

Most important, I. V. Polozkov, who was soon to be elected as the first secretary of the CP/RSFSR, launched a full-scale orthodox assault on Gorbachev's leadership as general secretary and his definition of party officials' priorities. Polozkov declared that the leadership's growing incoherence on important ideological issues and its continued failure to provide local party officials with effective guidance were major sources of the USSR's growing difficulties. Polozkov assailed the Gorbachev leadership for its alleged failure to present a coherent program for the regeneration of socialism, to confront those who "opposed the theory of Marxism-Leninism and the practice of socialist construction," and its portrayal of the history of the USSR as a series of mistakes. In this context, he charged that the economy had been ruined by the Politburo's repeated insistence that party officials end their intervention in industrial administration even though no alternative system of management had been devised.[9]

But Polozkov was either unwilling or unable to outline a detailed alternative strategy for the new Communist Party at this juncture. He declared that it should "expose" the activities of anti-Communist political forces and oppose all efforts to "depoliticize" the army and police. He insisted that it should unite all those interested in the preservation of socialism, defend the interests of workers and peasants at all costs, and establish disciplined Communist factions in all of the soviets.

When the Congress turned to the election of its first secretary, the general secretary discovered to his immense disquiet that he was no longer able to control this process. He subsequently reported in his memoirs that this was the "first time" that the recommendations of the general secretary to a subordinate party organization had not been automatically adopted![10] Medvedev later revealed that the Politburo had immense difficulty responding to the new world of electoral politics and had been unable to agree on the nomination of a "leading figure" for the position.[11]

I. V. Polozkov was nominated from the floor but initially withdrew his own name on the grounds that he did not enjoy the support of the general secretary. But when he decided to run after all, Polozkov adopted a position that was more moderate than his initial broadside against the Gorbachev regime. He did not refer to the question of officials' priorities, and he seemed to endorse both reformist and orthodox formulations in an apparent effort to broaden his support. On the one hand, he defined the new party in orthodox terms as the defender of the "socialist choice on a Marxist-Leninist basis," called for additional state support to collective, and state farms and warmly welcomed an endorsement from Communists in the military. On the other hand, he expressed his willingness to cooperate with all democrats and denied that he was an "extreme conservative" similar to Andreeva.[12] Polozkov was elected first secretary of the Central Committee of the Communist Party of the RSFSR on the second ballot.

With his election, Polozkov was initially very conciliatory toward the leadership of both the RSFSR and the USSR. In his first brief press conference, he explicitly declared that he sought to cooperate with both Gorbachev and Yeltsin on the basis of perestroika and an improved life for the Russian people, and that he favored a "regulated market economy." He insisted that he had excellent relations with Yeltsin and expressed great interest in working with President Gorbachev.[13] In a more elaborate interview with *Pravda*, he seemed to be extremely tolerant of ideological diversity. He asserted that there were "positive" elements in both the Democratic platform and Marxist platform being circulated before the forthcoming 28th Congress of the CPSU and he pledged to eliminate the "conservative structure" of the party. He once again distanced himself from the orthodox orientation supported by Andreeva, and emphasized his desire to operate within the framework of the RSFSR's new parliamentary structure and to cooperate with Communist parties in other republics.[14]

Speaking on the eve of the 28th Congress of the CPSU, Polozkov seemed intent on avoiding a split within the party. He made no direct assault on the general secretary, did not refer to the divisive issue of party officials' proper role, and he stressed the possibility of cooperation between the new Communist Party of the RSFSR, Chairman Yeltsin, and President Gorbachev. Furthermore, Polozkov sought to demonstrate that he was well prepared for work at the apex of the political system. He implied that he had a long-standing personal relationship with Gorbachev and a full understanding of the complex relationship between the general secretary and other leaders, and expressed considerable admiration for Yeltsin and his objectives. He also declared his interest in a "dialogue" with all except those who sought to liquidate the CPSU, and pledged to cooperate with religious organizations in order to improve standards of morality and to foster national harmony. He also claimed to be the natural ally of all segments of the intelligentsia and seemed to soften his previous criticism of the drift toward a "market economy."[15]

Ligachev also adopted a conciliatory position on the eve of the 28th Congress. He had muted his criticism of the Gorbachev leadership in the spring of 1990, and he now seemed willing to overlook fundamental ideological differences in the interests of party unity. For example, he reported that he had congratulated Yeltsin on his election as chairman of the Supreme Soviet of the RSFSR and expressed the hope that Yeltsin would be able to cooperate with the new Communist Party of the RSFSR.[16]

While Polozkov and Ligachev tactfully avoided discussion of party officials' responsibilities in the interests of party unity, A. Yakovlev did not. On the eve of the Congress he charged that the refusal of party officials to give up their immense authority to the "people, the state and the soviets" had made it impossible to transform the CPSU into a "social-political organization" responsive to society's needs. While he claimed that the incorporation of "social-democratic experience" into its theory and practice might allow the CPSU to act "in a new way," he implied that it could well be swept from power because of its abiding failure to respond to existing needs.[17]

When the 28th Congress convened, the general secretary adopted a very conciliatory position toward both his orthodox and radical opponents. Gorbachev's report to the 28th Congress seemed to be designed to prevent a split in the CPSU and the breakup of the USSR. He repeatedly stressed the need for national unity and harmony and did not criticize either the orthodox leadership of the Communist Party of the RSFSR or the increasingly anti-Communist chairman of the Supreme Soviet of the RSFSR. In the same spirit, he sought to respond to the criticism of both the orthodox and radical opposition by vigorously defending both the process of democratization and a rapid shift to a market economy and by recognizing that the Politburo shared responsibility with the government for the failure to implement the economic reforms as originally planned.

But the general secretary reiterated the main elements of his revisionist stance on crucial ideological questions. He insisted that "socialism" would grow out of evolving practice rather than from any preconceived "blueprint," that the CPSU would retain its "vanguard" role only on a parliamentary and democratic basis, and defined it as the "party of socialist choice and a communist future" and as the supporter of "universal human and humanist ideals." Gorbachev warmly supported the introduction of a market economy and a sharp reduction in the state's administration of industry. He called for the elimination of the branch ministries in the near future and the introduction of an administrative system based entirely on horizontal linkages between independent production units operating on the principle of self-financing. While he muted his previous criticism of party officials, he clearly implied that they no longer had the right to impose their views on Soviet or state agencies and were now expected to "convey" ideas which enjoyed popular support to the appropriate state bodies.[18]

After Gorbachev had presented his report, the Congress moved in unprecedented directions. In response to demands that had been made at the founding congress of the Communist Party of the RSFSR, each member of the Politburo was obliged to report on his own activities. The reports of the leading secretaries of the Central Committee demonstrated that the conflict over party officials' priorities had been muted in the interests of party unity, but remained unresolved. While Secretaries Yakovlev, Razumovsky, and Medvedev endorsed the primacy of officials' "political" work with varying degrees of explicitness, Secretary Ligachev indirectly endorsed a more orthodox view of officials' responsibilities and explicitly called for the restoration of the Secretariat's previous authority.

Secretary Yakovlev's report focused on his role as the chairman of the Central Committee's commission on international affairs and the newly formed commission examining repressions under Stalin. While he did not criticize party officials as he had on the eve of the Congress, he clearly endorsed the primacy of their "political work" by vigorously defending his own previous role in fostering the development of glasnost and limiting party officials' control over the media and cultural affairs. Yakovlev adopted an openly anti-Stalinist stance, eloquently assailed the cynicism and careerism that hampered the party's activities, and charged that conservative elements within the party had thus far successfully blocked its regeneration.[19]

Secretary Razumovsky's survey of his activities as the director of the department of organizational-party work of the Central Committee and the chairman of its commission on questions of party construction and cadre work was extremely lackluster and dispirited. Razumovsky had not made any public comments during the first half of 1990 despite his broad responsibilities for personnel management. Razumovsky's silence may have been prompted by his absorption in the preparations for the 28th Congress of the CPSU. At the Central Committee meeting in February 1990 he had been named to the working group charged with developing a new version of the party's rules and a platform for the Congress.[20] During the following months he evidently had played an active role in these discussions and in April he was named to the special party commission preparing for the Congress.[21]

In his report to the Congress he emphasized the efforts of the personnel agencies of the Central Committee to accelerate the democratization of the CPSU and to revive the "political principles" in the activity of all of its local units. While he claimed that the democratization of personnel management had been extended widely within the CPSU, he also ruefully acknowledged that the "nomenklatura approach" to the problem had not been eliminated. He underlined the importance of the reform of the apparatus in 1988 in eliminating party officials' perennial "interference" in and "duplication" of the efforts of both Soviet and state economic agencies.[22]

Secretary Ligachev did not criticize the Gorbachev regime in his report to the Congress and he reaffirmed his support for a more gradual pace for reform. At the same time he refused to endorse Gorbachev's conclusion that the CPSU would now have to compete with other organizations to retain its "vanguard role" or his enthusiastic support for a market economy. He reminded his audience that perestroika had originally been designed to regenerate socialism, he assailed the transfer of control of the means of production to private owners, and he was particularly derisive of Gorbachev's tortured ideological rationalization of this basic shift in policy.

Ligachev did not overtly defend orthodox definitions of party officials' priorities as he had so often in the past, but he now insisted that the Secretariat and its apparat of party officials should be granted full responsibility for the supervision of all aspects of party members' activities. He lauded the role of the Secretariat during the first three years of perestroika in dealing with "questions of every day life," in monitoring the fulfillment of the decisions made by both the Central Committee and Politburo, and its management of personnel. He criticized the temporary "halt" in the Secretariat's activity after the establishment of the commissions of the Central Committee in 1988, and he insisted that the Secretariat be restored as a permanently operating body dealing with "urgent questions" of the party's life.[23]

Secretary Medvedev's report as the chairman of the Central Committee's commission on ideology revealed that he and his colleagues had failed to create a "new definition" of ideological work or a "new conception of socialism." Medvedev was clearly totally exhausted. He contended that the constant criticism of the regime from both "left and right" had made ideological work a "hazardous zone" and he adopted a remarkably defeatest position. He announced that the leadership had decided to narrow the scope of ideological work to "enlivening" the party's own publications and to the working out of a new definition of socialism that would be "grounded in Marxism-Leninism," free of "deformation," and based on "world wide experience." Medvedev declared that the citizens' faith in perestroika could be restored only if they believed that it was not "alien" and by appealing to their "deep patriotic feeling."[24]

Medvedev also attempted to respond to the widespread criticism that the Gorbachev regime had not created a coherent ideology to replace the orthodoxies of the past, but this proved to be a complete failure. He assailed those who awaited some "messiah" or some group of scholars to devise a new conception of socialism, and insisted that the "ideology and theory of perestroika" would emerge in the process of reform. But he then lapsed into incoherence. He concluded that it had become impossible to define the "boundaries of party opinion," and that the Congress would have to "broaden its program" and then sharply define its "ideological political boundaries."[25]

In addition to reports by the general secretary and members of the Politburo, both Polozkov and Yeltsin, the newly selected leaders of the RSFSR, also addressed the Congress. The first secretary of the Communist Party of the RSFSR continued to adopt a conciliatory position toward the general secretary and his policies. He muted his criticism of Gorbachev, praised the Congress's programmatic documents, described perestroika in positive terms, and outlined a program for the Communist Party of the RSFSR that could hardly present a challenge to the leadership of the CPSU. Polozkov announced that the Communist Party of the RSFSR would attempt to defend citizens against the negative consequences of the transition to a market economy and to raise labor productivity and discipline in enterprises. He also pledged to provide more modern equipment for the peasantry, to support the law enforcement agencies in their struggle against crime, and attempt to improve living conditions for veterans and young people.[26]

While Polozov adopted a conciliatory position, Boris Yeltsin, the chairman of the Supreme Soviet of the RSFSR, did not. Yeltsin declared that the Congress of Peoples' Deputies had replaced the Congress of the CPSU as the main source of direction for the country and denounced party officials as the major obstacle to the transformation of the CPSU into a genuinely democratic and parliamentary party. Moreover, Yelstin moved in a radical fashion. Yeltsin called for the abolition of the primary party organizations (PPO) in all state institutions and declared that rank-and-file Communists should be free to decide the fate of the PPO in industrial enterprises. Finally, he charged that the proposed program statement and revised rules of the CPSU did not provide for the full democratization of the party and therefore did not deserve the support of the Congress.[27] Yeltsin demonstrably resigned from the CPSU at the very end of the Congress.

The Congress ignored Yeltsin's broadside and moved on to complete its agenda. The subsequent proceedings indicated that General Secretary Gorbachev, despite the widespread criticism of his policies, had sufficient authority to win election as the general secretary, to reform the leading organs of the CPSU, and to assure that his ideological formulations were adopted by the Congress. First of all, the Congress elected Gorbachev as general secretary by a vote of 3,411 to 501. Second, Gorbachev created a totally new position of deputy general secretary and proceeded to nominate V. A. Ivashko, the first secretary of the Central Committee of the Communist Party of the Ukraine, for the position. The Congress supported Ivashko over Ligachev by a wide margin. Gorbachev later asserted that he had created this new position to allow Ivashko to lead the Secretariat so that Gorbachev could lead the country as the president of the USSR.[28]

Finally, Gorbachev's views on party officials' priorities and his revisionist ideological formulations were incorporated in the program statement and a revised version of the party's rules adopted by the Congress. These documents stipulated that party officials should adopt "political methods of leadership" in dealing with the party's rank and file and should share authority with the new legislative bodies at all levels of the political system. The program statement explicitly repudiated the CPSU's ideological monopoly, proclaimed that it was transforming itself into a "real political party" representing the interests of all social classes, and would no longer "supplant" state and soviet administrative organs. It also explicitly committed the CPSU to a parliamentary path, called for the formation of Communist factions in all elected Soviet bodies, and put an end to the control of the CPSU over personnel decisions in state agencies! Personnel decisions within the party itself were to be transferred from higher organs to local levels. The statement's discussion of the party's "theoretical" and "ideological work" made no reference at all to Marxism-Leninism, and its survey of "political and organizational work" focused on its support of "humane democratic socialism."[29]

The Congress also approved a new version of the party's rules that incorporated Gorbachev's revisionist views. The rules came close to defining the CPSU as a purely parliamentary party, and seemed to imply that the party officials would henceforth do little more than provide "suggestions" to the new legislative bodies. The CPSU was described as "struggling for political leadership" of the society through free elections to the soviets, and the decisions of the CPSU were portrayed not as binding decisions but as "proposals" to be submitted to the Congress of Peoples' Deputies for approval or disapproval.[30]

The new regulations explicitly defined the republican Communist Party organizations as independent bodies free to develop their own programs and broadened the rights of subordinate party organizations, including the primary party organizations. The rules called for the election of party officials at every level of the CPSU and defined the role of the local branches of the apparatus as the provision of "mainly information and analysis, sociological forecasting, and consultative services" for the elected bodies of the party.

General Secretary Gorbachev was also sufficiently powerful to transform the composition and function of both the Central Committee of the CPSU and its Politburo without apparent opposition. Until the 28th Congress, the Central Committee had included a large number of ministers as well as a large complement of full-time party officials. This arrangement had assured that the leaders of both the "inner" and "outer" party had been able to participate in the development of important decisions on public policy. Gorbachev simply discarded this principle in the formation of the new Central Committee and the number of ministers was sharply reduced.

But by all accounts, the general secretary was unable to control the composition of the Central Committee. The members were chosen in a complicated fashion from two separate lists circulated among the delegates. While the number of regional party officials was reduced, the number of city party officials and secretaries of large industrial enterprises increased significantly.[31] The end result, according to Cherniaev, was that the "overwhelming majority" of the members proved to be supporters of Ligachev and Polozkov.[32] Boldin subsequently claimed that this reorganization destroyed the authority of the Central Committee.[33]

Gorbachev had far greater success in reforming the composition of the Politburo. In his report to the Congress he had referred vaguely to the need to coordinate the activities of the republican Communist parties. On July 13–14, 1990, the new Central Committee convened and elected a totally new type of Politburo that seemed designed to meet the general secretary's wishes. It included the general secretary, his deputy, a number of secretaries of the Central Committee, and the first secretaries of the republican Communist parties, and excluded the chairman of the Council of Ministers and other key ministers.

This reform of the Politburo ended its role as the undisputed center of direction for the political system in the USSR. Until the 28th Congress, the Politburo had brought together the Politburo/secretaries of the CPSU who led the "inner" party and the Politburo/ministers who directed the "outer party." This arrangement had assured the participation of both groups in the formulation of policy and the coordination of the activities of both full-time party officials and state employees in the implementation of that policy. The elimination of ministerial representation in the new Politburo brought this vital arrangement to an end.

By all reports, the new Politburo reportedly met infrequently as Gorbachev turned increasingly to his position as president of the USSR to rule the country.[34] Boldin later claimed that the Politburo did not really deal with the country's many problems when it actually was convened.[35] Chairman Ryzhkov later charged that the reform of the Politburo helped to break the CPSU into its "national-territorial" units and thus helped to set the stage for the subsequent breakup of the USSR.[36]

Notes

1. Ryzhkov, *Desiat*, 421–428.
2. Gorbachev, *Zhizn'*, 539.
3. Medvedev, *V komande*, 139–140.
4. Gorbachev, *Zhizn'*, 532.
5. *Izvestiia TsK KPSS*, no. 5 (1990), 3.
6. Gorbachev, *Zhizn'*, 533–534.
7. *Sovetskaia Rossiia*, June 22, 1990, 3.
8. Gorbachev, *Zhizn'*, p. 536
9. *Sovetskaia Rossiia*, June 21, 1990, 6.
10. Gorbachev, *Zhizn'*, 538.
11. Medvedev, *V komande*, 142–143. Gorbachev reports that he had nominated two party officials who were members of the Bureau for the RSFSR in the Central Committee—V. A. Kuptsov and O. Shenin. Gorbachev, *Zhizn'*, p. 537–538.

12. *Sovetskaia Rossiia*, June 23, 1990, 3.

13. *Izvestiia*, June 24, 1990, 1.

14. *Pravda*, June 24, 1990, 2.

15. *Sovetskaia Rossiia*, July 1, 1990, 1–2.

16. *Pravda*, June 30, 1990, 2.

17. *Pravda*, June 23, 1990, 4.

18. *Current Soviet Policies* 11 (1990), 12.

19. *Pravda*, July 4, 1990, 3.

20. *Izvestiia TsK KPSS*, no. 3 (1990), 43–48, 92.

21. *Izvestiia TsK KPSS*, no. 5 (1990), 5, 32–35.

22. *Pravda*, July 5, 1990, 3.

23. *Pravda*, July 5, 1990, 2.

24. *Pravda*, July 4, 1990, 2.

25. *Pravda*, July 11, 1990, 4.

26. *Pravda*, July 9, 1990, 2–3.

27. *Pravda*, July 8, 1990, 4.

28. Gorbachev, *Zhizn'*, 558–559.

29. *Partiinaia Zhizn'*, no. 15 (1990), 12–13.

30. *Current Soviet Policies* 11 (1990), 96–100.

31. For a detailed discussion of the selection process, see Evan Mawsley and Stephen White, *The Soviet Elite from Lenin to Gorbachev: The Central Committee and Its Members 1917–1991* (New York: Oxford University Press, 2000), 202–206.

32. Chernayev, *Gorbachevym*, 357.

33. Boldin, *Krushenie*, 250.

34. Brown, *Gorbachev Factor*, 200.

35. Boldin, *Krushenie*.

36. Ryzhkov, *Desiat*, 139.

CHAPTER SEVEN

❧

The Revival of the Secretariat: 1990–1991

But if the Politburo languished after the 28th Congress of the CPSU, the Secretariat of the Central Committee did not. In fact, it actually flourished and extended its authority in a particularly dramatic fashion in the year between the 28th Congress and the abortive coup against President Gorbachev in August 1991. The new party rules explicitly defined the deputy general secretary as the director of the Secretariat. It was expanded at the 28th Congress to include Ivashko, eleven secretaries of the Central Committee and five other officials. While the general secretary chaired the first meeting of the revived Secretariat in August 1990, he did not continue this practice on a regular basis and evidently allowed Ivashko to direct it throughout the following year.

Under Ivashko's leadership, the Secretariat not only worked vigorously to expand its own authority, but also sought to broaden the responsibilities of the departments and commissions of the Central Committee, and of local party officials. But it must be emphasized that the secretaries of the Central Committee were unable to turn the political clock back to the early days of the Gorbachev regime. It was clearly impossible for them to ignore the vast extension of authority to the elected soviets at each level of the system. Thus the Secretariat did increase its authority in comparison to its position in the years between 1988 and 1990, but it also was now clearly obliged to work within the framework of the new elected legislative bodies.

Ivashko and his colleagues were able to broaden their authority because of Gorbachev's preoccupation with the threats to his power posed by Chairman

Boris Yeltsin, the self-styled "leader" of the Russian republic, during the last year of his reign. The nature of Chairman Yeltsin's position and his challenge to the central government of the USSR led Gorbachev to rely on his role as president of the USSR rather than his position as general secretary. After Chairman Yeltsin had quit the CPSU he was no longer subject to the "party discipline" imposed by the general secretary. And since Yeltsin now acted as if he were the chief executive of the RSFSR, Gorbachev had to use his authority as president of the USSR to deal with Yeltsin and his supporters. During the last year of his reign, Gorbachev became obsessed with two major conflicts between the government of the USSR and the government of the RSFSR: the development of a coherent economic policy for the entire country, and the establishment of a "new type" of federal system that would prevent the USSR from blowing apart into its republican components.

The relationship between President Gorbachev and Chairman Yeltsin shifted dramatically a number of times in the year from mid-1990 to mid-1991. In the summer of 1990 they began to cooperate on the development of a comprehensive program to introduce a "market economy" into the USSR, but in the fall of 1990 they clashed sharply over economic policy and the relative authority of the governments of the USSR and the RSFSR. In early 1991, in the aftermath of the dramatic crisis in the Lithuanian republic, Yeltsin called on President Gorbachev to resign. But in the spring of 1991 they restored their cooperation in an effort to create a totally new type of federal system for the USSR.

During this period, the deputy general secretary and the secretaries of the Central Committee worked without much fanfare to restore the Secretariat's authority and to broaden the responsibilities of the party officials under its supervision. The first step in this process was the transformation of the editorial board of the new journal of the Central Committee, *Izvestiia TsK KPSS*, which had been established after the reform of the apparatus in late 1988. In August 1990 Ivashko replaced Gorbachev as the chairman of the editorial board and Gorbachev's reformist allies, Medvedev, Yakovlev, and Razumovsky, were replaced by far more orthodox officials. Two members of the new board became particularly powerful: A. S. Dzasokhov, who had been named a secretary of the Central Committee and Politburo at the end of the 28th Congress of the CPSU and given responsibility for ideological questions, and O. S. Shenin, who had been a member of the Russian Bureau of the Central Committee and named a secretary of the Central Committee and member of the Politburo at the 28th Congress, was given responsibility for personnel management.[1]

On July 28, 1990, the general secretary chaired the first meeting of the newly formed Secretariat. He reportedly urged it to "activate" the party in all spheres of the country's social life, stressed the need to work with the "masses in labor collectives," and to eliminate party officials' "technocratic approach" and "commandism."[2] Ivashko quickly followed the lead of the general secretary and declared that the Secretariat would focus on the "revival of the party."[3]

Leading orthodox officials quickly demonstrated what they meant by the "revival of the party." Y. A. Prokofiev, the first secretary of the Moscow *gorkom*, who had been named to the Politburo at the 28th Congress, not only insisted that "the party" remained responsible for the solution of all of the country's problems, but also explicitly declared that local party organizations should be willing to challenge the decisions of the Council of Ministers and the Congress of Peoples' Deputies![4] Most important, Prokofiev revealed that under his leadership the Moscow *gorkom* had created new institutions to revitalize the activities of its subordinate primary party organizations. He pointed with great pride to the *gorkom*'s convocation of regular meetings of the secretaries of one hundred of the largest primary party organizations within the capital and to the establishment of new party organizations at places of residence. He noted that the PPOs should vigorously defend the interests of the workers within the context of a "regulated market economy" despite the loss of their previous right to supervise the administration of the enterprise.

In September 1990 *Izvestiia Tsk KPSS* published a interview with A. S. Dzasokhov, one of the new secretaries of the Central Committee, that revealed their deep commitment to the restoration of the Secretariat's central role in the political system. He was particularly critical of the Secretariat's severe loss of authority after the reform of the apparatus in 1988. He charged that "during the last one or two years" the failure of the Secretariat to supervise the implementation of its own decrees had brought "disastrous results" to the party as a whole. He praised the 28th Congress for its decision to rejuvenate the Secretariat, and pledged that it would work with both party and state agencies to assure the implementation of the Congress's resolutions on economic affairs, agrarian questions, problems of youth, military, education, science, culture, and the media.[5]

He insisted that "the party" remained responsible for the development of social-economic policy and declared that the commissions of the Central Committee would work out its details with the aid of specialists, advisers, and other members of the Central Committee. He also pledged that the secretaries of the Central Committee would travel throughout the country to respond to regional problems and difficulties, and claimed that the establishment of a new Council of secretaries of primary party organizations would help to generate new ideas and improve their "links with the masses." Finally, he outlined the Secretariat's agenda in very inclusive terms. He reported that it would henceforth organize the meetings of the Central Committee, monitor the implementation of the resolutions of the 28th Congress, periodically examine policies in agriculture, military affairs, and the internal budget of the CPSU, and evaluate the activities of local party officials.

In August 1990 the Secretariat began to issue its own orders to local party organizations on a wide range of important issues. The scope of these orders varied from sector to sector. Party officials' direct responsibility for agricultural affairs had never been challenged and the departments for agriculture had never been dismantled. As a result, the Secretariat's orders on agrarian questions were directed solely to the local party apparatus. For example, on August 7, 1990, in accordance with a dramatic appeal issued by President/General Secretary Gorbachev dealing with shortages of food supplies, the Secretariat ordered local party officials to improve their "organizational work" in order to produce a major increase in the fall harvest.[6]

But in areas of public policy where party officials had been obliged to share authority with state and soviet agencies, the Secretariat had to operate in a more complex environment. It not only provided orders for local party officials, but also gave directives to the Communists in ministries, and called on local party agencies to introduce appropriate legislation in the corresponding soviet. For example, on August 14, 1990, in response to widespread outbreaks of vandalism against monuments to Lenin and other leaders, the Secretariat ordered all party committees to improve their ideological work dealing with Lenin and his legacy and the "party's policy at the present stage of perestroika." The Secretariat also called upon Communists within ministries to assure that they acted to protect these monuments, and recommended the introduction of appropriate legislation in the Supreme Soviet of the USSR.[7]

The Secretariat's decrees on "internal" questions sought to improve party officials' capacity to work with local soviets and other agencies. On August 14, 1990, the Secretariat ordered the Academy of Social Science to prepare a new curriculum for party officials to help them to understand the rapidly changing social-economic landscape in the country and the "transition to a regulated market economy." The Secretariat's decree was itself based on a joint report prepared by the departments of the Central Committee for party construction and cadre policy, social and economic problems, ideology, and administration of affairs. It called for the training of party officials in sociology, social psychology, political science, and in the use of "political methods of work" in order to improve their relationship with deputies to the soviets and with representatives of social organizations.[8]

By the end of August, the Secretariat, acting on the recommendations of the departments of the Central Committee, sought to extend party officials' responsibilities for economic problems. In August 1990 the departments on social-economic policy and agricultural affairs issued a scathing report on massive shortfalls in the production of consumer goods, tobacco products, and food. It assailed the responsible ministries in no uncertain terms, sharply attacked party officials for their failure to give sufficient attention to these shortages, and recommended that the Communist ministers responsible for these shortages should appear before the Secretariat to answer for their mistakes.[9]

Most significant, on August 28, 1990, the Secretariat issued a decree based on this report that challenged Gorbachev's repeated demands that party officials end their excessive interference in state agencies. The Secretariat now charged that party officials had avoided the critical shortages of consumer goods because of their overly zealous efforts to end their "substitution" for state agencies. It called on the party organizations within ministries to monitor the "Communist-ministers" more directly and to find "new ways" to cope with pressing economic problems. While the Secretariat's decree did not order responsible ministers to report to it directly, it did dispatch secretaries of the Central Committee throughout the country in order to persuade *obkom* officials to act more aggressively to assure the production and distribution of consumer goods.[10]

At the same time, the secretaries of the Central Committee worked assiduously to bolster the Secretariat's authority. In September 1990, Secretary O. S. Shenin implied that the Secretariat itself was no less powerful than the Politburo in its dealings with legislative bodies throughout the system. He insisted that both the Politburo and Secretariat should be more assertive in persuading local party committees to establish active Communist Party factions in the new legislatures. He also seemed to imply that the Secretariat itself should serve as the major source of suggestions for legislation by the Supreme Soviet.[11]

The Secretariat also issued a series of important decrees on educational and cultural matters. On September 11, 1990, it issued a decree (which was based on a series of reports by the Central Committee's departments on ideology and social-economic policy) dealing with the disastrous impact of the shift to a market economy on the development of culture in the USSR. The Secretariat called for a wide variety of urgent measures to defend Soviet cultural institutions from the growing "commercialization" fostered by the shift to market relations.[12] It ordered the Academy of Social Sciences of the Central Committee to appoint a task force of party and state officials to work out proposals for a coherent "cultural policy" for the USSR, and urged the departments for ideology, social-economic questions, and legal affairs of the Central Committee to call upon the Supreme Soviet of the USSR to enact legislation to defend Soviet culture and cultural institutions. The report also urged the Supreme Soviet to compensate for the decline in the state's financial aid by seeking support for cultural activities from a variety of new commercial and social organizations. The Secretariat urged local Communist organizations to deal with the legislative bodies within their own jurisdiction in the same fashion.

In early October, on the eve of a meeting of the Central Committee, the Secretariat sought to counter the efforts by "radical democrats" to limit the role of primary party organizations in educational institutions. On October 2, 1990, the Secretariat issued a resolution that sharply criticized Communists working in secondary and higher educational institutions for their failure to mount an adequate response to this threat, which had ostensibly increased after the election of Boris Yeltsin as the chairman of the Supreme Soviet of the RSFSR. It called upon members of the Central Committee to meet directly with both students and teachers to explain the educational philosophy of the CPSU and demanded that the party press give more attention to these problems.[13]

During the fall of 1990, while the Secretariat sought to restore its authority in a variety of areas, Gorbachev seemed unwilling to use the new Politburo and Central Committee to assert his own authority. During this period, Gorbachev turned increasingly to his new position as president of the USSR to deal with two major questions: the establishment of a "regulated market economy" and a fundamental reform of the federal system. In the process, Gorbachev repeatedly collided with both the chairman of the Council of Ministers of the USSR and the chairman of the Supreme Soviet of the Russian republic.

President Gorbachev, Chairman Ryzhkov, and Chairman Yeltsin adopted different orientations toward these issues as they became increasingly intertwined. Chairman Ryzhkov and other members of the USSR Council of Ministers sought to retain its primacy over the governments of the member republics and to develop a program of gradual transition toward a market economy. In direct contrast, Chairman Yeltsin and his supporters, who increasingly regarded the government of the RSFSR as the coequal of the government of the USSR, endorsed a far more radical program of rapid transition to a market economy and a dramatic change in the nature of the federal system.

The president's effort to develop a coherent economic policy for the entire country floundered in the face of these basic conflicts. It must be remembered that in the fall of 1990 the government of the USSR had not yet worked out an agreed-upon program of economic reform. In the spring of 1990 the Congress of Peoples' Deputies/Supreme Soviet had ordered the USSR Council of Ministers to submit a new program to the legislature by

September 1, 1990. As a result, during the summer of 1990 Chairman Ryzhkov, Vice Chairman Abalkin, and their colleagues were racing to prepare a new set of proposals.

At the same time, the leaders of the RSFSR had challenged the government of the USSR in an unprecedented fashion. In keeping with the declaration of sovereignty by the Supreme Soviet of the RSFSR in June 1990, the new government of the RSFSR headed by I. S. Silaev was preparing its own program for a more rapid transition to a market economy under the leadership of G. A. Yavlinsky, a young economist who served as deputy chairman of the RSFSR Council of Ministers from July to November 1990.[14]

President Gorbachev subsequently claimed that in the summer of 1990 he had sought to "merge" the programs of the USSR and RSFSR in order to prevent a clash between the "center and Russia" and to keep the other republics in the USSR from following the lead of the RSFSR.[15] Gorbachev intervened personally in the decision-making process in order to achieve this objective. He brought the leaders of the governments of the USSR and RSFSR together on July 27, 1990, to establish a working group to hammer out a single set of proposals by September 1, 1990. The working group, chaired by academician Shatalin, included some of the country's leading economists and representatives of the member republics of the USSR but excluded representatives of the government of the USSR. Chairman Ryzhkov later revealed that he had regarded the agreement as a direct assault on the primacy of the government of the USSR.[16]

Gorbachev then proceeded to go on his vacation. Without his direct supervision, the hoped-for cooperation between the Shatalin group and the government of the USSR broke down and both continued to work out their own programs. In a rather bizarre effort to overcome these differences, the president convened a joint meeting of the Presidential Council and the Federation Council and invited nearly two hundred ministers, scholars, and deputies from the legislatures of both the USSR and RSFSR for an "exchange of opinions" on the proper path forward.

Although this unwieldy assembly clearly led to an intensification of conflict between the government of the USSR, on the one hand, and the leaders of the RSFSR and other member republics on the other, in early September 1990 President Gorbachev blithely reported to the Supreme Soviet that the differences could be easily overcome![17] Chairman Yeltsin clearly did not share Gorbachev's optimism. On the same day as Gorbachev's address, Yeltsin explicitly called on the government of the USSR headed by Ryzhkov to resign and urged the Supreme Soviet of the RSFSR to begin its own deliberations on the Shatalin program.[18]

The leadership of the Communist Party of the RSFSR strongly opposed the Yeltsin leadership's decision to make the Shatalin program the basis for its own policy. In September, when its founding Congress was reconvened, First Secretary Polozkov charged that the proposed rapid transition to a market economy would produce inflation, increase unemployment, foster the growth of a mentality based on the defense of private property, and accelerate the development of social stratification. He declared that the Communist Party of the RSFSR would defend the working people against the government's economic policy and urged the Communist deputies in the new Supreme Soviet of the RSFSR to counter the Yeltsin government's efforts to restore a capitalist system.[19] Henceforth, the Communists of Russia, which included approximately 40 percent of the house, emerged as a powerful and vigorous opponent of the economic policies of the Yeltsin regime.

At approximately the same time, President Gorbachev renewed his personal efforts to create a single program of economic reform for the entire country. He simply ordered the two working groups (headed by Abalkin for the USSR and Yavlinsky/Shatalin for the RSFSR) to overcome their differences under the arbitration of the reformist economist A. G. Aganbegian. The new version that emerged from this process, which became known as the Presidential program, prompted diametrically opposed responses from the legislative bodies of the USSR and the RSFSR. On the one hand, the Supreme Soviet of the RSFSR refused to endorse it and instead adopted the Shatalin program, known as the "500 day program," as the basis for its own policy.[20] On the other hand, the Supreme Soviet of the USSR called on the government of the USSR to produce yet another version that would somehow incorporate the best elements from the Presidential program, the Abalkin program, and the Shatalin program by October 15, 1990.[21] At the same time, the Supreme Soviet of the USSR granted the president additional powers of decree to guide the transition to the market.[22] Gorbachev and his closest advisers assumed the responsibility for creating a new program by the appointed deadline.[23]

While Gorbachev and his advisers worked feverishly to draft this new program, the Central Committee was convened on October 8, 1990, to discuss the role of the CPSU in the transition to a market economy. Gorbachev did not present the report on the agenda but assigned this delicate task to his newly selected deputy. Ivashko was clearly in an extremely difficult position. He could hardly speak out directly against the general secretary but did not want to offend the orthodox members of the Central Committee. He therefore bracketed revisionist and orthodox formulations together in his report to the Central Committee.

As a result, Ivashko was unable to provide coherent guidance for the Central Committee and local party officials about the proper relationship between party and state bodies in guiding the transition to a market economy. On the one hand, he explicitly recognized the primacy of the state's executive authority. He endorsed the extension of the president's decree powers by the Supreme Soviet of the USSR and insisted that the CPSU was obliged to follow the lead of the president, the Council of Ministers of the USSR, the Supreme Soviet of the USSR, and all local state agencies in order to deal with an extremely threatening social and economic situation. In the same spirit, he also implied that the Central Committee had no right or authority to question the decision to move toward a market economy but was obliged to define the role of Communist Party organizations in stabilizing the economy and assuring the transition to a market.[24]

On the other hand, Ivashko continued to insist that the CPSU remained the "ruling party" and argued that the work of Communist deputies in the legislative bodies throughout the USSR was the key to retaining the party's "leading role." He also declared that the primary party organizations were obliged to defend the political and economic interests of the workers against all threats, including those posed by organs of the Soviet state!

Ivashko's discussion of the transition to a market economy was equally contradictory. On the one hand, he overtly recognized that many members of the CPSU resisted and resented this transition, admitted that both state and party agencies had bungled the initial efforts to move in this direction, and claimed that party officials' loss of "direct execution of economic functions" had contributed significantly to the growing difficulties. He also insisted that Communists were obliged to actively defend and support those segments of the population hurt by the transition, to reduce unemployment, to oppose the commercialization of culture, to provide state support for health, education, etc.[25]

On the other hand, Ivasho represented the transition to a market economy as the only way to solve the country's growing financial and economic problems and to produce the necessary level of goods and services for the population. He made a blistering attack on the orthodox view that state ownership of the means of production was the essential feature of socialism, and insisted that the fears and misgivings about the market had to be replaced by a "new type" of consciousness. He therefore demanded that the party's entire system of ideological work (including internal party education, self-study, and mass media) should henceforth be devoted to the education and preparation of party cadres for work under market conditions!

At the end of his report, Ivashko announced that new commissions were being formed in the Central Committee to assure that it would become the party's "center of political and organizational work" and turned the meeting over to Secretaries of the Central Committee Dzasokhov and Shenin to spell out the details. Their reports revealed that the authority and the activities of the Secretariat had grown considerably since the 28th Congress of the CPSU.

Secretary Dzasokhov reported that the Secretariat now met on a weekly basis and that each one of the eleven secretaries was responsible for a particular area of current party policy. He admitted that the Secretariat's linkages with local party units had been weakened seriously "during the past years," that many local officials were still waiting passively for orders from above and had found it difficult to shift from "commandism" to the use of persuasion when working with others. But he insisted that the Secretariat would be able to overcome these difficulties by dispatching the secretaries of the Central Committee throughout the country in order to improve their understanding of regional problems. He also announced that the Secretariat would also convene more frequent conferences for the local specialized secretaries on particular problems such as ideological questions and interethnic relations.

Secretary Dzasokhov declared that the "party" retained responsibility for the development of social economic policy, argued that the Secretariat would provide "party backup" for the transition to a market economy, that it would also play a role in the development of a new union treaty, and the improvement of the party's internal system of education and the decisions about the fate of its daily newspaper. But Dzasokhov had a far broader definition of "ideological work" than the one outlined by the deputy general secretary. While he did endorse Ivashko's conclusion that the party's internal educational institutions should devote more attention to the study of market relations, he urged them to give equal attention to nationality problems, and the fostering of both Soviet patriotism and "parliamentary culture."[26]

Secretary O. S. Shenin's report on the commissions and departments of the Central Committee clearly indicated that he wanted them to play a more significant role in the formation of public policy. He announced that the Politburo and Secretariat now regarded the "standing commissions" as "one of the main forms" of organizing the work of the members of the Central Committee, the "main component" in shaping party policy, and an essential link between the center and local party organizations.[27] Shenin reported that the existing commissions on ideology, on social-economic policy, on agrarian policy, and on problems of international policy had been made into standing commissions. He also announced the formation of a new sociopolitical commission that was designed to analyze the sociopolitical situation in the country, establish links with non-Communist sociopolitical organizations, monitor the Communist deputies in the soviets and the process of "state building," as well as other issues. The new commission on nationalities policy would focus on the negotiation of the new union treaty, and a new commission on women and family issues would train women for the new system of market relations and for new positions of leadership. A new standing commission on the revival of primary party organizations would establish a new Council of Secretaries of party organizations, and additional commissions would be established to deal with science, education, culture, youth, and military policy.

Shenin also discussed the role of the departments of the Central Committee in some detail. He declared that they would provide support for the commissions, fulfill the directions of both the Politburo and Secretariat, and coordinate the activities of central apparatus and local party organizations. (The party construction and cadre policy department was replaced by the organizational department to achieve that objective.) Shenin also reported that new departments had been created to strengthen party officials ties with non-Communist organizations. A new department for the humanities would establish closer links with the intelligentsia, and a new department on sociopolitical organizations would work with trade unions, youth organizations, and other movements.

Following Ivashko's lead, Shenin reported that the Politburo and Secretariat now expected local party officials to devote far more attention to the work of the Communist deputies in the soviets. He now charged that the Central Committee's "passivity" toward Communist deputies in the past had left them unprepared for parliamentary activity and resistant to the formation of organized Communist factions within the new legislative bodies. He now insisted that party officials' work with deputies was "fundamental" to the fate of the CPSU as the "leading party" in the country, and announced the formation of a new department for legislative initiative and legal matters to deal directly with the Communists in soviets.[28]

Following the reports by the secretaries of the Central Committee, local party officials who were members of the Central Committee took the floor. While Ivashko and other leaders of the Secretariat had seemed to endorse Gorbachev's view on the transition to a market economy, other leading party officials expressed their serious reservations. For example, Yu. Prokofiev, first secretary of the Moscow *gorkom* and a member of the Politburo since the 28th Congress, charged that both the government of the USSR and the RSFSR were wrong to believe that the establishment of a market economy would solve the country's economic problems. He insisted that the state still had an important role to play in the economy and that state property should be transferred to workers' collectives rather than be privatized in any fashion. He maintained that the country had to establish political stability before making this transition and that a new federal system had to be worked out before the transformation of the economic system. Finally, he faulted President Gorbachev for subordinating his responsibilities as general secretary to his role as president of the USSR.[29]

I. K. Polozkov, the first secretary of the Communist Party of the RSFSR also was extremely skeptical of the transition to a market economy. He was particularly disdainful of the leadership's failure to work out a coherent ideological stance and its cavalier combination of Communist slogans with support for capitalist entrepreneurship. He sharply attacked the Gorbachev leadership for its failure to consult with "the party" in its development of its economic program.[30]

Polozkov's complaint was apparently completely legitimate. General Secretary Gorbachev subsequently recognized that many members of the Central Committee had deeply resented the expansion of the role of the Supreme Soviet in the development of economic policy at the expense of both the Politburo and Central Committee. Gorbachev reports that in October 1990 he had explicitly told the members of the Central Committee that the president and the government rather than party organs now had the right to take concrete actions dealing with economic policies.[31]

In fact, shortly after the meeting of the Central Committee in October 1990, the president's "general guidelines" for a transition to a market economy were approved by the Supreme Soviet of the USSR by an overwhelming majority.[32] At first, this decision seemed to intensify the disagreement between President Gorbachev and Chairman Yeltsin over economic policy. But the very sharpness of this conflict evidently convinced both of them to make a serious effort to avoid further confrontation, and they met on November 11, 1990, to resolve these and other differences. On November 13, 1990, Chairman Yeltsin reported to the Supreme Soviet of the RSFSR that he and Gorbachev continued to disagree over the sovereignty of the RSFSR but had agreed to establish a number of working commissions to overcome the breach between the governments of the USSR and the RSFSR, and to confer on a regular basis in order to avoid future confrontations.[33]

This renewal of cooperation between President Gorbachev and Chairman Yeltsin enraged orthodox Communist deputies in the USSR Supreme Soviet who feared that this apparent rapprochement would lead inexorably to the collapse of the central government and the replacement of state socialism with a market economy. As a result, on the opening day of the Supreme Soviet of the USSR, the conservative "soiuz" faction (which included a number of party officials) demanded that the president report immediately on the current crises in the country and the means to overcome them.[34]

The president's initial report to the Supreme Soviet failed to provide a concrete program of action and was greeted with such hostility that Gorbachev evidently feared that he might be voted out of office by the parliament that had elected him as president of the USSR eight months earlier. In the face of this challenge, he decided to strengthen the executive branch of the USSR.

The president abruptly called for the establishment of three new centers of state executive authority, without, however, clearly defining the proper relationship between them. He demanded that the council of the federation, which included the heads of state of all of the republics, be transformed into a governmental body, that the appointed Presidential Council be replaced by a new Security Council including leading ministers and headed by the president, and that the Council of Ministers, whose members had been approved by the Supreme Soviet of the USSR, be replaced by a Cabinet of Ministers named by the president.[35] The president's report on these changes was very authoritarian in tone, demanding the establishment of law and order in all levels of the system and the creation of special new agencies to fight crime and to assure the implementation of decrees. He concluded with a call for the rapid renegotiation of a new union treaty that would preserve the USSR and an appeal to all members of the CPSU to support his proposals.

Gorbachev's decision to bolster the power of USSR's central government evidently encouraged orthodox leaders in the CPSU to launch a full-scale assault on the entire process of reform. For example, First Secretary Polozkov of the Communist Party of the RSFSR charged that the Gorbachev leadership had allowed anti-Communist "radicals" and "national separatists" to seize control of the policy-making process and to use their control over the mass media to wage a savage assault on "socialist values," the legitimacy of the CPSU, its primary party organizations, and against the military and the agencies of law enforcement. Polozkov also claimed that the party leadership's misguided economic policies had destroyed peoples' faith in socialism and had produced a virtual "civil war" between the supporters of socialism and the "new bourgeois forces" that sought its destruction. He denounced all proposals for the "privatization" of state industry, and insisted that the regime establish a "regulated market of the socialist type" to avoid the dangers and pitfalls of a capitalist market.[36]

Gorbachev's efforts to strengthen the authority of the central government also provided the Secretariat with an excellent opportunity to extend the scope of its directives. During the first half of November the Secretariat had focused on measures to counter growing anti-Communist sentiment and orientations in various areas. The resolutions of the Secretariat had dealt with efforts by anti-Communists to eliminate primary party organizations in a number of educational institutions in Moscow, the alleged overt persecution of Communists in western Ukraine, and the growth of antimilitary sentiment in various parts of the country.[37]

Immediately after the president's address, the Secretariat began to make more specific demands on local party organizations and their officials. On November 22, 1990, it dispatched an urgent telegram dealing with the problem of food supplies in urban areas to all party organizations. The telegram assailed the breakdown of the distribution system and widespread mismanagement and malfeasance in state agencies, ordered the "leader Communists" in these agencies to assure the fulfillment of existing agreements on the supply of foodstuffs to the all-union fund, and demanded the immediate establishment of local bodies of worker control to supervise the distribution of foodstuffs.[38]

On November 27, 1990, the Secretariat also ordered all party organs to "strengthen the struggle against crime." After citing the population's growing anxiety about all types of criminal activity and the apparent passivity of some law enforcement agencies, the Secretariat ordered local party bodies to assure that both party organizations and the executive committees of all soviets discussed the issue and improved the operations of the primary party organizations within law enforcement agencies. The Secretariat demanded that Communist leaders improve labor discipline in every area, and urged party agencies to revive and restore militia and volunteer organizations to supplement the activities of the regular law enforcement agencies.[39]

At the same time, the new commissions of the Central Committee also became more active. At least some of them adopted a reformist position. For example, the new commission on women and the family, led by Secretary of the Central Committee G. Semenova, sharply criticized the leadership's failure to advance women to important positions in the CPSU, called for the establishment of new educational programs to prepare women to become involved in independent enterprise, and the preparation of legislation to train them for leadership and to develop programs in defense of womens' interests.[40]

In contrast, the new commission on the revival of the primary party organizations and the new commission on nationality policy proved to be deeply divided and uncertain about the proper path forward. The members of the commission on the revitalization of the primary party organizations disagreed sharply over the proper role and function of the primary party organizations at its first meeting in November 1990. Some charged that the loss of *pravo kontroliia* by the primary party organizations had destroyed their sense of direction, while others claimed that their success would depend on their role in "shaping new economic relationships" at the enterprise. Disagreement also developed over priorities. Some members of the commission emphasized the need to establish new councils of primary party organizations within large industrial combines, while others wanted to establish new primary party organizations at places of residence in order to support the party's electoral activities. The commission did agree to convene zonal conferences of secretaries of primary party organizations throughout the USSR during the next two months.[41]

The commission on nationality policy, which was headed by Secretary Girenko, divided sharply over the nature and the proposed name of the new federal system.[42] Despite these disagreements the commission clearly regarded itself as the major source of public policy on the subject. The commission declared that it would elaborate the "theoretical basis" for nationalities policy, prepare programmatic documents on the subject, and provide "forecasting" of the state of interethnic relations in various parts of the USSR. V. A. Mihailov, the head of the department for nationality policy of the Central Committee, briefed the commission on the elaboration of a "conceptual approach" to the question for the forthcoming meeting of the Central Committee in December.[43]

In December 1990 the secretaries of the Central Committee publicized their own efforts to revitalize the Secretariat. Secretary A. N. Girenko reported that all of them were working to "strengthen the role of the Secretariat of the Central Committee as the organizer of the implementation of party decisions."[44] Girenko also reported that the Secretariat had embarked on a major campaign to improve the "style and method of work" of subordinate party organizations. He promised that the Secretariat would provide them with more complete analyses of the country's political, economic, and social problems and programs, and improve internal communication within the CPSU.

At this time, the general secretary suddenly lurched back to a more orthodox definition of the responsibilities of full-time officials. He did not attempt to explain why he had shifted his position, but the timing of his remarks suggests that they reflected his efforts to recentralize authority over the entire political system. In an address to the Moscow *gorkom* on December 2, 1990, Gorbachev not only again referred to the CPSU as a "vanguard" party and as a "ruling party," but declared that he had "never agreed" with those who wanted the CPSU to act as a purely parliamentary party! He also reverted to a more orthodox definition of ideology. He now made no reference to the importance of the "values of world civilization," as he had so often in the past, and declared that the CPSU had always supported socialist goals, peoples' power, and social justice. He also emphasized the link between the

CPSU and the working class, admitted that it had been a "mistake" to exclude labor collectives from representation in parliamentary bodies, and promised to rectify the situation. Finally, he also admitted that it had been a mistake for party officials to reduce their contacts with "economic leaders" and implied that party officials should give far greater attention to social and economic issues. (Gorbachev was very cagey on the subject of officials' economic role. He noted that "someone" had complained that party organizations had not maintained sufficient contact with economic leaders, that this had occurred in both the Central Committee and other organizations, but that the situation was now "correcting itself.")

Partiinaia Zhizn' published Gorbachev's discussion of the CPSU in his report to the form of a separate article,[45] as if to imply these formulations had extraordinary political significance. Immediately after Gorbachev's address, the Secretariat moved vigorously to dramatize local party officials' responsibilities for "social-economic questions," particularly at the level of the primary party organizations.[46]

Simultaneously, President Gorbachev sought to bolster the authority of the central government of the USSR. On the same day as his address to the Moscow *gorkom*, the president replaced V. Bakatin, the relatively liberal minister of internal affairs with B. Pugo,[47] who later became one of the leaders of the abortive coup against Gorbachev in August 1991. Gorbachev's newfound enthusiasm for an extension of executive authority won praise from leading orthodox Communists. In particular, First Secretary Polozkov of the Communist Party of the RSFSR warmly endorsed the restoration of a powerful central government led by a strong executive president to reestablish political and economic stability and to restore key elements of state socialism.[48]

In mid-December 1990 the Congress of Peoples' Deputies of the USSR was convened to approve the changes in the organization of the executive branch. In his report to the Congress, President Gorbachev made a vigorous plea for the restoration of law and order to prevent "intensified discord, a rampage of dark forces, and the disintegration of the state."[49]

But Gorbachev's successful extension of the central government's authority infuriated the chairman of the Supreme Soviet of the RSFSR. During the debate on the president's report to the Congress, Yeltsin angrily charged that the president was being granted unlimited authority, declaring that "neither Stalin nor Brezhnev had so much legislatively established power."[50] But the Congress clearly did not share Yeltsin's sense of outrage. At the very end of 1990, it adopted a resolution that granted the president even more authority over all spheres of public policy.[51]

In this context, the Secretariat and its leaders pressed hard to assert their authority. In early January the Secretariat issued a decree reminding local party officials that the repudiation of "substitution" had not eliminated their responsibilities for the improvement of the workers' standard of living. The decree ordered local party officials to establish systems of workers' control to assure the provision of food supplies, consumer goods, and the improvement in law and order. It also ordered them to improve their supervision of the "Communist leaders" in the various trusts and industrial combinations.[52]

Simultaneously, Deputy General Secretary Ivashko made a major effort to revive the morale of both party officials and the rank-and-file members of the CPSU. He urged them to discard the "self imposed inferiority complex" that was hampering their effectiveness at all levels of the system, and to "make the party work" rather than merely talk about solutions. He insisted that the CPSU remained the "most powerful and well organized political force" in the country and was responsible for leading it out of the current economic and political crisis. He praised the most recent meetings of the Central Committee for dealing with the country's most pressing problems, the revival of its various commissions, and the vigor of the Secretariat itself.[53]

Furthermore, other members of the Secretariat now openly attacked the general secretary. For example, V. A. Kuptsov, who had served as head of the Central Committee's department for work with social political organizations[54] and had been named to the Secretariat at the 28th Congress of the CPSU, sharply condemned the various mistakes of the Gorbachev leadership. He explicitly opposed those who supported the formation of factions within the CPSU, and demanded the restoration of party discipline and a more assertive stance against the growth of anti-Communist orientations. He urged his colleagues to remember that the CPSU was the country's "ruling party" and to assert their authority in every soviet. Finally, he praised the Central Committee for its effective opposition to the most radical programs for a transition to a market economy and insisting that "collective forms of property" be retained at its meeting in October 1990.[55]

Notes

1. *Izvestiia*, July 17, 1990, 2.

2. "Sekretariat TsK posle s'ezda: pervyi shagi" (Interview with Dzasokhov), *Izvestiia TskKPSS*, no. 9 (1990), 4, approved for publication September 10, 1990.

3. *Izvestiia TsK KPSS*, no. 8 (1990), 11, approved for publication August 10, 1990.

4. "Razryv v glubine demokratizatsii sushchestvenno sokratilsiia," *Partiinaia Zhizn'*, no. 16 (1990), 16, 19, approved for publication August 2, 1990.

5. "Sekretariat TsK posle s'ezsa: pervyi shagi," *Izvestiia TsK KPSS*, no. 9 (1990), 3.

6. "Postanovleniia sekretariata TsK KPSS, August 7, 1990," *Izvestiia Tsk K KPSS*, no. 9 (1990), 7–10.

7. "Postanovlenie sekretariata, August 14, 1990," *Izvestiia Tsk KPSS*, no. 9 (1990), 11–12.

8. "Postanovleniia sekretariata, August 14,1990," *Izvestiia TsK KPSS*, no. 9 (1990), 9–11.

9. The report was published in *Izvestiia TsK KPSS*, no. 10 (1990), 15–19.

10. "Postanovlenia sekretariata, August 28, 1990," *Izvestiia TsK KPSS*, no. 10 (1990), 11–12.

11. O. S. Shenin, "Prislyshivat'siia k pul'su strany i partii," *Izvestiia TsK KPSS*, no. 10 (1990), 3–6.

12. See *Izvestiia TsK KPSS*, no. 10 (1990), 19–26 for the decree and the supporting reports by the departments.

13. "Postanovlenie sekretariata October 2, 1990," *Izvestiia TsK KPSS*, no. 11 (1990), 12–13.

14. *Pravitel'stvo vlast rossii* (Moscow: Institut sovermennoi politiki, 1997), 157.

15. Gorbachev later charged that Yavlinksy's proposals had been designed to allow the RSFSR to "seize the initiative in the race to the market" from the USSR, to force the USSR government to accelerate its own efforts at reform and to place the assertive leadership of the RSFSR in a "no lose" situation. If the government of the USSR had accepted the Yavlinsky program, then the leaders of the RSFSR would win acclaim for their decisiveness. If, however, the USSR government did not follow the RSFSR's lead, the government of the USSR could be branded as "bankrupt." Gorbachev, *Zhizn'*, 571.

16. Ryzhkov, *Desiat*, 357–359.

17. *Izvestiia*, September 2, 1990, 1–2.

18. *Sovetskaia Rossiia*, September 2, 1990, 2.

19. *Pravda*, September 5, 1990, 1–2.

20. *Izvestiia*, September 12, 1990, 1.

21. *Pravda*, September 25, 1990, 2.

22. See Chronology in Mikhael Gorbachev, *Memoirs* (New York: Doubleday, 1995), 709.

23. Gorbachev, *Zhizn'*, 579–580.

24. *Pravda*, October 9, 1990, 2.

25. Ibid.

26. Pravda, October 10, 1990, 2.

27. Ibid.

28. Ibid.

29. *Pravda*, October 10, 1990, 3.

30. *Pravda*, October 10, 1990, 4.

31. Gorbachev, *Zhizn'*, 580.

32. *Izvestiia*, October 19, 1990, 1; October 20, 1990, 1.

33. *Izvestiia*, November 14, 1990, 2.

34. *Izvestiia*, November 15, 1990, 1–2.

35. Brown, *Gorbachev Factor* 275. *Pravda*, November 18, 1990, 1.

36. *Sovetskaia Rossiia*, November 16, 1990, 1–3.

37. For the resolutions on these issues, see *Izvestiia TsK KPSS*, no. 12 (1990), 12–24.

38. The telegram was published in *Izvestiia TskKPSS*, no. 12 (1990), 23–24.

39. *Izvestiia TsK KPSS*, no. 12 (1990), 25–26.

40. *Pravda*, November 26, 1990, 2.

41. *Pravda*, November 24, 1990, 2.

42. *Sovetskaia Rossiia*, November 22, 1990, 3.

43. *Pravda*, November 29, 1990, 2.

44. A. N. Girenko, "Ukrepliaia obratnyi sviazi," *Izvestiia TsK KPSS*, no. 12 (1990), 3–8.

45. "M. S. Gorbachev o KPSS," *Partiinaia Zhizn'*, no. 24 (1990), 3–4. It did not report that Gorbachev's comments were part of his address.

46. *Pravda*, December 4, 1990, 1–2.

47. *Izvestiia*, December 3, 1990, 3.

48. I. Polozkov, "Ziakel'nost," *Partiinaia Zhizn'*, no. 23 (1990), 33–34, approved for publication, December 14, 1990.

49. *Izvestiia*, December 18, 1990, 1.

50. *Izvestiia*, December 20, 1990, 6.

51. *Izvestiia*, December 26, 1990, 6.

52. "Postanovlenie Sekretariata, January 3, 1991, *Izvestiia TsK KPSS*, no. 1 (1991), 13–15.

53. V. A. Ivashko, "Vremia real'nykh deistvii," *Izvestiia TsK KPSS*, no. 1 (1991), 4–8.

54. *Pravda*, July 8, 1990, 1.

55. V. A. Kuptsov, "My obiazanyi splotitsiia," *Izvestiia Tsk K KPSS*, no. 1 (1991), 44–45.

CHAPTER EIGHT

～

From Orthodoxy to Reform:
January–August 1991

In the first months of 1991 President Gorbachev attempted to use his new powers to restore the authority of the government of the USSR over the Lithuanian republic. Gorbachev's efforts produced a severe crisis within the republic that threatened the integrity of the entire federal system. Moreover, his attempts to strengthen the authority of the chief executive of the USSR provided orthodox officials in the Secretariat and in the republican and oblast levels of the CPSU with an ideal context to reassert their own prerogatives.

The parliamentary elections in the Lithuanian republic in 1990 had brought anti-Communist nationalists to power, and their intense conflict with orthodox Communists had moved the republic to the edge of civil war. In January 1991 the president attempted to bring the nationalists to heel by publicly denouncing them for allegedly violating constitutional norms and by hinting that he might be forced to impose direct presidential rule. Gorbachev's demarche had a dramatic impact on political developments in the republic. It evidently encouraged orthodox Communists in Lithuania to establish a national salvation committee as a potential alternative to the government, and thereby set the stage for an assault on unarmed civilians by local units of the armed forces of the USSR.

This crisis prompted a sharp conflict between President Gorbachev and Chairman Yeltsin. While Gorbachev denied both knowledge and responsibility for the armed attack, Yeltsin not only publicly sided with the leaders of the Baltic republics against the government of the USSR, but also called on Gorbachev to resign. In late February, President Gorbachev, fearful of a complete breach between the Russian republic and the USSR, made a tentative effort to reach agreement with Chairman Yeltsin. But the orthodox leaders of the Communist Party of the RSFSR had a totally different agenda. They refused to follow the president's lead and instead in March 1991 launched a major effort to unseat Yeltsin as chairman of the Supreme Soviet of the RSFSR. This led to a dramatic confrontation between Yeltsin's supporters and Soviet military units in the streets of Moscow in late March 1991. At the last moment President Gorbachev decided not to allow the use of armed force against Yeltsin's supporters.

In the aftermath of this confrontation, the president began to openly cooperate with Chairman Yeltsin and the leaders of some of the other republics in a effort to establish a confederation to replace the existing federal system in the USSR. The restoration of cooperation between the revisionist president and the anti-Communist Yeltsin and their support for a massive reduction of the authority of the USSR's central government enraged orthodox officials at all levels of the system. Orthodox attacks on the president and his definitions intensified in the months between the spring of 1991 and the abortive coup against him in August 1991.

Orthodox party officials received a major boost from President Gorbachev's response to the crisis in the Lithuanian republic in the first weeks of 1991. The "Lithuanian question" had plagued the leaders of the USSR since the late 1980s. As the nationalist movement had gained ground, the leadership of the Communist Party of Lithuania had sought desperately to retain its influence in the republic. In December 1989 the leadership had declared the party to be independent of the CPSU while a minority faction had broken off to establish its own pro-CPSU Communist Party. General Secretary Gorbachev had visited Lithuania in early 1990 in an attempt to persuade the leaders of the independent party to change their mind, but his mission was to no avail. In March 1990 the newly elected Supreme Soviet of the Lithuanian republic, which was dominated by anti-Communist nationalists, had declared the republic independent of the USSR. Intensive political and economic pressure from the president of the USSR had forced it to rescind this declaration. As a result, conflict between the anti-Communists in power and the pro-CPSU Communist Party had intensified during the last months of 1990.

In January 1991 the pro-CPSU Communist factions organized a massive demonstration at the parliament building in the capital city of Vilnius to protest the government's economic policies. The clashes between the demonstrators and the nationalists defending the building[1] prompted President Gorbachev to dispatch an angry official note to the Supreme Soviet of Lithuania. The president charged that the Lithuanian government had violated the constitutions of both the USSR and the Lithuanian republic, was attempting to restore a "bourgeois" political system, and warned that there were "public organizations" within Lithuania that were legitimately calling for the imposition of direct presidential rule.[2] A few days later, a self-styled National Salvation Committee pledged to act on the basis of the president's appeal. Soviet military and security units in the republic attacked the television tower, inflicted casualties on its largely unarmed defenders, and the National Salvation Committee claimed to have seized power.[3]

President Gorbachev immediately denied responsibility for the armed attack on the television tower, and dispatched representatives from both the Federation Council and the Security and Defense Ministries to the scene.[4] Shortly thereafter the National Salvation Committee seemed to vanish. No attempt to impose direct presidential rule was ever made, and an uneasy status quo ante was restored.

This dramatic confrontation intensified the differences between Chairman Yeltsin, on the one hand, and the de facto alliance between President Gorbachev and orthodox Communist officials, on the other. Chairman Yeltsin not only sharply assailed the president, but also overtly defended the Baltic republics' aspirations for independence. Yeltsin demonstratively traveled to the Estonian republic where he explicitly acknowledged the sovereignty of the Baltic republics and joined with their leaders in an appeal to the United Nations to convene an international conference on the situation.[5]

While Chairman Yeltsin openly allied with the anti-Communist leaders in the Baltic republics, leading orthodox officials now rallied around President Gorbachev for his "defense of the integrity of the USSR." They also took advantage of the critical situation to defend the orthodox ideological formulations that the general secretary had openly repudiated at the 19th Conference of the CPSU. First Secretary Polozkov and Deputy General Secretary Ivashko took the lead. Polozkov published a lengthy defense of the "socialist character of perestroika" in *Kommunist* that derided the leadership's tendency to identify the market economy with the "advance of civilization" and to blur the vast differences between socialism and capitalism. He attempted to restore faith in orthodox definitions by portraying the USSR's introduction of a planned economy and an elaborate welfare state as in themselves "major contributions to civilization."[6] In the same spirit, Deputy General Secretary Ivashko now overtly supported a more orthodox definition of party officials' priorities. He explicitly attacked those who ostensibly sought to limit the Secretariat to "internal work" and insisted that it was concerned with *all* of the many issues facing the country.[7]

The Politburo also seemed to adopt a more orthodox position. On January 24, 1991, it issued a decree that implied that members of the CPSU should be wary of cooperation with non-Communist political organizations. At first glance, the decree seemed to be reformist in orientation. It endorsed political pluralism in the abstract and urged local party organizations to establish special commissions to foster cooperation with those who favored a "socially oriented" market economy. It also ordered the departments of the Central Committee and its internal educational programs to organize a conference on the training of Communists for dealing with a multiparty system by March 1991. But on a more specific level, the Politburo sharply condemned many of the new organizations for their anti-Communism, their efforts to destroy the USSR, their support for extremism of all sorts, and their attempts to take advantage of the country's economic crises in order to gain political power.[8]

In early February, the president and orthodox party officials seemed to form a de facto alliance. First Secretary Polozkov now praised President Gorbachev and his new Cabinet of Ministers for acting effectively against the "reactionaries" in the Lithuanian republic who had ostensibly restored the "dictatorship of private capital" and now sought to extend it to the entire USSR! Polozkov condemned the non-Communist regimes in the Baltic states as "totalitarian, nationalist and pro-Western" and defended the use of military force against such elements in the Lithuanian republic.[9]

In this context, Polozkov now portrayed the Communist Party of the RSFSR as a loyal supporter of the president and his government! He urged party members to support the president's efforts to restore economic and political stability, called on Communist deputies in the Russian parliament to "expose" their opponents more vigorously, and urged primary party organizations to focus on the problems of production. He also challenged the view that the CPSU should act primarily as a "parliamentary" party and warned that an overreliance on "electoral politics" could have dangerous consequences. In addition, Polozkov assailed the independent press for its anti-Communism, its accusations that the government of the USSR was "drifting toward dictatorship," and its misrepresentation of the Communist Party of the RSFSR as "conservative and obstructionist."[10]

While Polozkov lauded the president of the USSR, Chairman Yeltsin launched a fierce assault on Gorbachev and his new Cabinet of Ministers. In a television interview on February 19, 1991, Yeltsin charged that President Gorbachev sought to retain the old political system and to curtail the independence of the RSFSR and the other republics in the USSR. He assailed the government's use of armed force in the Baltic republics, accused Gorbachev of moving toward the establishment of a dictatorship, and demanded his resignation and the transfer of all state authority to the Council of the Federation.[11]

The Communist Party of the RSFSR responded very aggressively to Yeltsin's assault on the president. First of all, its faction in the Congress of Peoples' Deputies of the RSFSR called for and won support for the convocation of a special session for the following month to examine Yeltsin's role as chairman.[12] Second, First Secretary Polozkov actively cultivated the formation of an alliance between the Communist Party of the RSFSR and the USSR military against Chairman Yeltsin and his supporters. Polozkov condemned the demands of the "so-called democrats" for the elimination of Communist Party controls in the armed forces and urged local party agencies to give particular attention to the welfare of local military units.[13] Furthermore, on February 24, 1991, Polozkov attended a massive rally in support of the USSR's armed forces along with the USSR minister of defense, the chairman of the KGB, the minister of interior, and the first secretary of the Moscow *gorkom*.[14] Polozkov reiterated his harsh attack on Yeltsin's "radical democrats" in an address to a conference of nationalist organizations a few days later.[15]

In this context, the Secretariat intensified its efforts to broaden the responsibility of local party officials for "social-economic questions." This became particularly apparent in its discussion of the activities of the *obkom* in Orenburg. In early 1991 the major departments of the Central Committee had prepared a detailed report on the Orenburg *obkom*'s approach to "social-economic questions" that represented its activities as a model for all party officials. The report had praised the *obkom* leaders for (1) assuring that all of its subordinate party organizations prepared detailed programs for the improvement of housing, the supply of consumer goods and food products, and then submitting them to the appropriate soviet for discussion and approval; (2) providing leadership to the faction of Communist deputies within the *oblast* soviet to assure the implementation of these programs; (3) establishing various councils of secretaries of primary party organizations to coordinate activity and exchange information on the proper mobilization of work collectives; and (4) revitalizing agitprop work by effective use of the local media, press conferences, and meeting with local journalists.[16]

On February 28, 1991, the Secretariat issued a decree (based on this report) that ordered *all obkom* officials to plan all aspects of "party work" more carefully and to improve their communications with subordinate *gorkom* and *raikom*. In the process, it urged party officials at these levels and the leaders of primary party organizations to end their "estrangement" from the solution of social-economic questions, and to use "measures of a political character" to assure that both workers' collectives and state administrators responded to the needs of the working class and were prepared for the transition to a market economy.[17] Finally, the decree also demanded that party officials devote more attention to the soviets and the elections for local deputies. It urged them to nominate more workers and peasants as candidates, to improve agitprop work and their relationship with trade unions, women, veterans, and youth organizations.

While the Secretariat worked assiduously to restore the authority of its subordinates, the president of the USSR, faced with a series of insurmountable economic and political problems, attempted to diffuse the bitter conflict with Chairman Yeltsin. At the end of February Gorbachev hinted at the need for a truce with Yeltsin in an ambiguous speech to the Academy of Sciences of the Belorussian republic,[18] and cooperated with him during the all-union referendum on the future of the USSR that was held on March 17, 1991. As far as can be determined, President Gorbachev made no attempt to prevent Yeltsin from attaching a rider to the referendum on the desirability of an elected president for the RSFSR.

The president hailed the results of the referendum, in which 70 percent of the population supported the continuation of the USSR in some form, but the results did little to bolster the president's authority. This became painfully evident during the severe crisis that broke out on the eve of the convocation of an extraordinary session of the Congress of Peoples' Deputies of the RSFSR on March 28, 1991. This session had been convened on the initiative of the Communist deputies who hoped to oust Chairman Yeltsin from his position.

A few weeks before the session the first secretary of the Central Committee of the Communist Party of the RSFSR had assailed the Yeltsin regime in his address to the party's Central Committee. Polozkov had charged that the "radical democrats" who supported Yeltsin were acting as the agents of a coalition between the "new bourgeoisie," foreign companies, and the national separatists who sought to lead the USSR "to the edge of destruction under the nominal leadership of a Communist President" and then represent themselves as the country's only salvation. Polozkov had insisted that the Communists in the RSFSR should do everything possible to block this "unholy alliance."[19]

In this context, Yeltsin's supporters, fearful that the Communist deputies in the Congress of Peoples' Deputies would be able to mobilize support for a vote of "no confidence" against him, organized a mass demonstration on his behalf on the eve of the session of the Congress. The demonstration exposed the deep division between the governments of the USSR and the RSFSR in particularly dramatic fashion. While the president of the USSR and the Supreme Soviet of the USSR banned the demonstration, both the city government in Moscow and the Supreme Soviet of the RSFSR refused to implement the ban. The president responded to this extraordinary show of independence by dispatching regular army and security forces to Moscow as thousands of Yeltsin's supporters filled the streets and squares to defy the president's orders. Medvedev reports that President Gorbachev, faced with the threat of a bloody confrontation, decided to withdraw the armed forces at the last moment.[20]

The president's dramatic retreat seemed to convince Chairman Yeltsin to do the same. On March 29, 1991, he delivered a lengthy report to the Congress of Peoples' Deputies of the RSFSR that was highly critical of the USSR government's economic policy and its approach to the development of a new type of federal state. But Yeltsin did not directly attack President Gorbachev. In fact, Yeltsin now endorsed the concept of a new federal treaty based on the recognition of the republics' sovereignty, called for an end to conflict over this issue, and implied that he sided with Gorbachev against his orthodox opponents.[21]

Gorbachev needed all of the support he could muster. In the spring of 1991 his orthodox opponents were becoming increasingly aggressive. In early March the Central Control Commission (CCC), which was responsible for the maintenance of party discipline, suddenly issued a sharply worded decree that blamed the leadership of the CPSU for the collapse of party discipline. It charged that the Central Committee, its Politburo and its party committees (the Secretariat was not mentioned), had failed to provide the "theoretical, ideological, political and organizational work" needed to assure the implementation of decrees and effective communication between party units at various levels of the system. The CCC demanded the immediate restoration of internal discipline and the revival of communication between the party bodies.[22]

In April, Gorbachev's orthodox opponents began to mobilize their party organizations against him. Gorbachev later charged that in early April 1991 the *gorkom* in Kiev, the *obkom* in Leningrad, and the Central Committee of the Communist Party of Belorussia had all called for his resignation and the convocation of a special meeting of the Central Committee to deal with this question. He also charged that Prokofiev, the first secretary of the Moscow *gorkom*, Melnikov, a secretary of the Central Committee, and Gidaspov, the secretary of the Central Committee and head of the Leningrad *obkom*, had all worked assiduously to organize party meetings calling for the resignation of the general secretary.[23]

Circumstantial evidence suggests that these assaults helped to convince President Gorbachev of the need for closer cooperation with Chairman Yeltsin and the leaders of the other republics of the USSR. Medvedev reports that sometime in early April the newly appointed Security Council (it included the president, the vice president, the chairman of the cabinet of ministers, the ministers of internal affairs, foreign affairs, and defense, and the chairman of the committee on state security)[24] began to consider proposals for a "new type" of federation.

Medvedev also reports that at this critical juncture Gorbachev had become particularly confused about the proper path forward. Medvedev claims that Gorbachev had asked him whether he should seek an immediate agreement with the leaders of nine republics, which would enrage the Central Committee scheduled to meet later that month or reassert the authority of the government of the USSR over the republics and thereby win the support of an increasingly conservative Central Committee. Medvedev claims that he had convinced the president to work with the leaders of the nine republics on a new type of federal system and then present it to the Central Committee for approval. Gorbachev evidently agreed and ordered Medvedev to work with Shakhnazarov to prepare the platform for the conference with the republican leaders that was convened later that month.[25]

After considerable deliberation, on April 24, 1991, the conference issued a "joint statement of the President and leaders of nine republics" signed by Gorbachev and the heads of the governments of the RSFSR, Ukraine, Belorussia, and the five republics in Central Asia. The statement called for the acceleration of the negotiations for a new union treaty "among sovereign states" that would provide the juridical basis for a totally new constitution and new elections. It also called for the restoration of economic cooperation at all levels of the system, the reduction of the increases in prices that had been imposed the previous month, and an end to all "politically motivated" strikes. The statement closed with the declaration that the "fundamental enhancement of the role of the union republics" was the key to the solution of the country's political and economic crises.[26] Serious negotiations over the new treaty continued for the next three months.

But the general secretary was clearly in terrible trouble. On April 24, 1991, the Central Committee and the Central Control Commission convened in a joint session amidst speculation in the media that he was about to resign.[27] Gorbachev told the assembled officials that it was absolutely essential to support his agreement with the republican leaders and the latest "anti-crisis" economic program cobbled together by the new Cabinet of Ministers to assure the political and economic recovery of the USSR.[28]

But the orthodox members of the Central Committee were in no mood to support his position. S. I. Gurenko, the first secretary of the Ukrainian Communist Party, assailed Gorbachev for his failure to "rely on the party in his practical activity" and called for the restoration of "real participation of the party in working out policy and personnel management." A. M. Anipkin, the first secretary of the Vogograd *obkom*, followed suit.[29] A. M. Zaitsev, the first secretary of the Kemorovo *obkom*, criticized the leaders of the CPSU for their failure to counter openly anti-Communist actions, such as the activities of Democratic Russia in the country's mining regions.[30]

Gorbachev abruptly interrupted the debate to announce his resignation as general secretary. His dramatic gesture produced widespread panic among members of the Central Committee.[31] The Politburo was hastily convened, voted to instruct the Central Committee not to accept Gorbachev's resignation, and the Central Committee supported the Politburo by a wide margin. This vote revealed that many members of the Central Committee were terrified of a future without the general secretary, despite their hostility to him. The Central Committee dutifully endorsed his agreement with the leadership of the nine republics at the end of the plenum.[32]

But there were limits to the subservience of the Central Committee. While it endorsed the president's own project for a confederation of republics, the Central Committee simply refused to support the "anti-crisis program" worked out by the government of the USSR! On the eve of the Central Committee meeting, V. S. Pavlov, the new chairman of the Cabinet of Ministers, had presented his program to the Supreme Soviet of the USSR for its approval. The program was extremely eclectic and contradictory. It simultaneously called for a program of "controlled inflation," the privatization of the consumer sector of the economy, the continued use of state orders to assure the production of goods in vital sectors, and an increase in taxation to raise revenue.[33]

The Central Committee now openly opposed the policies of the government of the USSR! Although the CC/CPSU endorsed the program in general terms, it demanded that it be totally revised in order to meet the needs of the working population. The Central Committee now ordered the government to act immediately to prevent any further decline in the standard of living, to improve housing, to modify the recently adopted price reforms, to raise stipends for students, and to improve the lot of those on low fixed incomes. The resolution also charged that the shift to the market was being carried out far too quickly, demanded greater regulation of the process by the state, challenged the pace of liberalization of prices and the destatification of property, and called for stricter controls over the "shadow economy" and more government support for science and culture. Finally, the Central Committee called upon the leaders of the party and all party organizations to support its own program, insisted on the reimposition of discipline within the CPSU, and suggested a variety of ways to improve the linkages between higher party bodies and the primary party organizations.[34]

In the aftermath of the Central Committee's dramatic show of independence, a number of the secretaries of the CC/CPSU intensified their criticism of the general secretary and his program. V. A. Kuptsov (who had been named a secretary of the Central Committee at the 28th Congress), derided the regime's failure to develop an alternative to replace the command administrative system and openly declared that glasnost had created a new set of illusions to replace the old.[35] I. A. Manaenkov, the secretary of the CC/CPSU responsible for relations with the Communist Party of the RSFSR, now stressed the overriding importance of "democratic centralism" in assuring the unity of the CPSU.[36]

At the same time, the commissions and the departments of the Central Committee worked assiduously to bolster the authority of party officials in a variety of ways. The organizational department convened a conference of party secretaries that urged the Central Committee to establish closer links with the primary party organizations and to define their responsibilities with greater clarity.[37] In early May the Secretariat announced that the ideological department had established a new political information center to help local party organizations to improve their ideological work and their programs of political education for members of the party.[38] In mid-May 1991 the new commission of the Central Committee on questions of youth and the organizational department of the Central Committee issued a report that urged the restoration of the broken ties between the units of the party and the organization for youth. On May 16, 1991, the Secretariat issued a decree dispatching the report to all party organizations.[39]

On May 28, 1991, the Secretariat issued two decrees dealing with the primary party organizations. The first was based on the conclusions of a series of zonal conferences of secretaries of the primary party organizations sponsored by the commission of the Central Committee charged with their revival. The decree declared that the rejuvenation of the primary party organizations could provide the basis for a revival of the CPSU as a whole and outlined their responsibilities in very broad terms. They were henceforth expected to improve labor productivity, to tighten labor discipline, assure the implementation of both planned and contractual obligations, improve the standard of living, prepare for the transition to a market economy, and defend the workers' interests. The decree also called for the establishment of new agitprop groups specializing in primary party organizations to achieve these objectives and to counter efforts to blame the CPSU for the "mistakes and miscalculations" of state agencies in the development of economic policy.[40]

On the same day, the Secretariat issued a decree on the activities of primary party organizations in higher educational institutions that portrayed the activities of the primary party organization in Kharkhov University as a model for other Communists. The decree praised the leaders of the primary party organization for cooperating with the university administration in responding to students' needs, for fostering a revival of their interest in the study of Marxism-Leninism, and restoring broken linkages with the Komsomol. The Secretariat urged other primary party organizations to follow suit, and called for the con-vocation of a conference of secretaries of primary party organizations in higher educational institutions. It also called for the establishment of new commis-sions for science, education, and culture at all local party organizations, and ordered the Academy of Social Sciences to establish new training programs for the leaders of these commissions.[41]

The other commissions of the Central Committee also were particularly active in the spring and summer of 1991. The commission on agricultural policy headed by Stroev discussed measures to achieve some rough "parity" between the prices for industrial and agricultural products.[42] The social eco-nomic commission met under the leadership of Deputy General Secretary Ivashko, and issued a report that openly attacked the "destatification" poli-cies adopted by the Supreme Soviet of the USSR. The commission's report endorsed the policy of "destatization" in general terms but urged the govern-ment not to engage in total denationalization of property. It insisted that the state's pending legislation on the subject should strengthen rather than weaken the state's regulatory role, that the state should retain control of a "significant portion" of the country's national wealth, and retain its respon-sibilities for citizens' welfare. The report also urged local party organizations to be vigilant about any transfer of property to the "shadow economy."[43]

Other commissions and departments of the Central Committee were evi-dently convened about the same time. The published summaries of their de-liberations indicated that at least some of them continued to adopt reformist positions. For example, the commission on science, education, and culture, which was headed by I. T. Frolov, a member of the Politburo and former ed-itor of Pravda, as well as a close adviser to the general secretary, stressed the need to incorporate guarantees of cultural freedom into pending legislation on the USSR's cultural policy. It also endorsed the suggestion made by stu-dents in higher educational institutions to establish new councils of student-Communists under the auspices of the new humanities department of the Central Committee.[44]

In contrast, the department on social-economic policy of the Central Committee continued to support more orthodox priorities. It sponsored a conference of the secretaries of party organizations in all-union ministries that sought ways to rally the primary party organizations around the imple-mentation of the Central Committee's highly critical resolution on the gov-ernment's economic policy in April 1991.[45]

At this juncture, serious differences in orientation seemed to appear be-tween the Politburo and its Secretariat. While the departments of the Cen-tral Committee sought ways to improve party officials' "economic work," in early June the Politburo gave priority to certain elements of "political work." The Politburo's decree of June 3, 1991, may have been designed by the general secretary to counter the growing authority of orthodox officials. The decree explicitly defined parliamentary activity as "one of the most important forms of the political function of the CPSU" and ordered the social-political commission of the Central Committee to give it the highest priority.[46] (This decree seemed to put an end to a rather extended period of deliberation on this subject. In December 1990 Politburo/Secretary Yanaev had presented a report to the Central Committee on the role of Communist deputies in the Congress of Peoples' Deputies, but the Central Committee did not act on this issue until its meeting of April 1991. At that time, the Central Committee passed a vague resolution on the subject without providing any detail.)

The decree ordered the Secretariat to prepare legislative proposals for submission to the Congress of Peoples' Deputies/Supreme Soviet of the USSR and to establish closer links with the deputies who served in the USSR's legislative bodies. The Politburo urged the Communist deputies who served in the various committees and commissions of the parliament to develop legislation to improve the welfare of soviet citizens and ordered local party officials and their committees to focus on the activities of the Communist deputies in the soviets within their jurisdiction. Local party secretaries were told to work with the leadership of Communist factions to assure their internal discipline, to provide more coherent aid and support to their respective deputies groups, and to evaluate their performance. Finally, the Politburo ordered the internal educational institutions of the Central Committee to help to educate Communist deputies and to develop a program of research and "theoretical work" on the party's parliamentary activities by the fall of 1991.

The contrast between the Politburo's stress on parliamentary activity and the position of the orthodox secretaries of the CC/CPSU now became particularly sharp. For example, Secretary of the Central Committee Shenin, while endorsing the Politburo's position, gave higher priority to the restoration of a more centralized control of personnel within the CPSU. He charged that the higher party bodies' loss of control over the management of cadres had created an "abnormal situation" within the party and he insisted that local party officials had the right to demand an accounting of the "Communist leaders" who headed the administrative organs of the Soviet state. Finally, he insisted that local and primary party organizations should play the "leading role" in all trade unions, and youth and womens' organizations.[47]

Moreover, other party officials now freely criticized other aspects of the general secretary's revisionist position. M. Semenov, the first secretary of the Grodnenskii *obkom* in Belorussia, charged that the party's rules adopted by the 28th Congress had been written by those who sought to make the CPSU into an "amorphous organ" and had contributed significantly to the collapse of internal party discipline.[48] In the same spirit, P. K. Luchinskii, a Politburo/secretary, sharply criticized the new press laws for their failure to limit the "excesses" of the anti-Communist media and called for a return to closer cooperation between local party officials and the editors of local newspapers.[49]

While the Secretariat and the various commissions and departments of the Central Committee pressed for the restoration of officials' responsibilities, the president of the USSR and the new Council of the Federation had been struggling to redefine the USSR's federal system. On May 28, 1991, the Council of the Federation had convened to discuss the proposed new union treaty. Boldin later disclosed that conflict flared between the president of the USSR and the leaders of the union republics, on the one hand, and between the leaders of the union republics and the leaders of the autonomous republics, on the other. Boldin also reports that subsequent meetings of the Council of the Federation in June proved unable to resolve these conflicts.[50]

While the president struggled with these issues, his authority was being challenged by the leaders of both the Russian republic and the USSR. On June 12, 1991, Boris Yeltsin was elected the first president of the RSFSR with over 57 percent of the popular vote. Gorbachev dutifully congratulated Yeltsin on his victory, but the election of an avowed anti-Communist as the president of the RSFSR clearly produced immense anxiety within the Cabinet of Ministers of the USSR. This may help to explain the rather bizarre and halfhearted effort by Pavlov, the chairman of the Cabinet of Ministers to broaden its authority a few days after the election of Yeltsin as president of the RSFSR.

On June 17, 1991, when President Gorbachev was deeply engaged in the negotiations over the new union treaty, Chairman Pavlov reported on his government's activities to the Supreme Soviet of the USSR. In the process, he clearly implied that the Cabinet of Ministers should enjoy the right to initiate legislation and to act independently without first obtaining the consent of the president.[51] In responding to questions from the deputies about his intentions, Pavlov not only implied that he disagreed with the president, but also that he did not recognize his constitutional authority over the government.[52]

In the following days, Gorbachev's orthodox opponents in the legislature launched an offensive against him. Most important, a group of deputies from the conservative "soiuz" faction called for the transfer of authority from the president to the Cabinet of Ministers, while the Supreme Soviet asked for reports from the ministers of defense and the chairman of the KGB. These reports were delivered in a closed session and prompted rumors of a possible coup against the president. Although Gorbachev was able to reassert his authority, these actions seemed to indicate that the chairman of the Cabinet of Ministers and the leaders of the "power ministries" feared that the proposed new federal system would seriously undermine the authority of the government of the USSR.[53]

The members of the Cabinet of Ministers had good reason to be worried. The draft treaty for a "Union of Sovereign States" that was published on June 27, 1991, threatened to undermine the Cabinet's authority in a number of ways. The draft defined the republics as sovereign states with full control over all aspects of their internal affairs and granted the heads of the governments of the republics voting rights in the sessions of the cabinet. The draft made no reference to socialist values and gave prominence instead to such principles as the UN universal declaration of human rights. Finally, the draft limited the jurisdiction of the government of the USSR to defense, foreign affairs, union budget, and the direction of law enforcement, and gave the union and republican governments "joint authority" in all other spheres of public policy. In sum, it was reasonable for the leaders of the Cabinet of Ministers to regard the adoption of this treaty as a major step toward the elimination of the USSR and the destruction of socialism.

With the publication of the draft treaty, Gorbachev turned his attention to the critical question of composing a new party program for the CPSU. In mid-1990, the 28th Congress of the CPSU had appointed a commission to compose a new program, but it had made little progress by the middle of 1991. Medvedev later reported that the commission had been unable to agree upon a text because of constant conflict between the representatives of the ideological factions within the CPSU who had been named to the commission.[54]

General Secretary Gorbachev sought to jolt the commission into action. In an address to the commission on June 28, 1991, he implied that he wanted a program that was so revisionist that it would convince the orthodox members of the CPSU to leave the party.[55] (Some party officials claimed that the draft program submitted to the Central Committee in late July had been written by Gorbachev's assistant, Shakhnazarov, and was designed to be unacceptable to the conservative wing of the CPSU.)[56] Gorbachev later claimed that he had sought to speed up the work of the commission in order to counter the growing campaign of criticism from a group of powerful orthodox party officials. In his memoirs, he singled out Prokofiev, the first secretary of the Moscow *gorkom* and a member of the Politburo, Gidaspov, a secretary of the Central Committee, Gurenko, the first secretary of the Ukrainian Communist Party and member of the Politburo, and Shenin, the secretary of the Central Committee and member of the Politburo.[57]

In fact, circumstantial evidence suggests that Gorbachev may have been preparing to establish an alternative political organization for his own activities in the event of his ouster from his position as general secretary. The day before the publication of his comments on the commission, a number of leading reformists in the CPSU suddenly announced the establishment of a new political organization called the Movement for Democratic Reform. Their leaders claimed that this organization would mobilize the society in defense of Gorbachev's program and in support of individual rights against the efforts of "ultra-conservative forces" to consolidate their position in the society. A. Yakovlev, one of the founding members, declared that the new organization was essential to the implementation of Gorbachev's program because party officials had blocked it at "every turn."[58]

Three weeks later, on July 23, 1991, the draft program was published in the non-Communist *Nezavisimaia gazeta*, which had obtained an advance copy of the document. The draft must have enraged orthodox party officials. It repudiated basic elements of Bolshevik theory and practice and presented a social democratic program in its stead. It indirectly denigrated Lenin's Bolshevism by asserting that it had reflected the "insights and illusions" of the early twentieth century and portrayed Lenin's NEP as the basis for the development of socialism rather than as a temporary expedient forced on the Bolsheviks by the need to recover from the ravages of the civil war. It denounced the Stalinist political system as a totalitarian state based on the use of force, praised the 20th Congress of the CPSU for its efforts to reform the political system, and sharply criticized N. S. Khrushchev's successors for their indifference to the country's problems and their support for an "authoritarian bureaucratic regime."[59]

The draft simply dropped the concept of the CPSU as a "vanguard" party and instead stressed its commitment to individual freedom and to the values "common to all mankind" as the major source of its orientation. The program underlined the independence of all of the republican Communist parties, the broad autonomy enjoyed by local and primary party organizations, the right to form political factions, and discarded the conception of class conflict and defined the "ideas of humane democratic socialism" as the ideology of the CPSU.

The draft also portrayed the CPSU as the representative of the interests of all social classes in society (including those engaged in private business) and it explicitly repudiated the party's traditional hostility to religion. The program also pledged the CPSU to develop a democratic multiparty system based on the separation of powers between legislative, executive, and judicial branches. Finally, the program insisted that the CPSU would reorient the economy to meet the needs of consumers, and establish a "controlled market economy" that would limit privatization and provide the population with a wide range of social and educational services.

This revisionist program clearly challenged the ideological foundation for all aspects of party officials' leadership of Communists in state and soviet agencies. Its overt repudiation of a Marxist-Leninist ideological perspective and its support for social democratic theory and practice destroyed the rational for coherent "ideological work" at all levels of the CPSU. Its support for the complete decentralization of personnel management and the election of party officials by their respective committees seriously threatened the capacity of the Secretariat and local personnel departments to select and assign local officials as in the past.

But the proposed party program was never discussed on its merits. On July 23, 1991 (the same day as the publication of the program), Yeltsin, president of the RSFSR, made a frontal assault on the primary party organizations of the CPSU. He issued a decree banning the primary party organizations of the CPSU in all state organs and enterprises within the RSFSR and called on the Supreme Soviet of the RSFSR to submit legislation to the Supreme Soviet of the USSR to ban party organizations in the USSR's armed forces and security police.[60] Yeltsin's assault on the primary party organizations threatened to reopen the breach with General Secretary Gorbachev. Gorbachev had redefined the role of the party's officials and reformed both the Central Committee and the Politburo, but he had never questioned the need for the primary party organizations in state institutions and production enterprises.

But Gorbachev was faced with such widespread opposition from orthodox leaders at this juncture (thirty provincial Communist organizations had called for his resignation as general secretary on the eve of the meeting of the Central Committee in late July)[61] that he evidently concluded that he had to retain his alliance with Yeltsin against them.

As a result, when the Central Committee was convened in July, Gorbachev responded to Yeltsin's challenge with extraordinary circumspection. Gorbachev told the Central Committee that the Politburo had "evaluated" Yeltsin's decree (he did not report that the Politburo had condemned it in no uncertain terms) and agreed that the Central Committee should take a stand on the issue, but refused to do so himself. He simply acknowledged that Yeltsin's actions had "complicated" a difficult situation and noted that the chairman of the Supreme Soviet had asked the Committee of Constitutional Supervision for its opinion on the matter.[62]

While Gorbachev made no concession to orthodox members of the Central Committee in dealing with Yeltsin's dramatic action, he did retreat from some of the most revisionist formulations about the history of the USSR. In his report to the Central Committee on the draft program, he did not criticize the ideology of Bolshevism, toned down the draft program's direct assault on the Stalinist system, and now recognized that "major results" had been achieved during Stalin's reign. He made no reference to the regime's massive use of force or to Khrushchev's criticism of Stalin at the 20th Congress of the CPSU, and portrayed Khrushchev's successors in a far more sympathetic fashion. At the same time, he gave considerable attention to the role of the Central Committee in decision making, insisted that the CPSU still needed party discipline, and made no reference to the right of party members to form factions.

But Gorbachev refused to discard his revisionist definition of official ideology and of the role of the CPSU. He insisted that Marxism-Leninism had to be supplemented with other sources of socialist thought and he clearly defined the CPSU as a purely "parliamentary party." Most significant, he now explicitly recognized that it might even be defeated electorally and forced to act as a "constructive opposition." In that event it would be obliged to support the "sensible" measures of the authorities and oppose those actions detrimental to the working people when necessary. In the end, he implied that those members of the CPSU who could not accept the program should leave the party.[63]

The general secretary's ideological juggling did not mollify his most ardent critics. B. V. Gidaspov, the first secretary of the Leningrad *obkom* and secretary of the Central Committee, charged that the draft program would weaken the party because of its negative orientation toward Marxism-Leninism, its excessive enthusiasm for a market economy, its failure to provide a Marxist analysis of the current critical situation, or to confront the leadership's own responsibility for the problems facing the country. He reported that the Leningrad *obkom* had recently called for the convocation of an extraordinary Congress of the CPSU for the fall of 1991. He implied that it should not only change the party's leadership, but also "reexamine" the distribution of authority between the Central Committee and its Politburo and Secretariat.[64]

Y. A. Prokofiev, the first secretary of the Moscow *gorkom* and a member of the Politburo, charged that the draft program was designed to eliminate the "leading role of the CPSU." He called for a broader debate within the CPSU over the program to be based on a comparison of the drafts proposed by other segments of the CPSU and seconded the call for the convocation of a party congress in the fall of 1991.[65] Lesser known members of the Central Committee were extremely harsh in their assault on the general secretary. For example, A. P. Proskurin, a worker on a state farm, charged that Gorbachev's flaccid leadership had encouraged Yeltsin to make his assault on the primary party organizations, criticized the general secretary's obvious failure to denounce Yeltsin's actions, and urged him to focus on his responsibilities as the general secretary.[66]

At this critical juncture, the Central Committeee turned directly against its general secretary. First of all, it moved beyond Gorbachev's flaccid reaction to Yeltsin's abolition of primary party organizations and sharply condemned his action. The Central Committee explicitly endorsed the condemnation of Yeltsin made by the Communist Party of the RSFSR, and called on both the president and the Supreme Soviet of the USSR to provide a "legal assessment" of the actions of the Russian president. Second, it did not endorse the draft program (as Gorbachev later claimed) but merely recognized it as an "acceptable basis" for further work and discussion. The Central Committee returned the text to the program commission in preparation for a party-wide discussion of the document.[67]

At the very end of his address to the Central Committee, Gorbachev had announced that the new union treaty, which had been under negotiation for months, had been agreed upon on July 23, 1991. He claimed that the new treaty would restore stability to the USSR by its clear demarcation of authority between the member republics and the central government. In fact, the definitions of the authority of both the Council of Ministers of the USSR and of the president of the USSR provided in the treaty were extremely unclear.[68]

Boldin subsequently reported that some members of the Cabinet of Ministers of the USSR were convinced that the treaty would lead to the destruction of the economy, of the USSR's military capacity, the outbreak of ethnic conflict, and to the total destruction of the USSR.[69] And their anxieties must have been intensified by Gorbachev's revisionist program. On August 19, 1991, the leaders of the Cabinet of Ministers acted on their fears. They established a State Committee for the State of Emergency to run the USSR and placed President Gorbachev under house arrest. The State Committee included the vice president of the USSR and the leading members of the Cabinet of Ministers (the chairman of the Cabinet of Ministers, the chairman of the KGB, the minister of defense, the minister of internal affairs, the first deputy chairman of the defense council, the president of the association of state industries, and the chairman of the union of peasants).[70]

While it is obvious that the leaders of the government played the key role in the implementation of the abortive coup, leading orthodox party officials were also involved. O. Shenin, a member of the Politburo and secretary of the Central Committee, V. Boldin, who had served as Gorbachev's chief of staff, and O. Baklanov (who had served as the secretary of the Central Committee responsible for supervising the defense industry before becoming deputy chairman of the defense council) were arrested later. Most important, Gorbachev subsequently implied that Ivashko had collaborated with the emergency committee and revealed that the Secretariat had ordered local party officials to support it.[71]

Notes

1. *Izvestiia*, January 9, 1991, 1.

2. *Izvestiia*, January 10, 1991, 1.

3. *Pravda*, January 14, 1991, 1–2.

4. *Pravda*, January 15, 1991, 1.

5. *Izvestiia*, January 14, 1991, 2.

6. I. Polozkov, "Za sotsialisticheskii kharakter perestroika," *Kommunist*, no. 2 (1991), 10–11. Approved for publication January 11, 1991.

7. *Pravda*, January 26, 1991, 1.

8. "Postanovlenie Politburo TsK KPSS, January 24, 1991," *Izvestiia TsK KPSS*, no. 2 (1991), 25–26.

9. *Pravda*, February 4, 1991, 1.

10. *Sovetskaia Rossiia*, February 5, 1991, 1–3.

11. FBIS-SOV-91-034, February 20, 1991, 74–79.

12. *Izvestiia*, February 21, 1991, 2.

13. *Sovetskaia Rossiia*, February 22, 1991, 2.

14. *Sovetskaia Rossiia*, February 25, 1991, 1.

15. *Sovetskaia Rossiia*, February 28, 1991, 2.

16. See *Izvestiia TsK KPSS*, no. 5 (1991), 26–27.

17. "Postanovleniia sekretariata, February 28, 1991, *Izvestiia Ts K KPSS*, no. 5 (1991), 23.

18. For the full text, see FBIS SOV 91-040, February 28, 1991, 70–82.

19. *Pravda*, March 7, 1991, 1–3.

20. Medvedev, *V komande*, 179–182.

21. *Rossiiskaia Gazeta*, March 31, 1991, 1–3.

22. "O distsipline v kpss," *Pravda*, March 6, 1991, 1.

23. Gorbachev, *Zhizn'*, vol. 2, 528, 535.

24. Ibid., 531.

25. Medvedev, *V komande*, 181–182.

26. *Izvestiia*, April 24, 1991, 1.

27. *Izvestiia*, April 23, 1991, 1.

28. *Pravda*, April 25, 1991, 1–2.

29. *Pravda*, April 26, 1991, 3.

30. *Pravda*, April 29, 1991, 3.

31. Medvedev, *V komande*, pp. 184–185.

32. The resolution was published in *Partiinaia Zhizn'*, no. 10 (1991), 4–7.

33. *Pravda*, April 23, 1991, 2–3.

34. *Partiinaia Zhizn'*, no. 10 (1991), 4–5.

35. V. A. Kuptsov, "KPSS otkryta dliia sotrudnichestva," *Izvestiia TsK KPSS*, no. 5 (1991), 5–6.

36. I. A. Manaenkov, "Krepit nashe edinstvo," *Izvestiia TsK KPSS*, no. 6 (1991), 4–9.

37. "O chem govoriat sekretarii partkomov," *Izvestiia TsK KPSS*, no. 7 (1991), 65–66.

38. "Informatsionno-politicheskii tsentr TsK KPSS," *Izvestiia Ts K KPSS*, no. 7 (1991), 59–60.

39. See *Izvestiia TsK KPSS*, no. 7 (1991), 61–65.

40. "Postanovlenie Sekretariata, May 28, 1991," *Izvestiia Ts K KPSS*, no. 8 (1991), 44–46.

41. "Postanovlenie Sekretariata, May 28, 1991," *Izvestiia TsK KPSS*, no. 8 (1991), 39–40.

42. *Partiinaia Zhizn'* published brief summaries of the meetings of a number of commissions in issue no. 12 (1991), 14–15. Approved for publication June 7, 1991. Unfortunately, it did not provide the dates of these meetings.

43. "Osnovnyi polozheniia I rekomendatsii po realizatsii politiki kpss v oblaste razgosudarstvleniia sobstvennosti," *Izvestiia TsK KPSS*, no. 8 (1991), 20–24.

44. *Partiinaia Zhizn'*, no. 12 (1991), 12–15.

45. Ibid.

46. Postanovlenie Politburo TsK KPSS, June 3, 1991," *Izvestiia TsK KPSS* no. 8 (1991), 15.

47. O. S. Shenin "Kadrovaia politika partii," *Izvestiia TsK KPSS*, no. 8 (1991), 7–8.

48. M. Semenov, "Pozhinaia gorkie plody," *Izvestiia TsK KPSS*, no. 7 (1991), 39–41. Approved for publication, June 7, 1991.

49. P. K. Luchinskii, "Partiia I ee pressa," *Izvestiia TsK KPSS*, no. 8 (1991), 4–8.

50. Boldin, *Krushenie*, 400–402.

51. *Pravda*, June 18, 1991, 1–2.

52. *Izvestiia*, June 18, 1991, 1–2.

53. For materials on this episode, see *CDSP* 43, no. 25 (July 24, 1991), 1–9.

54. Medvedev, *V komande*, 186.

55. *Pravda*, July 3, 1991, 1–2.

56. See *CDSP* 43, no. 31, 9.

57. Gorbachev, *Zhizn'*, vol. 2, 542.

58. *Izvestiia*, July 2, 1991, 1–2.

59. *Nezavisimaia gazeta*, July 23, 1991, 2.

60. *Sovetskaia Rossiia*, July 23, 1991, 1.

61. *Rossiiskaia Gazeta*, July 31, 1991, 1

62. *Pravda*, July 26, 1991, 2.

63. *Pravda*, July 26, 1991, 1–2.

64. *Pravda*, July 27, 1991, 3.

65. Ibid.

66. *Pravda*, July 27, 1991, 5.

67. Ibid., 1.

68. See Boldin, *Krushenie*, 404–405; *Izvestiia*, August 15, 1991, 1–2.

69. Ibid.

70. Dunlop, *Rise of Russia*, 191.

71. Gorbachev, *Zhizn'*, vol. 2, 572.

Chapter Nine

Conclusion

The members of the Secretariat revolted against Gorbachev because of his actions as president of the USSR and his actions as general secretary of the CC/CPSU. First of all, they concluded that the president's effort to grant vast authority to the union republics of the USSR and to cooperate with the newly elected anti-Communist president of the RSFSR would destroy the USSR. Second, they believed that the general secretary's revisionist draft program for the CPSU had deprived it of any coherent ideological direction, and that his definition of the CPSU as a purely parliamentary party threatened to eliminate party officials' responsibilities for leadership. They concluded that a focus on electoral politics and on staff work for the elected Communist deputies would surely destroy party officials' leadership of the Communists in the executive and legislative branches of the Soviet state.

Gorbachev's position in 1991 was a far cry from his initial definition of officials' responsibilities in his report to the 27th Congress in 1986. At the time, he had argued that the full-time party officials should grant autonomy to the members of the CPSU who staffed state and soviet agencies. Gorbachev had claimed that the elimination of their "interference" would allow these officials to provide "political leadership" by continued control over the management of personnel and the definition of official ideology.

But the general secretary then proceeded to subvert both his initial design and to undermine his own authority over party officials. He used his position as general secretary to impose a series of political reforms that made it increasingly difficult for party officials to provide effective "political leadership."

His transformation of official ideology, his support for the "democratization" of both the CPSU and Soviet state, alarmed and alienated many officials who believed that their leadership of the Communists in state and soviet agencies was the essence of "party leadership" of the entire system.

Gorbachev's program of reform seemed to be based on a series of extremely optimistic assumptions about the capacities and orientation of the major actors in the system. First of all, he initially presumed that the limitation of party officials' direct intervention in the administration of industry (it is essential to remember that the general secretary did not challenge their authority in the agricultural sector) and the concomitant extension of the Council of Ministers' authority would improve industrial performance. The general secretary initally seemed to share Chairman Ryzhkov's views that the centralized economic administration of the Soviet state could in fact perform more effectively without the "horizontal" interference and direction of the "industrial branch" departments at all levels of the party's apparat. Gorbachev also seemed to presume that the limitation of officials' interference in industrial administration would free them to give more attention to the "social economic questions" that concerned Soviet citizens. He probably hoped that this shift in orientation might have helped to restore their faith in the utility of "party leadership."

Gorbachev also presumed that the limitation of officials' "interference" in industrial administration and the extension of their responsibilities for "social-economic questions" would oblige them to change their "style of work" in a significant fashion. Greater autonomy for state and soviet agencies, it was hoped, would force party officials to stop giving direct orders to those under their supervision and to learn how to use "persuasion" in their "work with people." In his view, if the party officials showed greater respect for the Communists who manned the state and their capacity to fulfill their immediate obligations without constant prodding, the party officials' "suggestions" would be accepted as binding.

Gorbachev initially seemed to believe that the Secretariat would be able to "steer" party officials in this direction by replacing the industrial branch departments (except for defense) with new departments for "social economic questions," and by retaining control over the management of personnel and over the definition of the nature and content of official ideology. It is at least possible that the introduction of a less dictatorial "style of work" might have established a more humane and responsive relationship between the members of the "inner" and "outer" party. It is also at least possible that party officials' focus on "social economic problems" may have won them greater support from citizens concerned with their standard of living.

But the general secretary then proceeded to undermine the Secretariat's capacity to provide this direction by calling for the transformation of the key sectors of "political work." The Secretariat's control over cadres at all levels of the system was severely weakened by the general secretary's insistence on the election of party officials by their respective party committees and his subsequent declaration that local party organizations were autonomous. This position not only fostered the independence of local officials, but also allowed them to make direct assaults on Gorbachev in the name of their respective party organizations.

In this context, Gorbachev's conception of "ideological work" is incomprehensible. He periodically insisted that the elimination of party officials' interference in administrative agencies would permit them to devote greater attention to "ideological work" that he often defined as the "most fruitful" sphere of party officials' activity. But he made these assertions at a time when his own revisionism had produced such sharp divisions within the leadership of the CPSU that it had become impossible to identify the boundaries of official ideology. His growing emphasis on the importance and utility of bourgeois democratic and social democratic ideology and practice so blurred the difference between "bourgeois" and "socialist" ideology that it crippled the efforts by Secretary Medvedev and others to create a "new definition of socialism." Under these circumstances, it became impossible for "ideological workers" to present a coherent version of ideology to party members throughout the political system.

The general secretary's approach to the democratization of the state structure is equally difficult to understand. His decision to transform the soviets into democratically elected legislatures clearly undermined party officials' capacity to provide "party leadership" to the Communists who manned state and soviet agencies. But Gorbachev was evidently so sanguine about party officials' capacity to work effectively within the new framework of electoral politics that he refused (at least in public) to recognize that these new legislatures might threaten the authority of party officials.

As a result, the general secretary defined officials' relationship with the newly empowered soviets as merely another component of their "political work." He evidently believed that they would quickly learn how to extend their authority into the new and powerful legislative bodies, to prepare electoral programs that could appeal to increasingly restive citizens, and to move out of their offices to debate their political opponents. As a consequence of the general secretary's optimism, the leadership actually made little effort to prepare party officials for electoral politics and many of them were defeated in the elections for the USSR Congress of Peoples' Deputies in 1989.

Gorbachev's failure to recognize the inherent conflict between the newly elected legislatures and the party's full-time officials reflected his unwillingness or inability to define the proper relationship between the "democratization" of the state structure and the "democratization" within the CPSU. He had repeatedly applauded the introduction of alternative candidates for election to the soviets, their transformation into genuine legislative bodies, and had pressed hard for the election of party officials by their respective party committees. But his comments in the period between 1989 and the middle of 1991 revealed that he found it extremely difficult to define the proper relationship between the Secretariat, the party officials elected by their own committees, and the Communists elected as deputies to the new soviets. On the one hand, his repeated emphasis on the "leading role" of the CPSU implied that the Secretariat and its subordinates would continue to provide some form of guidance to Communists in state and soviet agencies. On the other hand, his repeated assertions that the leading role of the CPSU was totally dependent upon its electoral success implied that the Secretariat and its subordinates should give priority to the local party organizations' electoral campaigns and preparations for the legislative actions of Communist deputies.

In mid-1991, Gorbachev evidently sought to resolve this issue by stressing the parliamentary responsibilities of both the Secretariat and its subordinate party officials. In June 1991, the Politburo ordered them to focus on the development of proposed legislation for the new legislative bodies and told local officials to work more closely with the elected Communist deputies to the soviets. While the decree did not explicitly subordinate the Secretariat and its officials to the soviets, it clearly implied that party officials were now expected to assure that the CPSU served as a "parliamentary party." This definition was incorporated into the revisionist draft program that Gorbachev sought to impose upon the CPSU in July 1991.

Gorbachev's optimistic conception of the capacity of party officials to lead by focusing on their "political work" was matched by his optimistic conception of the orientation of the Communists who manned the state and soviet bodies. He seemed to conclude that they had so completely internalized the party's values and program that they could therefore be given greater independence without threatening the party officialdom's "leadership" of their own activities. Gorbachev seemed oblivious to the possibility that party members who held important state positions might take advantage of their newly found autonomy to press for even greater independence. For example, N. I. Ryzhkov, Gorbachev's own appointment as chairman of the Council of Ministers, worked assiduously to broaden the government's role in the development of the USSR's industrial policy and consistently resisted what he regarded as undue interference of party officials. Furthermore Ryzhkov ardently defended the government's prerogatives against Gorbachev's efforts to dismantle ministerial authority and to grant ever greater autonomy to individual enterprises. Chairman Ryzhkov clashed repeatedly with the general secretary from mid-1987 onward and regarded the decisions of the 19th Conference of the CPSU as sanctioning greater independence for the Council of Ministers and its subordinates. Despite these serious differences, Gorbachev seemed to presume that Ryzhkov would still continue to follow the general secretary's lead. Ryzhkov's spirited resistance to the general secretary's views intensified the divisions within the Politburo and undermined its own capacity to provide coherent guidance.

Gorbachev also seemed to have a sanguine perspective on the behavior of Communist deputies in the newly elected legislatures. He did not seem to consider the possibility that without close supervision by party officials the Communist deputies in the various newly empowered parliaments might act in an increasingly independent fashion. For example, despite Gorbachev's explicit opposition, the deputies to the new Congress of Peoples' Deputies of the RSFSR used the independence granted this new institution to elect Boris Yeltsin as chairman of the Supreme Soviet of the RSFSR in the spring of 1990.

Gorbachev's orthodox critics and opponents clearly did not share his optimistic views. At the 27th Congress in early 1986 they began to express their skepticism toward his vision of a "new type" of relationship between party officials and the Communists under their supervision. During the next few years they increasingly argued that Gorbachev's efforts to persuade party officials to engage in "political methods of leadership" would destroy the basis for "party leadership" of both state and society. Gorbachev's critics concluded that slackening of close supervision and control would make it impossible for the top leadership of the CPSU to impose its program and goals on the members of the party or to prevent them from moving off in a variety of directions.

Gorbachev's critics were therefore extremely distressed by his effort to limit party officials' traditional role in the administration of industry, his loosening of the Secretariat's control over the appointment of local party officials, his total destruction of a coherent official ideology, and his effort to transform the soviets into elected legislative bodies. Ligachev, Polozkov, and others argued repeatedly that party officials' close supervision of Communists' activities was vital to the maintenance of "party leadership," that constant ideological vigilance against the attractions of "bourgeois democratic" and "social democratic" theory and practice was essential to prevent dangerous ideological and political backsliding. They correctly concluded that the general secretary's growing enthusiasm for various forms of nonsocialist ideology had immense implications for the future of political institutions. In particular, they realized that Gorbachev's support for a "bourgeois" multiparty system and a parliamentary order would undermine both the ideological and institutional basis for officials' leadership of Communists in both the executive and legislative organs of the Soviet state.

Gorbachev's orthodox critics in the Secretariat launched a serious counter-attack on Gorbachev's definitions after the 28th Congress of the CPSU in mid-1990. Although they were obliged to work within the new framework created by the transformation of the soviets into elected legislatures, the selection of Ivashko as deputy general secretary and the restoration of the Secretariat's authority at the Congress allowed the secretaries of the Central Committee to attempt to restore party officials' responsibilities in many areas in the year between the 28th Congress and the abortive coup against Gorbachev in August 1991. The secretaries' support for the coup was the ultimate reflection of their hostility to Gorbachev's efforts to reform the role of party officials.

A leading specialist on perestroika has recently declared that it is extremely difficult to determine Gorbachev's conception of "the party" despite the revelations provided by the memoirs of his closest lieutenants. This study suggests that the effort to determine the general secretary's view of "the party" is not a particularly fruitful line of inquiry because it blurs the vast differences between the party's full-time officials and the Communists who manned the state.

In their generalizations about the major actors in the political system in the USSR, many Western scholars fail to differentiate between the party's officials and the CPSU as a whole. Some refer to "the party" and "the state" as if their members did not overlap and they were totally distinct and separate bureaucratic structures. Others refer to the USSR as a "party-state" as if the overlap in membership between party and state was somehow complete. Neither of these formulations gives adequate attention to the efforts of the Secretariat of the CC/CPSU and its subordinate full-time officials to provide leadership for Communists who staff the state and soviet agencies.

This study has differentiated between the "inner" and "outer" segments of the CPSU in order to highlight this process. The members of the "inner" party led by the Secretariat of the CC/CPSU had no positions in the state. They sought to supervise and lead those members of the "outer" party who held these positions, and who were subject to the party discipline imposed by the party's officials.

Western specialists on the political system of the USSR have disagreed over the nature of the relations between the members of the "inner" and "outer" divisions of the CPSU. Some scholars have stressed the party officials' efforts to provide guidance, while some leading studies of the USSR have stressed the development of coalitions between supervisor and supervised in the interests of common objectives. No doubt such cooperation did exist, but this study lends support for those who argued that the party's officials sought to lead the other members of the CPSU who held positions throughout the political system. While it is impossible to determine the extent to which this leadership proved successful, the effort to provide direction was unmistakable.

Gorbachev's effort to redefine the nature of this leadership, which seriously threatened to undermine party officials' capacity to "command" Communists in other agencies, was resisted by important party officials at every level of the CPSU. Secretaries of the CC/CPSU such as Ligachev and Sliunkov, republican leaders such as Polozkov, and regional and city leaders such as Gidaspov and Prokofiev clearly regarded Gorbachev's insistence on "political methods of leadership" as subversive to what they regarded as normal practice.

The concerted effort of the members of the Secretariat to restore its authority and to strengthen the position of its subordinates after the 28th Congress of the CPSU is instructive in this respect. Gorbachev's increased emphasis on the autonomy of party officials and his constant diatribes against "commandism" had clearly undermined the direct communications between the Secretariat and its subordinates. After the revival of the Secretariat at the 28th Congress, leading secretaries complained that it had failed to engage in the "verification of fulfillment" of its own decrees and pledged to correct the situation immediately. The secretaries not only worked to tighten the links of communication with subordinate party organs, but also pledged to travel throughout the country acting as "trouble shooters" for hard-pressed party organizations.

In addition, the Secretariat established new commissions and departments of the CC/CPSU to deal with new constituencies, to counter the decline in membership, and to improve the ideological capacities of local officials. The establishment of new agencies for the revival of primary party organizations, for dealing with women, youth and non-Communist organizations, the newly established legislative bodies, and for ideological questions, was designed to broaden officials' capacity to influence an increasingly complicated political system.

Most important, after the 28th Congress of the CPSU, the Secretariat increased the number and scope of its *direct orders* to local party bodies, to Communists with important positions in the state, and to the newly established legislative bodies. The Secretariat issued far more decrees than the newly reorganized Politburo during the last year of Gorbachev's tenure, and may actually have replaced it as the major source of direction for the CPSU as a whole.

Certain characteristics of these decrees deserve attention. They were not represented as "suggestions" that could be accepted or rejected by their recipients, but as binding orders. Most important, the Secretariat's decrees were invariably based upon the recommendations contained in reports by the various departments of the CC/CPSU that had remained in place after the reform of the departments in 1988. Unfortunately, it has proved impossible to determine the exact role of these departments in the period from the reform until the 28th Congress. But there is no doubt that in the period after the 28th Congress, these agencies and their local subordinates played a critical role in the development of the Secretariat's binding orders. The departments of the CC/CPSU evidently often worked jointly on a particular problem, and their reports provided an analysis of the problem at hand, a determination of responsibility for "shortcomings," and recommendations for corrective action. The Secretariat's decrees did not always endorse the recommendations of the departments for corrective action. But the reports themselves indicated that the departments were not merely conduits for information on the activities of subordinate units, but provided the basis for the Secretariat's direct intervention. It is not possible to determine the extent to which these reports may have been commissioned by the secretaries of the CC/CPSU, but their importance cannot be underestimated.

Gorbachev's role in the development of these binding orders remains unknown. As noted above, the general secretary had evidently taken the initiative in the revival of the Secretariat, but published sources suggest that he then had allowed Deputy General Secretary Ivashko wide leeway in directing the Secretariat's activities. The substance of the Secretariat's decrees suggest that it was following its own agenda and not paying too much attention to the preferences of the general secretary/president.

The general secretary may have made an attempt to persuade the Secretariat to act as the legislative staff for the Congress of Peoples' Deputies rather than as the major source of direction for the party's officials. In June 1991 the Politburo issued a decree urging the Secretariat to focus on this role. The leaders of the Secretariat did not seem to oppose the general secretary's suggestion, but continued to act on their own far more inclusive and extensive conception of the Secretariat's role.

In July 1991, the general secretary sought to persuade the CC/CPSU to endorse a totally revisionist program for the CPSU. Its repudiation of Marxism-Leninism, of the "vanguard role" for the party, its endorsement of a multiparty political system based on a separation of powers, implied that the Secretariat had no role to play beyond the provision of staff work for the USSR's legislature. The secretaries of the CC/CPSU evidently concluded that the general secretary was bent on the total destruction of their authority. It is not surprising that they joined with the Communist/ministers who led the abortive coup against the general secretary/president in August 1991.

Bibliography

Books

Boldin, V. I. *Krushenie p'edestala*. Moscow: Respublika, 1995.

Brown, Archie. *The Gorbachev Factor*. New York: Oxford University Press, 1997.

Chernayev, A. S. *Shest let s Gorbachevym*. Moscow: Progress, 1993.

D'Agastino, Anthony. *Gorbachev's Revolution*. New York: New York University Press, 1998.

Dunlop, John. *The Rise of Russia and the Fall of the Soviet Empire*. Princeton, N.J.: Princeton University Press, 1993.

Fainsod, Merle. *How Russia Is Ruled*. Cambridge, Mass: Harvard University Press, 1953.

Gorbachev, M. S. *Zhizn' i reformy*. Moscow: Novosti, 1995.

Hahn, Gordon. *Russia's Revolution from Above*. New Brunswick, N.J.: Transaction Publishers, 2002.

Hough, Jerry. *Democratization and Revolution in the USSR, 1985–1991*. Washington, D.C.: Brookings Institution Press, 1997.

Hough, Jerry, and Merle Fainsod. *How the Soviet Union Is Governed*. Cambridge, Mass.: Harvard University Press, 1979.

Ligachev, I. *Inside Gorbachev's Kremlin*. New York: Pantheon, 1993.

Malia, Martin. *The Soviet Tragedy*. New York: The Free Press, 1994.

McCauley, Martin. *Who's Who in Russia since 1990*. London: Routledge, 1997.

Medvedev, Vadim. *V komande gorbacheva*. Moscow: Bylina, 1994.

Roeder, Philip G. *Red Sunset: The Failure of Soviet Politics*. Princeton, N.J.: Princeton University Press, 1993.

Ryzhkov, N. *Desyat' let velikikh potriasenii*. Moscow: Assotsiatsiya kniga, prosveshchenie, milosredie, 1995.

White, Stephen. *After Gorbachev*. Cambridge: Cambridge University Press, 1993.

Journal Articles

Agaponov, A. "Blizhe k liudam, bol'she zaboty o nikh." *Partiinaia Zhizn'* 3 (1990): 48–51.

Borovika, Z. "Raikom: deistvovat politicheskimi metody." *Partiinaia Zhizn'* 22 (1987): 53–54.

Bystrov, E. "Nekomandovat a sovetovatsiia." *Partiinaia Zhizn'* 3 (1990): 52–53.

"Byt v avangarde, rabotat po novomu.soveshchanie v tsk kpss." *Partiinaia Zhizn'* 23 (1987): 6–7.

"Demokratizatsiia-rukovodiashchiu deiatel'nost v vnutrennyi zhizn' partii." *Partiinaia Zhizn'* 22 (1989): 7–8.

Efimov, V., and A. Losik. "Kak perestraivat partinuiu rabotu." Partiinaia *Zhizn'* 17 (1989): 38–43.

Egovin, V. "Gorkom partii v tsentre vnimaniia rekonstruktsiia proizvodsta." *Partiinaia Zhizn'* 18 (1987): 36–40.

"Ekonomicheskaia reforma I partiinyi komitet." *Partiinaia Zhizn'* 19 (1989): 3–8.

"Energichno vesti perestroiku partiinoi raboty." *Partiinaia Zhizn'* 14 (1986).

Gerasimov, A. "Oblagevat novym stylem rukovodstva. uchit'siia deistvovat v novykh usloviiakh." *Partiinaia Zhizn'* 17 (1988): 15–21.

Girenko, A. N. "Ukrepliaia obratnyi sviazi." *Izvestiia TsK KPSS* 12 (1990): 3–8.

Hahn, Gordon M. "The First Reorganization of the CPSU CC Apparat under Perestroika." *Europe-Asia Studies* 2 (Spring 1997): 281–302.

Ivashko, V. A. "Vremiia real'nykh deistvii." *Izvestiia TsK KPSS* 1 (1991): 4–8.

Kapto, A. "Ideologiia I praktika obnovleniia." *Partiinaia Zhizn'* 14 (1989): 3–11.

Khomiakov, A. "Osvaivat politicheskie metody rukovodstva, otkazyviat'siia ot administrativno-kommandogo stiliia." *Partiinaia Zhizn'* 19 (1986): 29–34.

Kobelev, G. "Ubezhdat I deistvovat." *Partiinaia Zhizn'* 2 (1990): 60–63.

Kuptsov, V. A. "kpss otkryta dliia sotrudnichestva." *Izvestiia TsK KPSS* 5 (1991): 5–6.

Kuptsov, V. A. "My obiazanyi splotitsiia." *Izvestiia TsK KPSS* 1 (1991): 44–45.

Luchinskii, P. K. "Partiia i ee pressa." *Izvestiia TsK KPSS* 4 (1991): 4–8.

Manaenkov, I. A. "Krepit nashe edinstvo." *Izvestiia TsK KPSS* 6 (1991): 4–9.

Medvedev, V. "K poznaniiu sotsializma. otvety na voprosy zhurnala kommunist." *Kommunist* 17 (1988): 3–6.

Miakinnik, N. "Partiinoe rukovodstva ekonomiki." *Partiinaia Zhizn'* 21 (1988): 5–13.

Novikov, V. "Ovladevta politicheskimy metodamy." *Partiinaia Zhizn'* 16 (1989): 24–26.

———. "Potentsial kooperatsii-uskoreniiu sotsialno-ekonomicheskogo razvitiia." *Partiinaia Zhizn'* 9 (1988): 49–53.

"O rabote tsentral'nogo komiteta kpss." *Izvestiia TsK KPSS* 7 (1989): 3–4.

Pokrovov, V. "Obladevat politicheskimy metodamy rukovodstva." *Partiinaia Zhizn'* 1 (1989): 30–32.

"Politcheskaia I ekonomicheskaia ucheba trudiashchikhsiia: sluzhit delu revoliutsionnogo obnovleniia obshchestva." *Partiinaia Zhizn'* 19 (1987): 14–20.

Polozkov, I. "Na konkursnoi sostiazatel'noi osnove." *Partiinaia Zhizn'* 22 (1988): 30–32.

———. "Ne dliia parada," *Idet perestroika*. Moscow: Politizdat, 1987.

———. "Organizatsiia proverka ispol'neniia'" *Partiinaia Zhizn'* 11 (1987): 9–17.

———. "Za sotsialisticheskii kharakter perestroiki." *Kommunist* 2 (1991): 10–11.

———. "Politicheskoe rukovodstvo ot slov k delu." *Kommunist* 2 (1989): 12–21.

———. "Ziakel'nost," *Partiinaia Zhizn'* 23 (1990): 33–34.

"Proivliat politicheskuiu voliiu." *Partiinaia Zhizn'* 2 (1990): 55–56.

Prokofiev, Y. A. "Razryv v glubine demokratizatsii sushchestvenno sokratilsiia." *Partiinaia Zhizn'* 16 (1990): 16–19.

"Raikom, gorkom partii v perestroike." *Partiinaia Zhizn'* 6 (1988): 11–13.

Razumovsky, G. "Sovershenstvovat podgotovki I perepodgotovkii rukhovodiashchikh kadrov partii." *Kommunist* 4 (1987): 3–4.

———. "Partiinuiu raboty-na uroven zadachi perestroiki." *Partiinaia Zhizn'* 12 (1987): 6–10.

———. "Ustav kpss-nezyblemi zakon zhizn' partii." *Partiinaia Zhizn'* 12 (1986): 10–16.

Semenov, M. "Pozhenaia gorkie plody." *Izvestiia TsK KPSS* 7 (1991): 39–41.

Shenin, O. S. "Kadrovaia politika partii." *Izvestiia TsK KPSS* 8 (1991): 7–8.

———. "Prislyshivat'siia k pol'su strany i partii." *Izvestiia TsK KPSS* 10 (1990): 3–6.

Sitnikov, V. "Partiinyi komitet: osvaivat politicheskie metody rukovodstva." *Partiinaia Zhizn'* 23 (1986): 11–14.

"Vazhnyi etap perestroikei. K itogam s'ezd narodnykh deputatov sssr." *Partiinaia Zhizn'* 13 (1989): 3–4.

Wishnevsky, "Alesandr Yakovoev to Regain the Ideology Portfolio?" *Report on the USSR*, July 29, 1989, 9–11.

Yakovlev, A. N. "Glavny v perestroike segodniia-prakticheskie dela i konkretny rezultaty." *Partiinaia Zhizn'* 19 (1987): 7–16.

———. "Dostizhenie kachestvennogo novogo sostoianiia sovetskogo obshchestva i obshcheestvennye nauki." *Kommunist* 8 (1987): 4–20.

Zhil'tsov, "Otrkrytost glasnost, uchet mnenii kommunistov." *Partiinaia* Zhizn' 3 (1990): 46–47.

Documentary Collections

Current Soviet Policies IX: The Documentary Record of the 27th Congress of the Communist Party of the Soviet Union. Columbus, Ohio: Current Digest of the Soviet Press, 1986.

Current Soviet Policies X : The Documentary Record of the 19th Conference of the Communist Party of the Soviet Union. Columbus, Ohio: Current Digest of the Soviet Press, 1988.

Current Soviet Policies XI: Documents from the 28th Congress of the Communist Party of the Soviet Union. Columbus, Ohio: Current Digest of the Soviet Press, 1991.

Spravochnik partiinogo rabotnika 1986–1990. Moscow: Politizdat, 1987–1991.

Index

About the Author

Jonathan Harris is associate professor as well as associate chair for undergraduate studies in the Department of Political Science at the University of Pittsburgh. For the last twenty years, he has served as the editor of the Russian and East European Series published by the University of Pittsburgh Press. His current research focuses on the development of local self-government in the cities of Russia.